The Adaptive Character
of Thought

STUDIES IN COGNITION

A series of volumes edited by
Edward E. Smith, Allan Collins, and Kurt VanLehn

Anderson: The Adaptive Character of Thought

The Adaptive Character of Thought

John R. Anderson
Carnegie Mellon University

 LAWRENCE ERLBAUM ASSOCIATES, PUBLISHERS
1990   Hillsdale, New Jersey   Hove and London

Lawrence Erlbaum Associates, Inc., Publishers
365 Broadway
Hillsdale, New Jersey 07642

Library of Congress Cataloging-in-Publication Data

Anderson, John R. (John Robert), 1947–
    The adaptive character of thought / John R. Anderson.
        p.   cm.
    Includes bibliographical references.
    ISBN 0-8058-0419-6
    1. Cognition   2. Adaptation (Psychology)   3. Cognitive
psychology — Research — Methodology.   I. Title.
BF311.A585   1990
153 — dc20   90-35099
                                                                    CIP

Printed in the United States of America
10 9 8 7 6 5 4 3 2

10-7-93
RM
21335767

To Abe, Jay, and Lynne
with love

Contents

Preface *ix*

1. INTRODUCTION *1*
   Preliminaries *1*
   Levels of a Cognitive Theory *3*
   Current Formulation of the Levels Issue *17*
   The New Theoretical Framework *23*
   Is Human Cognition Rational? *31*
   The Rest of This Book *38*
   Appendix: Non-Identifiability and Response Time *38*

2. MEMORY *41*
   Preliminaries *41*
   A Rational Analysis of Human Memory *43*
   The History Factor *49*
   The Contextual Factor *61*
   Relationship of Need and Probability to Probability and
     Latency of Recall *72*
   Combining Information From Cues *77*
   Implementation in the ACT Framework *82*
   Effects of Subject Strategy *84*
   Conclusions *89*

3. CATEGORIZATION *93*
   Preliminaries *93*
   The Goal of Categorization *95*
   The Structure of the Environment *96*
   Recapitulation of Goals and Environment *100*
   The Optimal Solution *101*
   An Iterative Algorithm for Categorization *102*
   Application of the Algorithm *106*
   Survey of the Experimental Literature *111*

Conclusion *132*
Appendix: The Ideal Algorithm *138*

4. CAUSAL INFERENCE *149*
Preliminaries *149*
Basic Formulation of the Causal Inference Problem *151*
Causal Estimation *155*
Cues for Causal Inference *161*
Integration of Statistical and Temporal Cues *168*
Discrimination *172*
Abstraction of Causal Laws *177*
Implementation in a Production System *186*
Conclusion *187*
Appendix *187*

5. PROBLEM SOLVING *191*
Preliminaries *191*
Making a Choice Among Simple Actions *194*
Combining Steps *201*
Studies of Hill Climbing *215*
Means-Ends Analysis *221*
Instantiation of Indefinite Objects *228*
Conclusions on Rational Analysis of Problem Solving *229*
Implementation in ACT *230*
Appendix: Problem Solving and Clotheslines *232*

6. RETROSPECTIVE *244*
Preliminaries *244*
Twelve Questions About Rational Analysis *246*

REFERENCES *259*

AUTHOR INDEX *271*

SUBJECT INDEX *275*

Preface

The history behind this book illustrates the fact that science is an adventure and not a planned activity. When I finished my last major research monograph on the ACT* theory (Anderson, 1983), I set out to apply the theory to the acquisition of complex skills. As I described it in 1983, the goal of this endeavor was to "permanently break the theory." Much, but not all of this research involved the creation of intelligent tutoring systems and the study of students' behavior with these systems. Surely, I reasoned to myself, I would see the theory crumble as I tried to teach mathematics or programming based on the theory's analysis of skill acquisition. Well, our work on skill acquisition turned out better than I had any reason to believe. The theory did change a bit, and these changes are reported in Anderson, 1987, but much of the basic analysis stayed untouched.

In 1986, the course of action seemed clear. I needed to write a book that worked through the theory and elaborated on its foundations, but most of all organized and simulated the mounds of data that we had accumulated with our tutors on skill learning. I took a sabbatical, a 4-month jaunt in the beginning of 1987 to Flinders University in Adelaide, Australia. It was supposed to be an opportunity to get away from my lab, which was forever spewing out data, and put in the thinking time to get this process started.

Well, something happened to me on the way to Australia. Lynne Reder and I took it as a goal on the trip to write a short paper drawing out the implications of the human memory literature for the computer science field of information retrieval. It seemed that a necessary prerequisite was to read a little about the field of information retrieval. As I did so, an issue about memory started to eat at me again. For a long time, I had felt that there was something missing in the existing theories of human memory, including my own. Basically, all of these theories characterized memory as an arbitrary and nonoptimal configuration of memory mechanisms. I had long felt that the basic memory processes were quite adaptive and perhaps even optimal; however, I had never been able to see a framework in which to make this point. In the computer science work on information retrieval, I saw that framework laid out before me. Human memory was functioning as an optimal information retrieval system.

This idea ate at me as I celebrated Christmas in California, saw New Year's pass in Honolulu, and rushed through the maddening Sydney airport. By the time I started working at Flinders University, I had a whole new image of the book. The A in ACT had stood for Adaptive. Perhaps now I could make good on that claim, not just for human memory but for all of human cognition. It seemed that much of human cognition could be understood on the assumption that it was an optimal solution to the information-processing problems posed by the environment. I dubbed such attempts to understand human cognition as "rational analyses" out of analogy to the rational man approach in economics. All my arguments with my father-in-law, the economist, had left some mark.

Another factor besides my doubts about memory fed this move to a rational analysis. Just after writing my 1983 book I read David Marr's (1982) monograph on vision. (It was my beach reading in a brief vacation in the South Pacific in 1983, just to continue this Southern Hemisphere theme.) That book had been highly critical of the approach to human cognition that focused on mechanism and highly critical of production system architectures like ACT* in particular. Although, initially, I just took offense at the criticisms, there were enough grains of truth in them that they haunted me throughout the subsequent years. My new insights about an adaptionist approach to human cognition offered me a way of reconciling the Marr criticisms with my own work.

My brief stay at Flinders was intellectually liberating. Freed from the daily demands of running a large research laboratory, I could spend a week or two struggling with one idea until I understood it. In that period, I wrote no less than two drafts of six chapters of the projected book. In my mind, it was a revolutionary new book that merged synergistically the original conception of the book with my growing insights about the adaptiveness of human cognition.

I doubt that one sentence from these drafts remains in this book. The two books, the old on cognitive architecture and the new on rational analysis, did not mix, despite my illusions. The result of the attempted mixture was confusion. I returned to Carnegie-Mellon University and spent another year revising and rewriting, trying to solidify that which would not be solidified. This is what was sent out to a first round of reviewers. Their comments were extremely valuable and helped me to see the flaws in my conception of the book.

I had been invited to give a presentation at the 1988 Carnegie Symposium on Cognition, which was devoted to architectures. I thought I would have fun with the opportunity and try to develop an extreme argument. I would present some of my work on rational analysis and argue that we could predict human cognition from assumptions of rationality without any assumptions about architecture. To my surprise, the lark had more truth than I had suspected, although the point was probably a bit too extreme.

It was this lark that convinced me that I had to abandon my original conception of the book in 1986 and write something totally centered on providing a rational analysis of cognition. Essentially, three old chapters were thrown out, and three new ones were written. With the help of my research group, I carefully stepped through those chapters in 1988-1989, and the current book emerged. It develops what I hope is both a clear and strong case for a rational analysis of human cognition. I think it is a shame that the original book disappeared under the urgency to pursue a new exciting idea. I still think it needs to be written in some form.

Developing such a book has been an interesting experience in intellectual honesty. The problem is that such a rational analysis is potentially a challenge to the cognitive architecture approach that I have largely followed and that most of my close associates have followed. There is danger in following these ideas, that they might lead to a renunciation of what I have spent most of my professional life building, and that I might wind up expelled from the intellectual school that has treated me so well. I have to confess that there were times when I ran away from ideas that seemed too threatening and that, at some points, I tried to deliberately distort the conclusions I was coming to in order to make them more palatable. But I was always driven back to the rational analysis, because it was just too good of an idea to be abandoned.

Although I have not yet come to a resolution of the architectures-versus-rational-analysis juxtaposition, I doubt that it will be resolved as decision between the two. It has become apparent to me that this rational analysis has assumed the general ACT framework, if not the ACT* theory (see Anderson, 1983, for a discussion of the distinction between theories and frameworks). I think Marr's analysis of the relationship between rational analysis and architecture (he did not actually use these terms, but for more on this read chapter 1) is basically correct: One should begin with a rational analysis to figure out what the system should be doing and then worry about how the prescriptions of a rational analysis are achieved in the mechanisms of an architecture. I think the rational analysis in this book provides a prescription for developing a new architectural theory within the ACT framework and one that will not be much different from ACT*. This will become clearer as I try to pursue these prescriptions in the future. However, as this book is evidence, a rational analysis can stand on its own without any architectural theory.

Although the implications of rational analysis for cognitive architecture still need to be played out, I suspect that this enterprise will not turn out to be self-destructive in terms of my ACT framework. However, in a peculiar sense, this rational analysis still may be, to some degree, self-destructive. As the reader will note, a rational analysis calls on a set of Bayesian statistical skills that are relatively sophisticated and that I have only patched together as the need arose. If rational analysis becomes a working methodology in psychology, surely students will come forth who know the Bayesian techniques much better than I. I fear that I will find myself replaced by them and the analyses offered in these chapters replaced by much more elegant ones and much more penetrating ones. If this happens and someone from that future generation reads this book, I hope they will forgive me for the roughness of a first endeavor.

The reaction of my colleagues to my efforts has been interesting. Predictably, some applauded me for pursuing an idea wherever it led and others cried that I was guilty of apostasy. I have rather predictable feelings about these two types of evaluations. However, it is interesting that, whatever their bottom-line evaluations, my colleagues' real contribution has been in how they backed up their evaluations. Whether telling me how to do it better or why I had it wrong, they gave me many pointers to ideas that made the final product much better. Intellectual dialogue has been working marvelously.

There is a general controversy about using optimality analyses to understand natural species. Fortunately, we have largely been spared this controversy in cognitive science. We have enough fruitless controversies of our own. I hope, perhaps vainly, that this book will not import the optimization controversies into our field. It would be nice if we could approach such analyses with an unbiased curiosity to see just what light they can shed on human cognition.

I don't know yet how successful a rational analysis will ultimately prove to be for different aspects of human cognition. This book is clearly written in the spirit of advocacy for rational analysis. It is a relatively new idea in the field, and a good case has to be made for it if others are going to take it seriously. I have taken the attitude that the way to make this case is not to argue generalities but to get down into the nitty-gritty of individual experimental paradigms and specific results. Rational analysis encourages one to take a particularly clear look at these experiments and ask just what subjects take to be their task and just how these experimental paradigms relate to what subjects have to do on a larger scale. So much of this book is an exercise in specifics. I have been surprised about how much data one can predict from a rational analysis. I hope the reader will be similarly impressed and that I will have achieved my advocate's goal of gaining serious consideration for a rational analysis. Despite what I regard as impressive progress, it is clear that much needs to be done on all fronts.

ACKNOWLEDGMENTS

My debt to the colleagues who read and commented on this book is enormous. My reviewers have included Gordon Bower, Bill Clancey, Gary Gillund, Mark Gluck, Keith Holyoak, Jill Larkin, Clayton Lewis, Jay McClelland, Timothy McNamara, Doug Medin, Allen Newell, Dick Nisbett, Roger Ratcliff, Lynne Reder, Paul Rosenbloom, Brian Ross, Allan Schoenfeld, Stephen Stich, and Kurt VanLehn. I also need to thank the members of the ACT research group who went through the book. Fred Conrad, Albert Corbett, Craig Kaplan, Irv Katz, Ken Koedinger, Lael Schooler, Emile Servan-Schreiber, Kevin Singley, and Ross Thompson all led discussions of the book and provided me with detailed feedback. The book is much better for all of the feedback it received.

I would like to thank NSF (Joe Young) and ONR (Susan Chipman) whose longstanding support makes such a monograph possible. I would also like to thank the hospitality of Flinders University, without which none of this would have happened. I need to thank the librarian there who pointed me to the material on library usage, which played a key role in chapter 2. I wish I could remember his name. I would also like to thank my secretary, Helen Borek, who struggled through a set of changes in drafts and plans that would have overwhelmed most people. Finally, I would like to thank Judith Amsel and Larry Erlbaum who patiently watched a book change and deadlines missed, provided encouragement, and got me ever more reviewers.

Finally, I thank my family, to whom this book is dedicated. It has been a trying time for me as I have had to struggle with a set of medical problems which, though hardly life threatening, were debilitating and just would not go away. Had it not been for the constancy and warmth of family life, I would not have had the emotional capacity to make it through this period. I love them.

John R. Anderson

1 Introduction

Contents
Preliminaries   1
Levels of a Cognitive Theory   3
    Marr's System of Levels   3
    Chomsky's Competence and Performance   8
    Pylyshyn's Distinction Between Algorithm and Functional Architecture   9
    McClelland and Rumelhart's PDP Level   11
    Newell's Knowledge Level and the Principle of Rationality   14
Current Formulation of the Levels Issue   17
    The Algorithm Level   18
    Behavioral Data   20
    The Rational Level   22
The New Theoretical Framework   23
    Lack of Identifiability at the Implementation Level   23
    The Principle of Rationality   26
    Applying the Principle of Rationality   29
    Advantages of Rational Theory   30
Is Human Cognition Rational?   31
    Computational Cost   32
    Is there an Adaptive Cost?   32
    Heuristics Need to be Evaluated in Terms of Expected Value   33
    Applications of Normative Models Often Treat Uncertain Information
        as Certain   34
    The Situation Assumed is not the Environment of Adaptation   37
    Conclusions   37
The Rest of the Book   38
Appendix: Non-Identifiability and Response Time   38

PRELIMINARIES

A person writes a research monograph such as this with the intention that it will be read. As a consumer of such monographs, I know it is not an easy decision to invest the time in reading and understanding one. Therefore, it is important to be up front about what this book has to offer. In a few words, this book describes a new methodology for doing research in

1

cognitive psychology and applies it to produce some important developments. The new methodology is important, because it offers the promise of
rapid progress on some of the agenda of cognitive psychology. This
methodology concentrates on the adaptive character of cognition, in
contrast to the typical emphasis on the mechanisms underlying cognition.

I have been associated with a number of theoretical monographs (Anderson, 1976, 1983; Anderson & Bower, 1973). The sustaining question in
this succession of theories has been the nature of human knowledge. The
1973 book was an attempt to take human memory tradition as it had
evolved in experimental psychology and use the new insights of artificial
intelligence to relate the ideas of this tradition to fundamental issues of
human knowledge. The theory developed in that book was called HAM, a
propositional network theory of human memory. The 1976 book was
largely motivated by the pressing need to make a distinction between
procedural and declarative knowledge. This distinction was absent in the
earlier book and in the then-current literature on human memory. The
theory developed in that book was called ACT. In ACT, declarative
knowledge was represented in a propositional network and procedural
knowledge in a production system. The 1983 book was motivated both by
breakthroughs in developing a learning theory that accounts for the
acquisition of procedural knowledge and in identifying a neurally plausible
basis for the overall implementation of the theory. It was called ACT* to
denote that it was a completion of the theoretical development begun in the
previous book.

In the 1983 book on the ACT* theory, I tried to characterize its
relationship to the ACT series of theories and my future plans for research:
". . . my plan for future research is to try to apply this theory wide and far,
to eventually gather enough evidence to permanently break the theory and
to develop a better one. In its present stage of maturity the theory can be
broadly applied, and such broad application has a good chance of
uncovering fundamental flaws" (Anderson, 1983, p. 19).

My method of applying the theory has been to use it as a basis for detailed
studies of knowledge acquisition in a number of well-defined domains such
as high-school mathematics and college-level programming courses. In
these studies, we have been concerned with how substantial bodies of
knowledge are both acquired and evolve to the point where the learner has
a very powerful set of problem-solving skills in the domain (Anderson,
Boyle, Corbett, & Lewis, in press; Anderson, Boyle, & Reiser, 1985;
Anderson, Conrad, & Corbett; in press).

The outcome of this research effort has certainly not been what I
expected. Despite efforts to prove the theory wrong (I even created a new
production system, called PUPS for Penultimate Production System, to
replace ACT*—Anderson & Thompson, 1989), I failed to really shake the

old theory. As I have written elsewhere (Anderson, 1987c; Anderson, Conrad, & Corbett, in press), we have been truly surprised by the success of the ACT* theory in dealing with the data we have acquired about complex skill acquisition with our intelligent tutors. ACT* proved not to be vulnerable to a frontal assault, in which its predictions about skill acquisition are compared to the data. This book contains some theoretical ideas that are rather different than ACT*, produced by the new methodology that the book describes. These ideas do not so much contradict ACT* as they address the subject of human cognition in a different way.

The A in ACT* stands for Adaptive, and this book results from an effort to think through what it might mean for human cognition to be adaptive. However, this book is not cast as an update on the ACT* theory, but rather is an effort to develop some points about human cognition from an adaptive perspective. The majority of the book, the next four chapters, tries to develop theory from an adaptive perspective in four related fields of cognition. This chapter is devoted to setting the stage for that development.

To state up front where this chapter is going, the argument is that we can understand a lot about human cognition without considering in detail what is inside the human head. Rather, we can look in detail at what is outside the human head and try to determine what would be optimal behavior given the structure of the environment and the goals of the human. The claim is that we can predict behavior of humans by assuming that they will do what is optimal. This is a different level of analysis than the analysis of mental mechanisms that has dominated information-processing psychology. Having raised the possibility of levels of analysis, the questions arise as to just how many levels there are and why we would want to pursue one level rather than another. It turns out that there have been many ideas expressed on these topics in cognitive science. Rather than just present my position on this and pretend to have invented the wheel, it is appropriate to review the various positions and their interrelationships. However, if the reader is impatient with such discussion, it is possible to skip to the section in the chapter that presents "The New Theoretical Framework," where the discussion of rational analysis begins.

LEVELS OF A COGNITIVE THEORY

Table 1-1 is a reference for this section, in that it tries to relate the terminology of various writers. I start with the analysis of David Marr, which I have found to be particularly influential.

Marr's System of Levels

No sooner had I sent in the final draft of the ACT* book to the publisher than I turned to reading the recently published book by Marr (1982) on

TABLE 1-1
Levels of Cognitive Theory According to Various Cognitive Scientists

Marr	Chomsky	Pylyshyn	Rumelhart and McClelland	Newell	Anderson
Computational Theory	Competence	Semantic Level		Knowledge Level	Rational Level
Representation and Algorithm	Performance	Algorithm	Macrotheory/ Rules	Program Symbol Level	Algorithm
		Functional Architecture	Microtheory PDP models	Register Transfer Level	Implementation
Hardware Implementation		Biological Level		Device	Biological

vision. It contained a very compelling argument about how to do theory development. I read over and over again his prescription for how to proceed in developing a theory:

> We can summarize our discussion in something like the manner shown in Figure 1-4 [our Table 1-2], which illustrates the different levels at which an information-processing device must be understood before one can be said to have understood it completely. At one extreme, the top level, is the abstract computational theory of the device, in which the performance of the device is characterized as a mapping from one kind of information to another, the abstract properties of this mapping are defined precisely, and its appropriateness and adequacy for the task at hand are demonstrated. In the center is the choice of representation for the input and output and the algorithm to be used to transform one into the other. And at the other extreme are the details of how the algorithm and representation are realized physically—the detailed computer architecture, so to speak. These three levels are coupled, but only loosely. The choice of an algorithm is influenced, for example, by what it has to do and by the hardware in which it must run. But there is a wide choice available at each level, and the explication of each level involves issues that are rather independent of the other two (pp. 24–25).

Although algorithms and mechanisms are empirically more accessible, it is the top level, the level of computational theory, which is critically important from an information-processing point of view. The reason for this is that the nature of the computations that underlie perception depends more upon the computational problems that have to be solved than upon the particular hardware in which their solutions are implemented. To phrase the matter another way, an algorithm is likely to be understood more readily by understanding the nature of the problem being solved than by examining the mechanism (and the hardware) in which it is embodied.

In a similar vein, trying to understand perception by studying only neurons is like trying to understand bird flight by studying only feathers: It just cannot

TABLE 1-2
Marr's Description of the Three Levels at Which Any Machine Carrying out an Information-Processing Task Must be Understood

Computational Theory	Representation and Algorithm	Hardware Implementation
What is the goal of the computation, why is it appropriate, and what is the logic of the strategy by which it can be carried out?	How can this computational theory be implemented? In particular, what is the representation for the input and output, and what is the algorithm for the transformation?	How can the representation and algorithm be realized physically?

be done. In order to understand bird flight, we have to understand aerody-
namics; only then do the structure of feathers and the different shapes of
birds' wings make sense. More to the point, as we shall see, we cannot
understand why retinal ganglion cells and lateral geniculate neurons have the
receptive fields they do just by studying their anatomy and physiology. We
can understand how these cells and neurons behave as they do by studying
their wiring and interactions, but in order to understand *why* the receptive
fields are as they are—why they are circularly symmetrical and why their
excitatory and inhibitory regions have characteristic shapes and distributions—we have to know a little of the theory of differential operators,
band-pass channels, and the mathematics of the uncertainty principle (pp.
27–28).

Marr's terminology of "computational theory" is confusing and certainly
did not help me appreciate his points. (Others have also found this
terminology inappropriate—e.g., Arbib, 1987). His level of computational
theory is not really about computation but rather about the goals of the
computation. His basic point is that one should state these goals and
understand their implications before one worries about their computation,
which is really the concern of the lower levels of his theory.

Marr's levels can be understood with respect to stereopsis. At the
computational level, there is the issue of how the pattern of light on each
retina enables inferences about depth. The issue here is not how it is done,
but what should be done. What external situations are likely to have given
rise to the retinal patterns? Once one has a theory of this, one can then
move to the level of representation and algorithm and specify a procedure
for actually extracting the depth information. Having done this, one can
finally inquire as to how this procedure is implemented in the hardware of
the visual system.

Marr compared his computational theory to Gibson's (1966) ecological
optics. Gibson claimed that there were certain properties of the stimulus
which would invariantly signal features in the external world. In his
terminology, the nervous system "resonates" to these invariants. Marr
credited Gibson with recognizing that the critical question is to identify
what in the stimulus array signals what in the real world. However, he
criticized Gibson for not recognizing that, in answering this question, it is
essential to precisely specify what that relationship is. The need for
precision is apparent to someone, like Marr, working on computer vision.
This need was not apparent to Gibson (see Shepard, 1984, for an extensive
analysis of Gibson's theory).

I tried to see how to apply Marr's basic admonition to my own concern,
which was higher-level cognition, but it just did not seem to apply.
Although Marr's prescription seemed fine for vision, it seemed that the
representation and algorithm level was the fundamental level for the study

of human cognition. It was certainly the level that information-processing psychology had progressed along for the last 30 years.

What I initially failed to focus on was the essential but unstated adaptionist principle in Marr's argument. Vision could be understood by studying a problem only if (a) we assumed that vision was a solution to that problem, (b) we assumed that the solution to that problem was largely unique, and (c) we assumed that something forced vision to adopt that solution. For instance, in the case of stereopsis, we had to assume that vision solved the problem of extracting the three-dimensional structure from two two-dimensional arrays, and there was usually a single best interpretation of two two-dimensional arrays. Analysis of the visual environment of humans suggests that there is usually a best interpretation. To pursue Marr's agenda, it is not enough to argue that there is a unique best solution; we also have to believe that there are adaptive forces that created a visual system that would deliver this best solution. Perhaps other aspects of cognition deal with problems that have best solutions, and the organism is similarly adapted to achieve these best solutions. Once I cast what Marr was doing in these terms, I saw the relevance of his arguments to cognition in general.

Marr's hardware-implementation level may still be inapplicable to the study of cognition. It made sense in the case of vision, where the physiology is reasonably well understood. However, the details of the physical base of cognition are still unclear.

Marr's analysis of these levels is very much motivated by the issue of how to make progress in cognitive science. As he saw it, the key to progress is to start off at the level of computational theory. As he bemoaned about the practice of theory in vision:

> For far too long, a heuristic program for carrying out some task was held to be a theory of that task, and the distinction between what a program did and how it did it was not taken seriously. As a result, (1) a style of explanation evolved that invoked the use of special mechanisms to solve particular problems, (2) particular data structures, such as the lists of attribute value pairs called property lists in the LISP programming language, were held to amount to theories of the representation of knowledge, and (3) there was frequently no way to determine whether a program would deal with a particular case other than by running the program. (Marr, 1982, p. 28)

These problems certainly characterize the human information-processing approach to higher level cognition. We pull out of an infinite grab bag of mechanisms, bizarre creations whose only justification is that they predict the phenomena in a class of experiments. These mechanisms are becoming increasingly complex, and we wind up simulating them and trying to understand their behavior just as we try to understand the human. We almost never ask the question of why these mechanisms compute in the way they do.

Chomsky's Competence and Performance

Marr related his distinction to Chomsky's much earlier distinction between competence and performance in linguistics, identifying his computational theory with Chomsky's competence component. As Chomsky (1965) described the distinction:

> Linguistic theory is concerned primarily with an ideal speaker-listener, in a completely homogeneous speech-community, who knows its language perfectly and is unaffected by such grammatically irrelevant conditions as memory limitations, distractions, shifts of attention and interest, and errors (random or characteristic) in applying his knowledge of the language in actual performance. This seems to me to have been the position of the founders of modern general linguistics, and no cogent reason for modifying it has been offered. To study actual linguistic performance, we must consider the interaction of a variety of factors, of which the underlying competence of the speaker-hearer is only one. In this respect, study of language is no different from empirical investigation of other complex phenomena.
>
> We thus make a fundamental distinction between *competence* (the speaker-hearer's knowledge of his language) and *performance* (the actual use of language in concrete situations). Only under the idealization set forth in the preceding paragraph is performance a direct reflection of competence. In actual fact, it obviously could not directly reflect competence. A record of natural speech will show numerous false starts, deviations from rules, changes of plan in mid-course, and so on. The problem for the linguist, as well as for the child learning the language, is to determine from the data of performance the underlying system of rules that has been mastered by the speaker-hearer and that he puts to use in actual performance. (pp. 3–4)

The competence–performance distinction has been the source of a great deal of confusion and controversy. The relationship between competence and performance is really not the same as the relationship between Marr's level of computational theory and his lower levels.[1] In Marr's case, the lower levels achieve the goals of the computational level. Chomsky's competence level is a theory based on a certain subset of data that is thought to be a direct and reliable reflection of the person's linguistic knowledge. For instance, judgments of whether a sentence is grammatically well formed

---

[1]Consequently, some people have questioned why I mentioned Chomsky's distinction at all. The answer is that Chomsky and Marr relate their distinctions to one another, and Chomsky's distinction is very well known.

provide key data for a theory of competence, but time to understand a sentence is thought to be less stable and is consigned to a theory of performance. Performance is somehow constrained to reflect the competence, but it reflects other factors as well. Unlike Marr's case, performance is not just a matter of implementing the goals of competence. Indeed, unlike Marr's computational-level, Chomsky's competence is not concerned with the goals of the system. A computational-level theory of language would have to be concerned with the functionality of language—a concern that Chomsky explicitly rejected. In fact, in contrast to all the other proposals for a higher level, Chomsky's competence is unique, in that it explicitly eschews concerns with functionality. Therefore, it is removed from the other levels in Table 1-1. It is better not thought of as a level in the sense of Marr's levels.

Still, Chomsky used the competence level to serve the same role in theory building as Marr used computational theory. Under both analyses, the scientist should first work out the higher level. Both felt that this was a key to making progress. Also, the lower levels are constrained somehow to reflect the higher levels.

Pylyshyn's Distinction Between Algorithm and Functional Architecture

Pylyshyn (1984) distinguished between three levels that are quite analogous to Marr's three levels. These he called the semantic level, the symbolic level, and the biological level. He developed the semantic level with respect to Newell's concept of a knowledge level, and we turn to reviewing that concept extensively at the end of this section. He had little to say about the biological level beyond making standard arguments for its inadequacy as the sole level of psychological explanation. Of major interest is a distinction he developed within the symbolic level, between mental algorithms and the functional architecture (Pylyshyn, 1980). These are two levels sandwiched between the biological and the semantic. They are very important levels, because they are the levels at which most cognitive psychologists have aimed their research.

The algorithm level is an abstract specification of the steps a system must go through to perform a process. This specification is abstracted away from the functional architecture that actually implements the steps of the algorithm. As Pylyshyn (1984) described the functional architecture:

It includes the basic operations provided by the biological substrate, say, for storing and retrieving symbols, comparing them, treating them differently as a function of how they are stored, (hence, as a function of whether they represent beliefs or goals), and so on, as well as such basic resources and constraints of the system, as a limited memory. It also includes what computer scientists refer to as the "control structure", which selects which rules to apply at various times (p. 30).

Despite his reference to biology, Pylyshyn's functional architecture is an abstraction above the biological level. The analogy Pylyshyn used is that the distinction between the algorithm level and the functional architecture corresponds to the distinction between a canonical computer program and its machine implementation. Pylyshyn's assertion is that there is a particular distinguished algorithm level, rather than the situation in computers where there can be layers of languages each compiling into a lower level. As he wrote: "Rather than a series of levels, we have a distinguished level, the level at which interpretation of the symbols is in the intentional, or cognitive, domain or in the domain of the objects of thought" (Pylyshyn, 1984, p. 95).

One of the examples Pylyshyn used to illustrate the distinction between algorithm and functional architecture is the process of answering questions like "If John is taller than Mary and John is shorter than Fred, who is the tallest?" At the algorithm level, one could imagine a procedure for answering such questions in which each of the premises (e.g., John is taller than Mary) requires placing the terms in an ordered list, and answering the question involves reading off the person at one end of the list. Such a procedure could be implemented in one of many programming languages that would involve a set of instructions. Pylyshyn's interpretation of the algorithm level seems to be, really, the specific programming language rather than the general procedure. The functional architecture would be concerned with the implementation of the instructions of that programming language on a particular machine. Thus, the functional architecture might tell us how long it takes to insert an element into a list or how long it takes to read off the item at the end of the list.

As argued in Anderson (1987a), the assumptions of the ACT* theory can be sorted into assumptions about the algorithm level and assumptions about functional architecture. In ACT*, there is one set of production system principles for representing knowledge states and determining transitions among these knowledge states and another set of principles for computing activation levels for the knowledge structures that determine how these knowledge structures map onto the specifics of behavior like response time. The first set of assumptions is about the algorithm level, and the second is about the functional architecture. Amazingly, I did not realize that the assumptions of my theory were at two levels until 1984 (Anderson, 1984), when I began to think about the implications of the theory for intelligent tutoring. Curiously, it seemed that only the algorithm level had implications for intelligent tutoring, and intelligent tutoring only had implications for the algorithm level.

Pylyshyn introduced an interesting principle to distinguish what belongs to the functional architecture from what belongs to the algorithm level:

Cognitive Impenetrability. **The operations at the functional architecture level are not affected by the organism's goals and beliefs.**

Thus, to call up the standard Sternberg (1969) model of memory scanning, although goals and beliefs determine what digits the subject will compare with what digits, the actual process of comparing one digit to another (the famous 35–40 msec) is not affected by goals and beliefs. Thus, the process of incorporating the experimenter's instructions is at the algorithm level, whereas the actual memory scan is at the level of functional architecture. Cognitive impenetrability gets at the essence of the difference between a symbolic and a subsymbolic level. Only the symbolic level should be influenced by the semantic contents of our knowledge.

McClelland and Rumelhart's PDP Level

A major new surge (to say the least) in cognitive science has been the appearance of connectionist theories, which try to model cognition in terms of units thought to reflect some aspects of neuronal functioning. Some question has arisen as to the level at which such connectionist theories are cast. It might seem obvious that they should be identified with the hardware level of Marr. However, Rumelhart and McClelland (1985), in their reply to Broadbent (1985), noted that their connectionist models (which they call PDP models — see McClelland & Rumelhart, 1986; Rumelhart & McClelland, 1986) are considerably abstracted from the hardware level and are really at the algorithm and representation level. As noted with respect to Pylyshyn's levels (see Table 1-1), Marr's representation and algorithm level can be broken into at least two levels, the levels that Pylyshyn called the algorithm level and the level of functional architecture. In Pylyshyn's terminology, connectionist models are theories at the level of the functional architecture.

Rumelhart and McClelland (1986) argued that the algorithm level is not a real level, but rather that emergent properties of their functional architecture may approximate the rules that other theorists propose for the algorithm level. As they wrote:

There is still another notion of levels which illustrates our view. This is the notion of levels implicit in the distinction between Newtonian mechanics on the one hand and quantum theory on the other. It might be argued that conventional symbol processing models are macroscopic accounts, analogous to Newtonian mechanics, whereas our models offer more microscopic accounts, analogous to quantum theory. Note, that over much of their range, these two theories make precisely the same predictions about behavior of objects in the world. Moreover, the Newtonian theory is often much simpler to compute with since it involves discussions of entire objects and ignores much of their internal structure. However, in some situations Newtonian theory breaks down. In these situations we must rely on the microstructural account of quantum theory. Through a thorough understanding of the relationship between the Newtonian mechanics and quantum theory we can understand that the macroscopic level of description may be *only an approximation* to the more microscopic theory. Moreover, in physics, we understand just when the macrotheory will fail and the microtheory must be invoked. We understand the macrotheory as a useful formal tool by virtue of its relationship to the microtheory. In this sense the objects of the macrotheory can be viewed as *emerging* from interactions of the particles described at the microlevel. (p. 125)

Under some interpretation, McClelland and Rumelhart must be right that the brain only approximates the symbolic rules we ascribe to it. However, the interesting question is, "Under what interpretation?". A computer only approximates the program it is implementing—there are failures of memory, interrupt device processes, overhead of operating systems, small surges of voltage, and so on. However, the approximation in the case of the computer is clearly both good and faithful. The Rumelhart and McClelland enterprise is based on the belief that the brain approximation of the algorithm level is neither good nor faithful. Thus, their point is not just that it is an approximation (surely their own PDP models are approximations in some sense) but that the algorithm level often can be a bad approximation that misses the essence of the behavior at hand.

Their basic reason for believing that the algorithm level is a bad approximation is their belief that learning is defined at the lower level. They used a compiler analogy to make their point. In their analogy, the algorithm level corresponds to a PASCAL program and the lower level to assembly code. Their view is that the mind programs itself at the assembly code level, and the assembly code can only be approximated by PASCAL code.

As they wrote in Rumelhart and McClelland (1985), "Because there is presumably no compiler to enforce the identity of our higher level and lower level descriptions in science, there is no reason to suppose there is a higher level description exactly equivalent to any particular lower level description" (pp. 195-196). Or, as they wrote in Rumelhart and McClelland (1986), "Since there is every reason to suppose that most of the programming that might be taking place in the brain is taking place at a 'lower level' rather than a 'higher level' it seems unlikely that some particular higher level description will be identical to some particular lower level description" (pp. 124–125).

I think they are wrong in this point and that their arguments in the quoted passages are so weak as to be vacuous. The reasoning implicit in both of these passages is basically, "We don't know how the brain does it, therefore it cannot" (i.e., an argument from ignorance). The psychological reality of the algorithm level is very much an empirical question to be decided by whether there are phenomena that can only be explained at this level. A great many phenomena of higher level cognition currently only have explanations at the algorithm level. This includes much of syntactic processing (Pinker & Prince, 1988), almost all of problem solving (Newell & Simon, 1972), learning of problem-solving skills (Anderson, 1981a), and human deduction (Johnson-Laird, 1983). Indeed, there is very little of what is conventionally called "thinking," which has been treated by connectionist models, let alone successfully treated. On the other hand, when we turn to the implementation of these thinking processes, such as memory for the facts being used, connectionist models enjoy great success.

The connectionists are focused on the level of functional architecture, because they believe that this level offers the key insights for making progress towards a successful scientific theory. Rather than the Marr-Chomsky approach of trying to guarantee some overall correctness or well-formedness of the computation, their concern is that the computation takes place in something at least approximating neural elements. As they wrote:

> We have found that information concerning *brain-style* processing has itself been very provocative in our model building efforts. Thus, we have, by and large, not focused on *neural modeling* (i.e., the modeling of neurons), but rather we have focused on *neurally inspired* modeling of cognitive processes. Our models have not depended strongly on the details of brain structure or on issues that are very controversial in neuroscience. Rather, we have discovered that if we take some of the most obvious characteristics of brain-style processing seriously we are led to postulate models which differ in a number of important ways from those postulated without regard for the hardware on which these algorithms are to be implemented. We have found that top-down considerations revolving about a need to postulate parallel, cooperative computational models (cf. Rumelhart, 1977) have meshed nicely with a number of more bottom-up considerations of brain style processing. (Rumelhart & McClelland, 1986, p. 130).

In writing the ACT* book, I was much concerned with this argument and tried to make that theory neurally realistic. I have since come to seriously question the force of the neural constraint for two reasons. As they noted in the preceding quote, our knowledge of neural mechanisms is weak. Thus, it is not clear what are "the most obvious characteristics of brain-style processing," and their neural assumptions may not correspond to what actually happens in the brain, as Crick and Asanuma (1986) complained with respect to PDP models. On the other hand, we may think certain things cannot happen that do and so unnecessarily restrict ourselves. So, we may very well be misguided by a premature insistence on neural fidelity.

However, my deeper concern is that it is not clear that the neural concerns provide much constraint, misguided or not. It is unclear what one cannot predict by a suitable arrangement of neural elements given that they are computationally universal. Even more disturbing, it seems that there are multiple arrangements of neural-like elements that will produce the same phenomena. That is, even if we restrict ourselves to some circumscribed class of neural models, like the PDP class, we will have the identifiability problems that have haunted all cognitive science theorizing at this level. Rather than too much constraint, it is likely to be, once again, a matter of too little.

Newell's Knowledge Level and the Principle of Rationality

As stated in the discussion of Pylyshyn and the PDP models, it is standard practice in cognitive psychology to work at what is variously called the symbol level (Pylyshyn), or the level of representation and algorithm (Marr). No one doubts the existence of a biological level below the symbol level, but we choose to work at the higher level, either because we believe we do not have adequate evidence about the biological level or because we believe we can make progress on psychological issues more rapidly by working at a higher level of abstraction. However, few until Marr and Newell had suggested that it was possible that there was a useful level of analysis above the symbol level. Newell formulated this as his knowledge level hypothesis.

The Knowledge Level Hypothesis. **There exists a distinct computer systems level, lying immediately above the symbol level, which is characterized by knowledge as the medium and the principle of rationality as the law of behavior (Newell, 1982,p. 99).**

As the preceding quote indicates, Newell's development of the knowledge level was originally with respect to computer systems, but he extended it to the human situation. Newell saw a lot of similarity between levels of analysis for the computer and levels of analysis for the human. When speaking of computers, he used the terms *program* or *symbol level* to refer to what Pylyshyn called the *algorithm level,* the term *register-transfer level* to refer to *functional architecture,* and *device level* to refer to the *biological level.* However, our focus is on his *knowledge level,* which corresponds to Pylyshyn's *semantic level.* His statement of this level has proven to be quite influential in artificial intelligence.

The concept that gives precision to Newell's knowledge level is the principle of rationality. As Newell (1982) stated it,

Principle of Rationality. **"If an agent has knowledge that one of its actions will lead to one of its goals, then the agent will select that action,"** (p. 102).

There are a number of undefined terms in this specification, but he did develop what he meant by each:

Goals. The organism is assumed to want certain states of affairs to come to be.

Selection. The claim is that the organism will perform one of the actions it knows to achieve its goals. An important complication is that it is possible that multiple actions will achieve a goal or that multiple goals will conflict in the action they will call for. Here, the knowledge level is silent (although lower levels will not be). It just places constraints on actions, it does not uniquely prescribe them.

Implication. What does it mean to have knowledge that an action will lead to a goal? Newell had in mind the idea that the knowledge logically implies the goal, although he did not want to commit himself at this knowledge level to a particular symbol system to implement the logic.

Knowledge. An obvious definition for knowledge might be something like "whatever the person has encoded from experience," but Newell avoided this, perhaps because it seems impossible to know or even set bounds on what a person might encode from an experience or perhaps because he was writing about computers and not about people. Rather, he offered the following definition: "Whatever can be ascribed to an agent, such that its behavior can be computed according to the principle of rationality" (Newell, 1982, p. 105).

Many people suspect circularity upon reading these various assertions of Newell. Newell's basic position may be summarized thusly: "Knowledge and goals imply behavior." Basically, there are three terms related by the principle of rationality — goals, knowledge, and behavior. Given any two, one can infer or predict the third. Thus, if we know a person's goals and observe his behavior, we can infer his knowledge. Now that we have determined his knowledge, if we manipulate his goals, we should be able to predict his new behavior. Thus, we see that this implicational structure allows us to infer knowledge from one situation and make potentially disconfirmable predictions in a new situation. The appearance of circularity is only illusory.

The important feature of the knowledge level is that it allows an analysis of human behavior abstracted away from any assumptions about the symbols or processes in the human head. For instance, it does not matter whether the person knows *Spinoza was a human* and *Humans have color vision* and infers *Spinoza has color vision,* or whether the person has that fact directly represented. In either case, we can predict what the person will say to the question "Did Spinoza have color vision?" This is because we assume that we know the person's goal (to answer the question) and because, in either case, the principle of rationality predicts the same answer. The difference between these two knowledge representations is a non-distinction as far as the knowledge level is concerned. Note that the knowledge level only predicts the behavior, not how long it takes to calculate it.

Analysis at the knowledge level leads to considerable predictive force. Thus, we can predict that the thirsty person will drink the water offered to him quite independent of any psychological theory at the symbol level. Similarly, we can predict what answer my son will give to a subtraction problem. Indeed, what is amazing to me as a cognitive psychologist (perhaps not amazing to any other type of person) is just how much of human behavior can be predicted without recourse to any of the standard machinery of cognitive psychology. However, there are clear difficulties for the knowledge level. Their clarity is further testimony to the fact that the level has precision.

The example Newell used to show the problems at the knowledge level is the fact that the knowledge level analysis would imply that someone who knows the rules of chess would play a perfect game, because such a game logically follows from this knowledge. To this, Newell acknowledged that the knowledge level is a "radical approximation," and, at many points, predictions derived from it would be overriden by considerations from a lower level, such as the impossibility of searching the game tree for chess in finite human time.

The knowledge level has much in common with Marr's computational level. Both are concerned with the issue of how the goals of the system constrain the behavior of the system. Newell's essential insight is that in the case of cognition, in contrast to vision, a major constraint takes place through the knowledge the person has acquired. However, in contrast to Marr, we do not find Newell making any claims that understanding the knowledge level is a prerequisite to doing research on other agenda in the study of cognition. Indeed, most of Newell's efforts have focused on the symbolic level and the constraint of having this system match the universal computability of the human system.[2] He has taken both biological and rational considerations simply as further constraints on his development of the symbol system.

As mentioned earlier, Newell avoided defining knowledge in terms of experience. As becomes apparent throughout the book, I think a principle of rationality should be defined in terms of a person's experience and not knowledge. The implications of experience are uncertain and fundamentally probabilistic, whereas the implications of knowledge are certain. Because it is experience that people have direct access to and not knowledge, our analysis of what behavior is rational has to face up to the probabilistic structure of uncertainty. As is argued in this chapter, some of the claims about human irrationality make the fallacy of treating uncertain experience as certain knowledge.

CURRENT FORMULATION OF THE LEVELS ISSUE

It is possible to amalgamate the ideas in the literature into a summary formulation that starts with the three levels of Marr's formulation and incorporates Pylyshyn's division of the second level into a level of algorithm and functional architecture. Thus, there are four levels of analysis that I call the rational level, the algorithm level, the implementation level, and the biological level. The highest level is called the rational level both because it is defined in terms of a principle of rationality (not quite Newell's; my principle of rationality is introduced shortly hereafter). The next level is called the algorithm level. The third level is called the implementation level, rather than Pylyshyn's level of functional architecture, because of difficulties with the use of the word architecture.[3] The lowest level is the biological level. Pylyshyn's term *biological level* is preferable to Marr's *hardware level* or Newell's *device level,* because it makes clear that we are talking about what is in the brain and not what is in the computer.

Having settled on names for these levels, however, does not settle the issue of their psychological reality. First, I begin with a bold assertion: When all is said and done and we know the truth about what is happening in the human brain, there will turn out to be only two levels of analysis that are psychologically real (i.e., in the brain). They are the algorithm level and the biological level. Marr had it right, and, despite practice in cognitive psychology, there is no intermediate implementation level except as an approximation useful in calculation. That is to say, Rumelhart and McClelland have it just wrong—it is not the algorithm level that has the

---

[2]Indeed, Marr (1982) was quite critical of Newell for this emphasis.

[3]As discussed in Anderson (1987a), architecture is better used to refer to the interface between the algorithm level and the implementation level.

status of Newtonian mechanics; it is the implementation level. The implementation level is an approximation to the biological level. We need it because we do not begin to know enough about the brain to specify the biological level. Thus, we need the implementation level as a computational approximation and as a holding position. Without it, as Pylyshyn has argued, we would not have any interpretation of the costs of the operations at the algorithmic level and would not be able to predict the temporal or reliability properties of various mental algorithms. However, it should be recognized as an approximation. There is no convincing evidence or argument that there is any real level between the biological and the algorithm level.

Not only does the implementation level lack true psychological reality, it has identifiability problems. That is to say, it is not possible to decide between many claims about the implementation level, such as whether processes are going on in parallel or serial (Townsend, 1974), the format of the knowledge representation (Anderson, 1978), or whether there is a distinct short-term memory (Crowder, 1982a). Of course, if implementation level theories are just crude approximations, there will be real limitations on our ability to discriminate among theories, because one cannot perform exacting tests of an approximate theory. However, the identifiability problem goes beyond this approximation limitation: The relationship of the implementation level to behavioral data is too indirect to allow identifiability, even if it were not an approximation. I expand on this issue of identifiability in the next section.

The Algorithm Level[4]

Given my pessimism about the reality and tractability of the implementation level, it might seem remarkable that I am optimistic in both senses about the algorithm level. The fundamental reason for my optimism about the reality of the algorithm level is my belief in Newell and Simon's (1976) physical symbol hypothesis, which Newell (1980a) stated as "The necessary and sufficient condition for a physical system to exhibit general intelligent action is that it be a physical symbol system" (p. 170). A physical symbol system is a system that manipulates symbols. Symbols, as they are used in the physical symbol hypothesis, are tokens that in essence are pointers to knowledge stored elsewhere. For instance, a variable, as it is used in a computer program, is a symbol. Symbols are basically the structures out of which the algorithm level is defined. This physical symbol hypothesis is basically a conjunction of two observations: (a) The only way we know how

---

[4]For a more complete discussion of the research issues at the algorithm level, read Anderson (1987a).

to achieve intelligence is by use of symbols, and (b) we now know a (growing) number of ways in which symbols can be implemented and manipulated in physical systems. From (a) and (b) the argument is made that the only way physical systems (including humans) can achieve their intelligence is by use of symbols.

The argument for the physical symbol hypothesis could be strengthened if we could argue that symbols are the only way to achieve intelligence, rather than the only *known* way, as just argued. The best argument that I have read to this effect is one that was recently made by Newell (in press):

It is a law of nature that processing in the physical world is always local, that is, always takes places in a limited region of physical space. This is equivalent to there being no action at a distance, or, somewhat more specifically, that causal effects propagate with an upper velocity of c, the speed of light in vacuo. Consequently, any computational system ultimately does its work by localized processing within localized regions in space. What guides or determines this processing task must then also be local. If the task is small enough or simple enough, then the processes could have been assembled within the local region and the task accomplished. Ultimately, there is no alternative to doing it this way. However, with complex enough processing, additional structure from outside the local region will be required at some point during the processing. If it is required, it must be obtained. If it must be obtained, then some process must do it, using structure within the local region to determine when and how to go outside.

The symbol token is the device in the medium that determines where to go outside the local region to obtain more structure. The process has two phases: first, the opening of *access* to the distal structure that is needed; and second, the *retrieval* (transport) of that structure from its distal location to the local site, so it can actually affect the processing. When to go outside is determined by when the processing encounters the symbol token in a fashion that requires the missing structure. . . .

Hidden in this account is the basic proposition behind information theory, namely, that for a given technology there is a limit to the amount of structure that can be obtained in a given region of physical space. In information theory this is expressed as the channel or memory capacity, and it is measured in bits. But its foundation is the amount of variety in physical structure, given that there is a limit to the amount of energy that is available to detect it. It applies to all systems, discrete and continuous (Shannon, 1949). Thus, as the demands for variety increase—corresponding ultimately to the demands for variety in functions to be composed, the local capacity will be exceeded and distal access will be required to variety elsewhere. Thus, there must be something within the local site that indicates what additional knowledge is needed.

To summarize: All processing must be done locally. Only so much knowledge can be stored locally. True intelligence can require using unbounded knowledge. Hence, we need the access and retrieval functions that are the essence of symbols. Newell's argument leaves open the question of how much of human cognition involves symbols, because much of human cognition does not involve unbounded use of knowledge.

Given that the algorithm level is tied to symbols, it is the level at which Pylyshyn's principle of cognitive penetrability applies. It is here that knowledge is brought to bear with full force and so can influence cognition. In addition to cognitive penetrability, my conception of the algorithm level is distinguished by the fact that steps of cognition at the algorithm level are correlated with observable behaviors. It is this issue of relationship to behavioral data that we turn to next.

Behavioral Data

Under the ACT* theory and many other theories, steps of cognition at the algorithm level correspond to points of discrete changes in working memory. In ACT*, these discrete changes are produced by a production firing that enters new information into working memory. In contrast, a step of cognition at the implementation level in ACT* corresponds to a change in activation pattern. In ACT*, these changes in activation pattern are continuous, and even when simulated discretely there will be 10–100 of these steps at the implementation level before there is a step at the algorithm level (i.e., a production firing).

It is important that different states at the algorithmic level are correlated with changes in working memory states. A change in the state of working memory can result in external behaviors. Thus, one can use the steps of behavior of a subject to infer the steps of cognition at the algorithm level. Of course, steps at the algorithm level can pass by without any behavior, but much of the methodology of cognitive science can be aimed at bringing out behavioral indicants. I have used the term *protocol* to refer to any rich sequence of behaviors elicited by the experimenter to try to trace changes in working memory. Verbal protocols are the most common protocol methodology and succeed in situations where states of working memory are verbally reportable. However, other protocol methodologies include use of streams of terminal interactions (keystrokes, mouse clicks) or eye movements, and, in many situations, such methodologies might be preferable. The essence of a protocol is that it provide a running series of responses that can be used to infer the sequence of mental states.

Protocols, at their best, offer the prospect of providing a state-by-state description of the transitions at the algorithmic level, and the scientist is simply left with the task of inducing the rules that determine these transitions. Protocols in real life are never so fine-grained as to report every state, nor are the reports sufficiently rich to discriminate between all possible pairs of states; however, they are a major advance over the situation at the implementation level. There are problems with the use of protocols and many more incorrect criticisms of their use (see Ericsson & Simon, 1984, for a thorough discussion of the issues). Many of the false criticisms of protocols stem from the belief that they are taken as sources of psychological theory rather than as sources of data about states of the mind. To serve the latter function, one need not require that the subject accurately interpret his mental states, but only that the theorist can specify some mapping between his behavior and states of the mind.

Note that the argument is not that the algorithm level has behavioral consequences and the implementation level does not. Rather, it is that the transitions at the algorithm level have direct behavioral indicants, whereas the transitions at the implementation level are only indirectly inferable from the behavioral indicants at the algorithm level. As an example of this point, consider the Sternberg task. In this task, subjects are shown a small study set of digits and then asked to decide whether a particular test digit is in that set. At the algorithm level, this can be modeled as a rather trivial task (e.g., see the ACT* model in Anderson, 1983): A single step is involved in deciding whether the test digit is in the memory set or not. A unique behavioral indicant of this is given—the subject says "yes" or "no." The Sternberg task has been of interest as a domain in which to study the implementation level. Many theories (Baddeley & Ecob, 1973; Glass, 1984; Sternberg, 1969, 1975; Theios, Smith, Haviland, Troupmann, & Moy, 1973) have been proposed in which detailed comparisons are being carried out between the test digit and the items in memory set either in serial or parallel. The behavioral data that has principally been used to decide among such theories is reaction time—the time for subjects to make this judgment. This does not give us a behavioral indicant for each step in the process but rather only a final datum. As a consequence of the poverty of the data relative to the complexity of the implementation level theories, it is generally regarded as impossible to decide such issues as whether the comparisons are being performed in serial or parallel.

This identification of the algorithm level with the behavioral function of the cognitive system is more abstract than the interpretation advocated by Anderson (1987a) or by Pylyshyn (1984), who basically identified it with a programming language. A programming language comes with a commitment to a particular syntax and potentially has implementation constraints. Rather, our use of algorithm is at a level of abstraction more like its typical use in computer science where it is an abstract specification of computation that can be realized in many computer languages. Issues of syntax are issues of architecture, namely the notation that interfaces the algorithm level and the implementation level.

The Rational Level

So far, I have discussed three levels of analysis: a biological level, which is real but almost inaccessible to cognitive theorizing, the approximate but essential implementation level, and the real and accessible algorithmic level. Is there a higher level where we should begin our inquiry, as Marr and Chomsky have advocated? As indicated in Table 1-1, I think there is a higher level, called the rational level, which is close in character to Marr's computational level. This book is mainly devoted to developing theory at the rational level, although it contains some speculations about how this relates to issues at other levels.

The rational level of analysis offers a different cut at human behavior. It is not an attempt to propose an information-processing analysis of mind at some level of aggregation from the molecular to the behavioral. It is not "psychologically real," in the sense that it does not assert that any specific computation is occurring in the human head. Rather, it is an attempt to do an analysis of the criteria that these computations must achieve to assure the rationality of the system. This turns out to be an important level at which to develop psychological theory, but a theory at this level is not directly about what the mechanisms of the mind are. Rather, it is about constraints on the behavior of the system in order for that behavior to be optimal. If we assume that cognition is optimized, these behavioral constraints are con-straints on the mechanisms. This level of analysis is important, because it can tell us a lot about human behavior and the mechanisms of the mind. The function of this book is to demonstrate the usefulness of the rational level of analysis.

The idea that we might understand human behavior by assuming it is adapted to the environment is hardly new. It started with the functionalist school in the beginnings of American psychology (e.g., Dewey, 1910; James, 1892). More recently, it has been associated with psychologists such as Brunswik (1956), Campbell (1974), and Gibson (1966). We have already discussed at length the adaptionist basis of Marr's contribution to vision. Neisser's (1976; 1982) emphasis on understanding cognition in ecologically valid situations has adaptionist components to its motivation. Cosmides (1989) and Shepard (1987) represent recent efforts to develop analyses with very explicit evolutionary connections. Shepard's work is particularly close to the material in Chapter 3 and we will include there some specific discussion of his theory.

Thus, in proposing a rational analysis of human cognition I can hardly claim to have invented the wheel. However, there is something quite different about the wheel that is being described in this book. This is a result of both how rational analysis is related to the various levels of a cognitive theory and because of the particular research program attached to rational analysis. It is more in keeping with the spirit of the rational-man analysis in economics (from which it borrowed its name) than with most other applications in psychology (the spirit is similar, however, to Marr and Shepard). In particular, it leads us to formal models of the environment from which we derive behavior. Thus, its spirit is one which focuses us on what is outside the head rather than what is inside and one which demands mathematical precision. The next section of this chapter describes the new theoretical framework associated with rational analysis.

THE NEW THEORETICAL FRAMEWORK

Although the proposals in this book differ in some details from other proposals advanced in the ACT* book, the more substantial difference concerns the philosophy from which they are developed. This philosophy comes from merging a negative conclusion about the goals of cognitive science with a positive conclusion about its prospects. On the negative side, I have come to appreciate the profound lack of identifiability in the enterprise of cognitive science. On the positive side, I have come to realize the considerable guidance that rational considerations provide. I first consider the negative point and then the positive.

Lack of Identifiability at the Implementation Level

Cognitive psychology would be a rather unreal science if we worked only at the algorithm level. Our minds are not abstract algorithms left to compute away but have significant temporal and reliability properties. Thus, one has to consider implementation-level issues, but it is rather dissatisfying to pursue implementation-level theories in face of their identifiability problems. Because the rational level offers a different cut at cognition (rather than a higher level of abstraction), it allows one to pursue issues of the temporal and reliability properties of human cognition in a way that is free from problems of approximation and identifiability. It also allows one to view these properties as design features of the human mind, rather than as design flaws. Thus, the issue of identifiability proves to be a substantial part of the motivation for the rational analyses of this book. This subsection is devoted to making that point in more detail.

If we confine ourselves to behavioral data, then by definition all we can see are the steps of mind at the algorithm level. Even here we do not really see the steps of the mind, but rather their behavioral consequences. Any theory of cognition that confines itself to behavioral data has to be judged by how well it does at predicting the specific behaviors that occur in response to specific experiences. That is, we are limited to what goes into the system and what comes out — where "what comes out" includes things like response latency or intensity. A large fraction of cognitive psychologists — myself included — have taken as our goal to induce what is happening in the mind at the implementation level from this information. Recall that the implementation level is concerned with a model of the mental steps that take place between overt behaviors.

I have tip-toed around the feasibility of this enterprise for the last 10 years, because it would be unpopular to say it could not be done. However, the pretense can no longer be maintained, and so I will bluntly say that it is just not possible to use behavioral data to develop a theory of the implementation level in the concrete and specific terms to which we have aspired. A number of people have argued elaborate special cases of this non-identifiability (Anderson, 1978; Townsend, 1974). The general case can be argued so simply that it is hard to believe that the field has not accepted the conclusion long ago.

Basically, what we are trying to induce is the function that maps input to output. We choose to specify this function as a set of mechanisms, but this should not obscure the fact that these mechanisms compute an input-output function, and it is this function that we can empirically test. Said another way, if two different sets of mechanisms compute the same input–output function, there is no way to discriminate among them. Now, one of the simple things we know from work on formal machine theory is that there is an infinite number of mechanisms that compute the same input–output functions. That is, there is a many-to-one mapping from mechanisms to behavioral functions, and, consequently, identifying the behavioral function will not identify the mechanism. So, behavioral data will never tell us what is in the mind at the implementation level. It is time we stopped fooling ourselves.[5]

Responses to Lack of Identifiability.   There are three standard responses to this dilemma. One is to appeal to parsimony and assume that the simplest set of mechanisms is correct. This might offer some hope of deciding within a circumscribed class of machines like Turing machines, but parsimony is meaningless when we compare different classes of computing mechanisms, such as PDP models and production systems. It is not possible to define an objective and acceptable metric to compare the parsimony of theories in such different formalisms. The inability of advocates of either class to make headway in arguing against the other should convince us of that. Second, as has been argued elsewhere (Anderson, 1983), it stretches credulity beyond any reasonable bounds to assume that nature chose the

---

[5]In the Appendix, I deal with counter claims based on considerations of computational complexity and processing time.

most parsimonious design for the mind. Thus, even if parsimony were capable of settling scientific disputes, it has no chance of telling us what is in the human head.

The second response is to argue optimistically that if we have enough data from enough phenomena of sufficient complexity, then the identifiability problem would go away. The supposed insight is that if we have enough behavioral constraints, there will be only one mechanism that satisfies them. However, identifiability problems do not go away with behavioral complexity. Again, this is easy to see in formal function and machine theory. There are lots of equivalent versions of complex Turing machines. All the complexity does is make it harder to choose. In general, identifiability problems are simpler when the behavior is simpler. There are a lot fewer programs that might be reasonably written[6] to write "hello" than to parse a sentence. Indeed, my reason for optimism about identifiability at the algorithm level is that at that level of abstraction we have to account for simple one-step transitions between reportable states rather than complex sequences of unobserved computations.

The third response to the identifiability problem is to appeal to physiological data to help tell us what is going on. The advantage of physiological data is that it offers the potential of providing a one-to-one tracing of the implementation level, just as protocols provide the potential for that kind of tracing of the algorithm level. Our knowledge of the mechanisms of early vision has developed because of physiological data. The right kind of physiological data to obtain is that which traces out the states of computation of the brain. Although there is still far to go, there has been considerable recent progress on this score (Dawson & Schell, 1982; Donchen, McCarthy, Kutas, & Ritter, 1983; Farah, 1988; Phelps & Massiotta, 1985; Posner, Peterson, Fox, & Raichle, 1988; Roland & Friberg, 1985). The wrong kind of physiological constraint is to make arguments based on things like speed of neural processing. As witness that this is the wrong kind of constraint, three very different theories (ACT* – Anderson, 1983; SOAR – Newell, in press; and PDP – McClelland & Rumelhart, 1986; Rumelhart & McClelland, 1986) have been proposed and defended in terms of neural timing.

Conclusion About the Identifiability Issue.   The study of cognitive behavior is an interesting and worthwhile endeavor, despite the identifiability problem at the implementation level. We are making important progress in the absence of physiological data. For many purposes, such as application to education, such a physiological base would be excess

---

[6]By "reasonable" I mean to exclude programs with useless steps. If we were to allow them, the identifiability problem would only be worse.

baggage. However, when we are inducing a scientific theory from behavioral data, we should not lose track of what we are doing. We are inducing an *abstract* function that maps input to output. We need a notation for codifying that function so we can communicate it to others, reason about it, and derive predictions. This is what our cognitive architectures and implementation theories provide us with—a system of notation for specifying the function. We should not ascribe any more ontological significance to the mechanisms of that architecture than we do to an integral sign in a calculus expression. If two theorists propose two sets of mechanisms in two architectures that compute the same function, then they are proposing the same theory. There are still bases for choosing among notations such as simplicity and tractability, but we are not choosing among scientific theories when we do so; we are choosing among notations for the same theory according to their convenience. To summarize, the argument is not that we should abandon developing implementation theory, but rather that their scientific claims should be read as the abstract behavioral functions they compute, not the specific mechanisms proposed. Part of the attraction of a rational approach is that it provides a way of specifying these functions without commitment to mechanism.

It should be clear how this position resembles behaviorism and how it differs. Behaviorism was correct in its usually unstated assumption that you cannot infer the mechanisms in the black box from what goes in and what comes out. It was incorrect in going from that to its claims that there should be restrictions on the notation with which theories are stated. The consequences of these restrictions was to produce theories that were incapable of computing the complex cognitive functions that people could. Said another way, the inadequacy of behaviorism was not its claim that a scientific theory was a mapping from stimulus to response but in the unnecessary restrictions it placed on the computational power of the mapping. All successful criticisms of behaviorist theories have focused on their computational power. The success of modern cognitive psychology stems from the computational power of our theories.

The Principle of Rationality

One of the consequences of our excessive concern with mechanism is that we often act as if God created the mind more or less arbitrarily, out of bits and pieces of cognitive mechanisms, and our induction task is to identify an arbitrary configuration of mechanisms. Of course, this is not the modern scientific understanding of human nature. The human is not a random construction but a construction that has been, to some degree, optimized to its environment by evolution. The behavior computed by our cognitive mechanisms must be optimized to some degree and in some sense. If we could only specify that degree and sense, we would be in a position to place enormous constraints on our proposals for cognitive mechanisms, both at the implementation level and the algorithm level. This is the strongest appeal of a rational approach.

Evolutionary Optimization.   It is a hard issue to specify to what degree and in what sense we would expect to see human cognition optimized. I have tried to work through current ideas about evolutionary optimization (a very controversial area – see Dupre, 1987, for a representative set of readings). Here is my summary of the consensus (such as there is one) cast in terms familiar to a cognitive scientist rather than the terms from that literature: At any stable point in evolution, a species should display a range of variability in traits. The differences in this range are not sufficiently important in their adaptive value that any have been selected out. There may be some change in the species during this stable stage because of a phenomenon known as genetic drift, in which the distribution of nonsignificant variability changes. The optimization process might get called on if some truly novel genetic variation is created by some random mutation. However, it is generally thought that optimization is more generally called in when the environment undergoes some significant change after which the former range of traits is no longer equivalent in terms of adaptive value. This is the view that sees changes in the environment as more significant in driving evolutionary history than are random changes in genetic code.

The significance of this viewpoint is that it characterizes evolution as a local optimizer. I understand this in terms of a hill-climbing metaphor in which the set of possible traits defines the space, and the adaptive value defines height. At a stable point in time, the species is at some point or plateau of a local maximum. When there is an environmental change, the contours of the space change, and the species may no longer be at a maximum. It will climb along the slope of steepest ascent to a new maximum and reside there. Extinction of a species occurs when it is not possible to adapt to the environmental changes. New species appear when different members of one species evolve to adapt to different environments. This means that the optimum that any species achieves is a function of the constraints of its past. Maybe humans would be better adapted with the social structure of insects, but given our mammaliam origins, there is no path of hill climbing from where we are to this hypothetical global maximum.

Within the hill-climbing metaphor, there are two major constraints on prediction by optimization analyses. One is the proximity structure on the space of traits, and the other is where the species currently is in that space. Only certain variations are reachable from its current location. So consider the case of the moths of Manchester that serve as a standard illustration of evolutionary optimization. When pollution became a major factor in Manchester, the former peppered gray moth was no longer optimal in avoiding predators, and a mutant black moth largely replaced it. There are other conceivable morphological responses to predators as effective—or more so—than changing color. For instance, one could imagine the development of offensive weapons such as possessed by other insects. However, moth mutants with offensive weapons do not occur, but color mutants do. Thus, color was a direction that was open for hill-climbing, but offensive weaponry was not.[7]This means that any species or aspect of a species is optimized, subject to some constraints that depend on evolutionary history and that can be pretty arbitrary and complex. The more arbitrary and complex these constraints, the less explanation there will be in appealing to optimization. The general lesson we can take from optimization explanations is that, in some cases, much explanatory power is achieved by appealing to optimization, and, in other cases, little explanatory power is achieved. Optimal foraging theory (e.g., Stephens & Krebs, 1986) is a field where we see a full range of explanatory outcomes from an optimization analysis. My book explores the question of how much explanatory power can be achieved in the case of human cognition. In particular, this book is an exploration of the following hypothesis.

General Principle of Rationality. **The cognitive system operates at all times to optimize the adaptation of the behavior of the organism.**

I have called this the principle of rationality, because it has a lot in common with the economist's position that people are rational agents and their economic behavior can simply be predicted on the assumption that they optimize their economic self-interests. This is a controversial position and one that it seems most people view as wrong, at least in detail (Hogarth & Reder, 1986). It is also generally viewed in psychology that people are anything but rational creatures and that their intellectual functions are shot through with intellectual fallacies. I try to reconcile the current position with this general wisdom in psychology in the last section of this chapter.

Part of the problem is with the term *rationality*. It has evolved two senses in social science. Perhaps the more obvious sense (which is close to Newell's sense) is that humans explicitly engage in logically correct reasoning in deciding what to do. Criticisms of human rationality are often arguments that humans do not do this. The second sense is that human behavior is optimal in terms of achieving human goals. This is the position in economics and the position advanced in this book. It explicitly disavows

---

[7]My 4-year-old son, who is enamored with "Teenage Mutant Ninja Turtles," has a different view about the plausibility of mutating offensive weaponry.

any claims about the mechanisms in the human head that achieve this optimization—they certainly do not have to involve logical calculation. (Only the theorists' predictions about human behavior require logical calculations.) It would have, perhaps, been less contentious and also perhaps clearer if I had chosen to call my principle the "principle of adaptation." However, I chose the terminology by analogy to economics before I appreciated its unfortunate consequences. Now I am stuck with it. At least I have tried to choose the right title for the book.

The principle should be taken as a scientific hypothesis to be judged by how well it does in organizing the data. One should not be surprised to find it doing well at explaining some aspects of cognition and not others. Obviously, I would not be writing this book if I did not believe I had achieved some success. My own sense is that cognition is likely to be one of the aspects of the human species that is most completely optimized and optimized in a clean, simple way so that it will yield to scientific analysis. This is because cognition seems one of the more malleable of human traits and, hence, more easily optimized and not as much subject to the constraints of evolutionary history. However, this is merely bias. The proof or disproof of the conjecture should not come from a priori considerations, but from how well the principle of rationality does in leading to successful theory.

Applying the Principle of Rationality

How does one use the principle of rationality to develop a theory of cognition? Developing a theory in a rationality framework involves the following six steps:

1. Precisely specify what are the goals of the cognitive system.
2. Develop a formal model of the environment to which the system is adapted (almost certainly less structured than the standard experimental situation).
3. Make the minimal assumptions about computational limitations. This is where one specifies the constraints of evolutionary history. To the extent that these assumptions are minimal, the analysis is powerful.
4. Derive the optimal behavioral function given items 1 through 3.
5. Examine the empirical literature to see if the predictions of the behavioral function are confirmed.
6. If the predictions are off, iterate. In my own experience, my problems have been with the mathematical analyses required in step 4, which can often be quite complex.

The theory in a rational approach resides in the assumptions in items 1 through 3, from which the predictions flow. I refer to these assumptions as the *framing of the information-processing problem.* Note that this is a nearly mechanism-free casting of a psychological theory. Ideally, most of the interesting assumptions in this theory come in step 2, because the structure of the environment is what is easiest to verify. One can, in principle, look and see if these assumptions are objectively true of the world. To the extent that assumptions in step 3 play a significant role, this ideal is only approximated. The reader will find in subsequent chapters that the computational assumptions are indeed weak, involving claims that almost all information-processing theories would agree on (such as a short-term memory limitation of some sort or that it takes time to process an alternative.)

It is worth commenting on the fact that this process of theory building is iterative. If one framing does not work, we have to be prepared to try another. Such iterative behavior has often been seen as a sign that an adaptionist enterprise is fatally flawed (Gould & Lewontin, 1979). However, as Mayr (1983) noted in response to Gould & Lewontin, iterative theory construction is the way of all science. Certainly, in cognitive science, we have seen a long iteration of mechanisms to explain cognition. Hopefully, we understand in cognitive science that a theory is to be evaluated by how well it does in organizing the data and not by whether it is the nth theory that has been tried. Having acknowledged this, I must note that my own experience with theory construction in the rationalist framework is less iterative than my experience with theory construction in the mechanistic framework. This is what we would hope for—that rational considerations would provide more guidance in theory construction.

Advantages of Rational Theory

In summary, let me list the advantages of the rational approach in order of increasing importance:

1.   It offers a way to avoid the indentifiability problems of the mechanistic approach. One has a theory that depends on the structure of an observable environment and not on the unobservable structure in the head.

2.   It offers an explanation for why the mechanisms compute the way they do. We do not have to view the human mind as a random set of postulates let loose on the world.

3.   It offers real guidance to theory construction. If the mind is not a random set of mechanisms, but is structured to optimize its adaptation, one can use the hypothesis of optimization to guide the search for a scientific theory. Otherwise, one has to rely on very weak methods to search a very large space of psychological hypotheses.

As Marr stressed, a special case of the third point is the role that a rational analysis can have in guiding the design of mechanistic theories at the algorithm and implementation levels. I hope to be able to follow up the analysis in this book with a new theory within the ACT framework to update the ACT* theory (see Anderson, 1983, for a discussion of the distinctions between frameworks and theories). Such a new theory will take advantage of the guidance of a rational theory.

Although a rational explanation is more satisfying than a mechanistic explanation in terms of point number 2 in the preceding list, there is another sense in which mechanistic explanations are more satisfying: For whatever reason, we enjoy having an image of what might be happening in the head. Thus, even if a rational theory could predict all the relevant data, we would want to pursue a mechanistic theory. Rational and mechanistic approaches need not be in conflict. We can take Marr's view that the rational analysis provides the needed guidance for the mechanistic approach. We can emerge from our scientific endeavor with both an answer to what is happening (modulo identifiability limitations) and why it is happening (modulo the relativism of adaptation because of evolutionary history and biological constraint).

IS HUMAN COGNITION RATIONAL?

As indicated earlier, it is common wisdom in psychology that humans are irrational, and this seems to go to the heart of the proposal in this book. Many a person has, in effect, said to me, "Your analyses are interesting, but they must be wrong, because human thought has been shown not to be rational." Most of these demonstrations of human irrationality come from the fields of decision making and social judgment and are not from the more basic cognitive domains that are the focus of this book. The basic resolution of this apparent contradiction between the results of these other fields and the current book is that rationality is being used in two senses and that rationality in the adaptive sense, which is used here, is not rationality in the normative sense that is used in studies of decision making and social judgment. For an extensive discussion of these two views of human rationality and their relationship to evolution, see Stich (in press).

It is possible that humans are rational in the adaptive sense in the domains of cognition studied here but not in decision making and social judgment. However, in this section, I argue that many of the purported demonstrations of human irrationality are demonstrations in the normative sense and not the adaptive sense. I enumerate in the following subsections some of the ways in which criteria of normative rationality can deviate from criteria of adaptive rationality.

Computational Cost

One problem with normative definitions of rationality is that they ignore computational cost. This is nicely illustrated in the application of Newell's principle of rationality to chess. There, the observation was that knowledge of the rules of chess plus Newell's principle of rationality implied playing a perfect game of chess. As Newell noted, this ignores the astronomical cost of searching the entire game-tree of moves. In an adaptive analysis, one has to place the cost of performing the computation into the equation to be optimized (step 3 in our prescription for developing a theory on a rational framework). This makes the principle of rationality developed here more like Simon's (1972) theory of bounded rationality, although Simon has insisted that there is a difference (see Simon, in press, and the discussion in Chapter 6).

This observation is one of the potential Achilles' heels of a rational approach. If we have to know computational cost to know what is rational, we may have to specify the mechanisms of cognition in advance of rational analysis. This is just what we are trying to avoid. However, I hope to be able to illustrate that we can progress with very weak assumptions about computational cost. This is certainly the case in the analysis of the chess dilemma.

Is There an Adaptive Cost?

A question that is rarely asked is whether there is really a cost associated with the purported irrationality. If a person prefers A to B, B to C, and C to A, but there are no differences among A, B, and C in their adaptive value, then the intransitivity does not violate the adaptive principle of rationality. It is important to stress that adaptation in the genetic sense is measured in number of surviving offspring (which is what controls evolutionary selection) and not money, power, or happiness. Thus, the gambler's fallacy may lead someone to lose money in Las Vegas, but if it leads him or her to try for a third child after two boys (because a girl is due), then it is quite adaptive.

Nisbett and Ross (1980), after documenting the abundance of experimental evidence for a number of intellectual fallacies, noted that some of them may have little cost. A good example is the primacy effect, where people give too much weight to initial evidence and discount later evidence. Suppose, for example, that primitive man is trying to decide which of two fishing spots yields a better chance of catching a fish. Suppose he samples one and succeeds. The primacy effect means that he is going to tend to discount later evidence about the efficiency of the two fishing holes and continue with the first. Conversely, if his first experience is bad, he will tend to avoid that fishing hole, irrespective of later experiences. Such behavior is not rational in a normative sense.

The interesting question is "How irrational is it in an adaptive sense?". On careful analysis, Nisbett and Ross concluded that it is not very costly at all. If the fishing holes yield a very similar probability of a fish, then it would not matter which hole was chosen. If one hole had a near-one probability of yielding a fish and the other had a near-zero probability, primitive man would choose the right one, despite the primacy effect, because it is very unlikely that his first experience would be misleading, and even if it was it would be quickly overwhelmed by subsequent experience. (The primacy effect is not so strong that we totally ignore all subsequent experience).[8]

Heuristics Need to Be Evaluated in Terms of Expected Value

People act according to principles that cannot be guaranteed to be correct and can fail in specific cases. Such principles are called heuristics, and there is no reason why normatively irrational heuristics cannot be adaptive. For instance, many people are likely not to believe an argument if they perceive that the arguer does not believe it. According to normative models, the validity of an argument is a function of the argument and not the beliefs of the arguer. However, it is an open question whether, given the fallibility of validity judgment, people are more likely to come to erroneous beliefs behaving in accord with this heuristic.

---

[8]To explore this more systematically, one must make some assumptions about the distribution of successful fishing holes. Suppose that there is a uniform distribution from zero to one of successful fishing holes in terms of probability of catching a fish on a given day. That is to say, the chances that a new fishing hole will yield a probability p of catch each day is the same for all p. This means that if our primitive man chose randomly which hole to fish at, his expected probability of catching a fish any day would be .50. On the other hand, if he were omniscient and knew which of the two holes was best, he could expect to catch a fish 2/3 of the time. Said another way, the omniscient primitive man would catch 1/3 more fish than the random primitive man, giving him a considerable survival advantage. Of course, primitive man could not be omniscient. But let us suppose he was rational, took a modest sample, and went with the evidence of that sample. Suppose he tried the first hole three times and the second hole twice, and went with whichever hole yielded the most fish, choosing the second hole if there was a tie. This would yield him an expected .625 chance of a fish per day, or 94% of the omniscient maximum. However, primitive man is not rational. Suppose he showed such a strong primacy effect that he would choose the second hole after a successful first catch only if he failed on his other two samples of the first hole and succeeded with his two samples of the second. Similarly, he would only choose the first hole after a failure to get a first catch if his next two tries at the first hole were successful and his two tries at the second hole both failed. It turns out that his expected catch per day would be .603, or 96% of the rational man's catch. Presumably, this does not convey much of a survival disadvantage.

A case that Nisbett and Ross discussed in detail is the fallacy in human judgment that causes should resemble their effects. J.S. Mill (1843/1974) wrote, "The most deeply-rooted fallacy . . . is that the conditions of a phenomenon must, or at least probably will, resemble the phenomenon itself" (p. 765). Nisbett and Ross (1980) documented some of the mispractices of medicine that derive from this. For instance, in medieval times the lungs of foxes were prescribed as a cure for asthma, because the animal was regarded as remarkable for its strong power of respiration. People ridiculed the hypothesis that yellow fever might be caused by mosquitoes. Much human suffering has been created or prolonged by the insistence that causes must resemble their effects.

However, use of similarity is, on the whole, rational — as is expanded on in chapter 4. We can reject many spurious correlations as noncausal because of total lack of similarity between purported cause and effect. We do not want to believe that roosters' crowing causes the sun to rise, that lying in bed causes one to vomit, or that being homosexual causes one to have AIDS. As Nisbett and Ross conceded, the similarity heuristic has probably guided medical discovery such as vaccination, the use of cold compacts to treat burns, and the relationship of smoking to lung cancer. The use of similarity is a heuristic, and any heuristic can sometimes lead one far astray. The only claim is that one will do better on average if one follows it than if one ignores it.

Applications of Normative Models Often Treat Uncertain Information as Certain

If I were to take issue with the validity of any demonstrations of human irrationality in the normative sense, it would be with certain applications of normative models in defining rational behavior. Normative prescriptions take the form of "If situation X holds, then action Y is prescribed." Many applications overestimate the certainty of knowing whether situation X holds. For instance, consider a recent set of medical decisions I had to make. I was told by an internist, and then by a surgeon, that I had an indirect hernia (it had no symptoms that I could detect), that there was a 5% chance it would become strangulated, and that strangulated hernias are fatal 30% of the time and result in serious complications 50% or more of the time. I was told that a hernia operation was nearly totally free of danger and complication. These facts were basically confirmed as common medical knowledge by a number of nonsurgeon physician friends who had no interest in the surgeon's fees and presumably some interest in my welfare. Simple mathematics showed that surgery reduced my chance of premature death by 1.5% (actually a bit more complicated) and a serious medical complication by 2.5% at little cost. These are small probabilities, but if we keep encountering such risks we are playing Russian roulette, according to decision theorists (Dawes, 1987), and assuring our early demise. I have to admit, I was ill at ease with this analysis, but I forced myself to behave rationally. Later, I learned that what was diagnosed as a hernia was not a hernia but rather what hernia experts call a "weakness"; that if it ever developed into a hernia it would have become a direct hernia; that strangulation is rare in the case of direct hernias; that there is a high probability (5–15%) that hernias will reoccur after an operation; that the probability is even higher for someone operated on for a weakness; and that there are substantially higher probabilities of strangulation with reoccurring hernias. I only found this out upon further research when my hernia operation did fail and I had a real symptomatic hernia. Thus, what had happened was I had read too many articles on rational decision making, treated the premises provided to me by physicians as certain, and proceeded to act in the rational manner.

The case in the literature that best illustrates this overemphasis on the certainty of the premises is the famous Kahneman and Tversky (1973) demonstrations concerning humans' failure to take into account base rates. For instance, they ask subjects to read descriptions of individuals and judge whether these individuals are engineers or lawyers. They also tell subjects information about the base rates of engineers and lawyers in the population (for instance, 70% of the population are lawyers). Subjects completely ignore this base rate information and make their judgment on how well the description matches a prototypical engineer or lawyer. However, the prescriptively normative Bayes Theorem says base rates should have strong effects.

Let us assume that subjects understood what they were told and took as their task the official task. Why should they believe the abstract information about base rates? As my medical experience testifies, information about base rates is typically unreliable. The instances of inaccurate base rate information abound. There were the famous polls that guaranteed Dewey's election. As another instance, a few years ago we were told that 1 in 100 people who tested positive for the AIDS virus would develop full-blown AIDS. Now, that estimate is up by more than a factor of 10. As a more humorous example, our local Pittsburgh magazine does a poll of local residents to get information about restaurants. Every year at least a plurality of people claim that Pizza Hut makes the best pizza. Should I really ignore personal experience and testimony of others to the contrary and accept this abstract base rate information gathered by a "reliable" source?

Believers in the need to use base rates are a die-hard crew, and whatever example I bring up they always say, "But, of course, you should have known that the information in that case was invalid. What you should pay attention to is *valid* information about base rates." Ignoring the problematical issue of whether there was any valid abstract information about base rates in our evolutionary history (from the village priests?), let me ask where is such valid information today, and how do we know it is valid?

I have asked bright colleagues where they think good information about base rates might be found. The most common answer is information like in *Consumer Reports* on things like repair statistics. Then I asked them how they know this is valid information in contrast to the AIDS information or the Dewey poll. It may well be that *Consumer Reports* does provide valid information, but none of my colleagues are in possession of reasons for believing so beyond an interesting "Well, if their information was bad, we would have heard about it," or "It proved reliable for me when I bought such-and-such a car."

Another comment I receive from colleagues who are less die-hard believers in abstract base rates goes something like this: "Well, all right, such base rate information is often invalid, but surely you cannot be arguing that one would be better off, on the average, to ignore such information." I am not arguing this, but, on the other hand, I can see no basis to argue that one would be better off to pay attention to abstract information about base rates. It is very much an open question that requires further analysis of how often base rate information is misleading and the costs and benefits of using frequently flawed information.

The only time it is clear that we should heed base rate information is for domains where we have personal proof that the information is valid. Thus, if one has personal experience that the reports from *Consumer Reports* have proven valid, then one should be influenced by them. On the other hand, when some high authority (medical, religious, political, or academic) has a pronouncement to make about something for which we have no personal experience or contradictory personal experience, we should be very suspicious. I wish I had been.

As a final observation, there is evidence that when our experience with base rates is concrete and not abstract (seeing is believing), and our behavior involves responding to the object in question, not engaging in a verbal exercise, people are extremely sensitive to base rates. A good example of this is the accuracy with which people probability match (see Kintsch, 1970b, for a review) when they are trying to predict an event in a random sequence. Interestingly, this probability matching has often been described as nonrational. If the probability is higher of a 1 in a random sequence of 0's and 1's, the subject should always predict 1 to maximize correct prediction. Upon close inspection, it turned out that subjects were not accepting the authoritative reports of experiments that these were random sequences, and they were searching out sequential patterns. Subsequent chapters in this book describe other instances in which people are very sensitive to concrete base rates, although, again, we often mischaracterize such sensitivity as irrational.

The Situation Assumed Is not the Environment of Adaptation

Adaptation is defined with respect to a specific environment. Often, the normative model assumes a different situation. Thus, human memory is often criticized because it cannot easily perform simple tasks, like storing a list of 20 words. However, human memory did not evolve to manage a list of 20 words but rather to manage a data base of millions of facts and experiences. In chapter 2, when we view memory in light of this situation, its behavior in a memory experiment appears quite adaptive.

Another example concerns the constant demonstration of human fallacies in experiments on deductive reasoning (Anderson, 1985, chapter 10). Deductive reasoning enables one to go from certain premises to certain conclusions. However, as discussed earlier, certain premises are rare or nonexistent in situations of adaptive importance. As a consequence, there is no reason why humans should have evolved to engage in correct deductive reasoning? Cosmides (1989) argues that we can understand the pattern of success and failure in reasoning about the Wason card-sorting task according to what situations are adaptively important.

An extension of this line of argument can be used to explain the apparent irrationality of modern life. Although it is important to avoid exaggerated doom-saying, we probably all agree that current human behavior is harming the prospects for human survival by creating huge nuclear arsenals and environmental disasters. A possible explanation is that human tendencies, adaptive in other earlier environments, are playing themselves out disastrously in the current modern technological age. One must be cautious of such rational explanations that make reference to past environments, rather than the current, because it is always possible to invent environments in which any behavior would be adaptive. This is not to say that one cannot make explanations by appealing to the past; however, they require independent evidence about what the past environments were really like.

Conclusions

Research comparing human behavior to normative models has been extremely useful; however, one must be careful in understanding its implications for adaptive rationality. It may well be that certain aspects of human cognition cannot be understood profitably in the framework I am advocating. However, I think we have grossly overestimated the irrationality of human cognition in this sense. Moreover, as I have begun to discover, there are aspects of human cognition that can be very profitably understood within the rationality thesis.

THE REST OF THIS BOOK

The next four chapters of this book are devoted to extensive analyses of a number of aspects of human cognition from the perspective of this rational framework. The fruitfulness of these analyses is the real evidence for the principle of rationality. Throughout the book, I briefly speculate on what the implications of these analyses might be for the ACT architecture, which is concerned with the algorithm and implementation levels. However, I have left working out these implications for another day. The fact that rational analyses can stand on their own is evidence that this is a level of theoretical analysis that can be pursued independently. I have not worked out the detailed architectural implementation, because it would be premature until I have fully worked out these rational derivations.

The book ends with a short chapter of general discussion. I wrote the chapter with some reluctance in response to those who felt the need to have general questions addressed after four chapters of detail. It should not be read without first reading the four contentful chapters.

APPENDIX:
NON-IDENTIFIABILITY AND RESPONSE TIME

In the main body of this chapter, the claim was made that behavioral data will not allow us to determine the underlying mechanisms at the implementation level. The reason for this is that there are many different sets of mechanisms that can mimic one another. This is a well-established fact in formal automata theory. However, in the conventional understanding of formal automata theory, the fact that two systems display the same input–output behavior does not guarantee that they will show the same timing behavior. That is, although the two systems may produce the same output, they may take different times to compute it. Indeed, a lot of work in automata theory is concerned with studying machines that compute the same behavior but with different temporal functions.

Suppose we had two implementation theories that agreed in the input–output behavior of the system. Both would claim that the mind went through some set of mental steps (largely unseen) to perform some task. They would be different because they claimed that the mind went through different sets of steps to achieve the same end state. The claim that might be advanced is that, even though the end states were the same, the time would be different because the two systems performed different internal steps.

Suppose system 1 takes n_1 steps to perform a task and system 2 takes n_2 steps, $n_1 < n_2$. It might seem simple to get timing mimicry despite the different number of steps. Let us just have system 2 take a fraction n_1/n_2 of the time to make its steps. This is the basic speed-up argument.

However, there is a well-known objection to such a speed-up proposal in automata theory. This objection involves the concept of computational complexity. System 1 and system 2 may take differing number of steps to perform their tasks, depending on the complexity of the problem. A simple example is that time to parse a sentence should vary with its length. Now if system 1 displays some function f_1 of complexity, and system 2 displays another function f_2 of complexity, it may not be the case for any constant speed-up factor a, $af_2(n) \leq f_1(n)$ for all n where n measures complexity (e.g., length of sentence). For instance, let f_2 be a squaring function and f_1 a linear function. For no $a > 0$ is it the case that $an^2 < n$ for all n. Basically, if n gets large enough, the system with the worse complexity function will start to lag behind the system with the better complexity function.

However, the whole problem with such arguments is that they depend on unbounded complexity, and people never deal with problems of unbounded complexity. As long as there is a bound on complexity, the argument vanishes. There are real and very sharp limitations on the complexity of human behavior. For instance, we can parse longish sentences only if they are basically linear concatenations of small phrases that we can parse separately. As another example, we can process in detail only a small part of a visual array at a time (that around the fovea). Again, we process a large array by a sequence of glances.

This complexity-bound argument is particularly forceful when one realizes that working-memory limitations and chunk-size limitations place very severe limitations on the number of elements that can be processed and, hence, on complexity functions. Any psychologically accurate model is going to have to involve linear concatenations of the processing of these limited-size chunks. With such severe limitations on complexity, mimicry of processing times would be particularly easy to achieve.

This observation has been discussed in Anderson (1979) and in Berwick & Weinberg (1984). Thus, the point of this argument is to say that, although the formal results are real problems for simulation of formal machines solving formal problems, they are not real problems for simulation of humans solving human problems.

I have been asked what happens to such speed-up arguments if one has physiological evidence that the operations of the brain can be performed only so fast. In principle, such considerations can serve to eliminate certain speed-up proposals. However, in practice, there are plenty of theories that do not push the brain beyond its limit. Typically, neurophysiological timing arguments, when they are invoked, are quite questionable. For example, J. A. Anderson (1973) has argued that the brain cannot do serial searches with 35 msec. comparison times per item, as was proposed by Sternberg (1969). Although I am inclined to believe that memory sets in the Sternberg task are not processed serially, there are no strong reasons for proclaiming 35 msec serial processing impossible. Perhaps certain schemes for processing an item could not be implemented in 35 msec, but Sternberg never (to my knowledge) made a commitment to a particular neural implementation.

2 Memory

Contents

Preliminaries   41
A Rational Analysis of Human Memory   43
   The Optimization Problem   46
   Estimation of Likelihoods of Memory Structures   47
The History Factor   49
   Burrell's Model of Usage   50
   Frequency and Recency   52
   Spacing Effects   53
   The Augmented Burrell Mode   53
   Simulation of Recency and Frequency Effects   55
   Simulation of Spacing Effects   59
The Context Factor   61
   Word Frequency Effects   64
   Priming Effects   66
   Fan Effects   68
   The Paradox of the Expert   70
Relationship of Need Probability to Probability and Latency of Recall   72
   Analysis of Latency of Recall   73
   Analysis of Probability of Recall   74
Combining Information from Cues   77
   Analysis of Latency   77
   Analysis of Accuracy   78
   Jones Experiment   80
Implementation in the ACT Framework   82
Effects of Subject Strategy   84
   Simulation of Free Recall   85
   Serial Position Effects   87
   Effects of Presentation Time and List Length   89
Conclusions   89
   Short-Term Memory Limitations   91

PRELIMINARIES

I begin my detailed application of rational analysis with human memory for a number of reasons. Human memory is the field of cognitive psychology with which I have had the longest association, going back over 20 years. It is also the area of cognition where I got my first glimmers of how a rational

41

analysis could apply. However, my main reason for starting with human memory is my belief that it is the field in cognitive psychology that is most in need of rational analysis. It has seen an amazing succession of mechanistic models, including a number of mine. It is almost taken as an axiom in the field that there is no rhyme or reason as to why human memory works the way it does. The task of the mechanistic theorist is to search an astronomical space of bizarre combinations of mechanisms to find something that fits the data.

This pessimistic characterization of human memory is not a discovery of the field of human memory. Rather, it is an importation into the field of the lay view of human memory. Simply put, human memories are seen as lousy systems, particularly in contrast to the marvelous memories of modern computers. For instance, over the years, I have participated in many talks with artificial intelligence researchers about the prospects of using models of human intelligence to guide the development of artificial intelligence programs. Invariably, the remark is made, "Well, of course, we would not want our system to have an unreliable human memory."

This view of human memory makes the classic error of oversimplifying the task that human memory faces. We present a subject with a list of 10 digits, note that the subject fails miserably, and contrast this with how marvelously a computer performs. But human memory did not evolve to give optimal performance in our silly laboratory task. Rather, it evolved to manage a huge data base of millions of complex facts and experiences. Its task is to dredge out of that huge data base facts that are relevant to the current situation. This is not an easy task—and not just because the data base is huge. It is also a difficult task because the current situation gives us such unreliable cues as to what memory is required. It would be nice if all of our retrieval needs were accompanied by "memory address" cues of the form "Retrieve the memory you formed 9:01:17 Monday, September 16, 1980." However, they don't. Rather, at their best, the cues are of the form "Why was Willie Stargell so great, Daddy?".

There is a field of computer science called information retrieval (Salton & McGill, 1983) that is concerned with solving a similar, although probably easier, task. My most typical encounter with such a computer-based information retrieval system is a library keyword system where I might type in a few keywords and get titles of books that are relevant to those keywords. Everyone's frustrations with such systems should disabuse us of the view that human memory is defective relative to computer memory. In fact, it was in reading about such systems that I first came to conceive of the analysis of human memory that appears in this chapter.

This chapter shows that a rational analysis can predict many of the significant phenomena of human memory with no real assumptions about memory mechanisms. The argument is that these memory phenomena and the mechanisms that produce them are caused by the goals of the system interacting with the structure of the environment. The argument is not that we do not need mechanistic models or that we do not need empirical research to understand memory. I have every intention of following this up with experiments to test the predictions of the rational theory and with an effort to develop a mechanistic model that satisfies the constraints of the rational analysis. At the end of this chapter I offer some initial speculations on implementations within an ACT framework.

This chapter and subsequent ones involve a substantial amount of mathematics. As a guide, Table 2-1 organizes the notation and symbols that are used in the chapter. This chapter is probably the most complex of the four substantive chapters of the book. This is because the documented empirical phenomena of human memory are very rich. In response to this richness, I have developed a rather elaborate analysis.

A RATIONAL ANALYSIS OF HUMAN MEMORY

In chapter 1, a general six-step procedure was given for conducting a rational analysis where the first three were key to defining the theory. Following are the first three steps for a rational analysis of memory.

Step 1. The first step is to specify the goal of the system. It is reasonably uncontroversial to claim that the goal of human memory is to retrieve knowledge that would allow us to solve the current problems we are facing. It becomes controversial only when we try to formalize this statement. I give a first approximation in terms of an expected utility analysis from decision theory. Memory has to balance the cost of memory search against the potential gain. The cost is to be measured in terms of the effort in sorting through memories. The gain is to be measured in terms of the value of the desired memory should it be retrieved. As a gross approximation, I assume throughout this chapter that there is a constant gain, *G,* associated with retrieving a desired memory. The search cost is specified under Step 3.

Step 2. The second step of a rational analysis is specifying the structure of the environment. The environment relevant to a memory analysis concerns how different memories are needed in different situations—for instance, when we need to recall a colleague's name and when we need to remember the quadratic formula. The major portion of this chapter is given over to developing a formal model of the structure of such retrieval needs. However, the basic idea is that, given the structure of the environment and

TABLE 2-1
Mathematical Notations Used in Chapter 2

Need Probability

$P(A)$	Probability that trace A is needed.
$P(\overline{A})$	Probability that trace A is not needed.
$P(A\|H_A)$	Probability that trace A is needed, conditional on history H_A.
$P(\overline{A}\|H_A)$	Probability that trace A is not needed, conditional on history H_A.
$P(A\|H_A \ \& \ Q)$	Probability that trace A is needed, conditional on history H_A and context Q.
$P(\overline{A}\|H_A \ \& \ Q)$	Probability that trace A is not needed, conditional on history H_A and context Q.
$P(A\|i)$	Probability that trace A is needed, conditional on an element i in the context.
$n(x)$	Probability that a trace with x as a component is needed.
$n(x\|i)$	Probability that a trace with x as a component is needed, conditional on element i in context.

Probability of Elements in Context

$P(i)$	Base probability of element i in context.
$P(i\|A)$	Probability element i is in context, conditional on the fact that A is needed.
$P(i\|\overline{A})$	Probability element i is in context, conditional on the fact that A is not needed.
$c(i)$	Base probability i is in context.
$c(i\|x)$	Probability element i is in context if a trace containing x is needed.

Conventions

A	Refers to traces.
x	Refers to components of traces.
Q	(For query) refers to the set of elements (cues) in context.
i	Refers to an element in the context.
H_A	History of trace A.
λ	Variable that varies over desirabilities (see Equation 2-6).
δ	Variable that varies over decay rates.
n	Number of uses.
t	Time.
p	Need probability.
P	Probability of recall.
o	Need odds.
O	Recall odds.
h	Log need odds.
H	Log recall odds.
Σi	A subscript denoting a set of elements, i.
B	$e^{-\theta/s}$ from Equation 2-22.

(*continued*)

TABLE 2-1 *(continued)*

Functions	
$r(t)$	Variation in desirability with time; if λ is initial desirability, desirability at time t is $\lambda r(t)$.
$p(n,t\|\lambda)$	Conditional probability of n uses in t time units if the initial desirability is λ (see Equation 2-7).
$M(t)$	Cumulative rate. If the initial desirability is λ, the expected number of uses in time t is $\lambda M(t)$ (see Equation 2-8).
$\pi(\lambda)$	Prior probability density of desirabilities (see Equation 2-6).
$\pi(\lambda\|n,t)$	Posterior probability density of desirabilities given that there has been n used in time t (see Equations 2-9 & 2-10).

Parameters	
C	Cost of retrieving a memory trace.
G	Gain associated with retrieving desired memory trace.
ν	Index of gamma distribution of desirabilities. (See Equation 2-6) Fixed at 2 throughout chapter.
b	Parameter of gamma distribution of desirabilities. (See Equation 2-6) Fixed at 100 throughout chapter.
α	Parameter for the exponential distribution of decay rates. Fixed at 2.5 throughout the chapter.
β	Parameter for the exponential distribution of revivals. Fixed at .04 throughout the chapter.
d	Exponent in Zipf's law used for converting need probability to latency (see Equation 2-21).
r	Multiplier in Zipf's law, used for converting need probability to latency (see Equation 2-21), set at .02 throughout the chapter.
l	Intercept in equation relating need probability to latency (see Equation 2-21), set at .3 seconds throughout the chapter.
θ	Threshold on log need odds for recall (see Equation 2-22).
s	Variance parameter for the distribution of log need odds (see Equation 2-22).

the current context, we can assign to a memory structure, A, a probability, p, that it will be relevant to solving the current problem. This I call the *need probability*, because it is the probability that A will be needed.

Step 3. The third step of a rational analysis is to specify computational constraints. As a first-order assumption, I assume that we consider the memories in an order and that the cost of a memory search is proportional to the number of memories we consider before we find the target memory. Or, said differently, there is a cost, C, associated with every irrelevant memory that we consider.

This statement of computational cost makes certain minimal assumptions about the nature of human memory, including that we can partition our memory into structures, that these structures are serially ordered, and that there is a cost associated with considering a memory. These should not be particularly controversial assumptions, and, indeed, they are true of the ACT* theory: Memories come packaged in cognitive units. Memories are retrieved by being matched to production conditions. Although the pattern matching takes place in parallel, the different memory structures are matched at different rates, placing an ordering on their retrieval (note that serial ordering of retrieval does not imply serial processing). Finally, there is a clear cost associated with that order, which is time. One might also speculate, although it is not part of the ACT* theory, that there is a metabolic cost.

The Optimization Problem

Now the optimization problem can be defined for human memory. Let G be the gain associated with retrieving the target memories. Let p be an estimated probability that memory structure A is relevant — that is, a target. A rationally designed information retrieval system would retrieve memory structures ordered by their probabilities p and stop retrieving when:

$$pG < C \tag{2-1}$$

That is, the system should stop retrieving when the probabilities are so low that the expected gain from retrieving the target is less than the cost of retrieving that item. A basic assumption is going to be that probability of being needed, p, is monotonically related to latency and probability of recall, which are the two major dependent measures used in the literature. It is related to latency because memory structures are ordered according to p, and it is related to accuracy because of the threshold on what items will be considered. To be able to predict speed and accuracy of recall, we need to inquire as to what factors memory can use to estimate p, and the prediction is that these factors determine memory performance. The optimization problem for the memory system is to come up with the best possible estimates of p.

Before turning to an examination of p, which is the major focus of the chapter, it is worth saying a little bit about C and G and how they might vary: G should vary with the importance of the task, implying that people should try longer before quitting in more important tasks and, consequently, recall more (recall is known to improve gradually as subjects try longer — Buschke, 1974); C should vary with the time spent inspecting an item before accepting or rejecting it as relevant to the current task. Varying it should lead to speed–accuracy trade-off functions where longer recall times are associated with more accurate memories.

This discussion of the optimization problem is framed in serial terms — first, the subject considers one target structure, then another, and so on.

However, given the equivalence between parallel and serial processes (Townsend, 1974), this is nothing more than an expository convenience. Indeed, I think of this all as being implemented in the parallel pattern-matching machinery of ACT* (Anderson, 1983). In ACT*, the system can assign resources to the structures it is processing according to their plausibility, and the system can effectively ignore structures below some threshold of plausibility. Thus, whether parallel or serial, the critical feature is that knowledge structures are ordered in terms of plausibility until they become too implausible to consider. It is not the goal of this chapter to inquire in detail as to the mechanisms that achieve this, only to inquire whether we can predict memory performance assuming that memories are so ordered.

Estimation of Likelihoods of Memory Structures

We are now one big step from having a theory that specifies the behavior of memory from purely rational considerations. That one big step is to specify the p in the preceding discussion. In developing this analysis, we assume that memory has access to the patterns of use of information in the past and the elements being attended currently but not the goals or intentions of the cognitive system. This rather encapsulated view of human memory corresponds to a typical computer information-retrieval system (Salton & McGill, 1983), which has access to statistics about past retrievals and the current keywords a user is providing but does not really know what the user "wants." This is the typical conception of memory in our field, which sees it as a general module to be used by various cognitive systems. In particular, this corresponds to the conception of memory in ACT*.

One solution to the estimation of p that appears in the computer information-retrieval literature (Bookstein & Swanson, 1974, 1975) is to use Bayesian estimation procedures. The two obvious pieces of information for evaluating whether a memory structure will be relevant are its past history of usage and the items in the current context. Thus, each structure A has some history H_A of being relevant in the past. The current context consists of a set of terms, called cues, and denoted by indices i. The *set* of cues are denoted herein as Q, for query. In doing Bayesian estimation, we are trying to calculate the posterior probabilities, giving us the following equation:

$$\frac{P(A|H_A \& Q)}{P(\overline{A}|H_A \& Q)} = \frac{P(A|H_A)}{P(\overline{A}|H_A)} \times \prod_{i \in Q} \frac{P(i|A)}{P(i|\overline{A})} \qquad (2\text{-}2)$$

where p from the previous discussion is $P(A|H_A \& Q)$ above. The odds ratio for item A is the product of the odds ratio for item A given history H_A times the product of the ratio of the conditional probabilities for each cue in the context. This equation makes certain assumptions about conditional independence, namely that the degree to which A affects the probability of i in the context does not depend on A's past history or the other cues in the context. Formally, the assumption is:

$$\frac{P(i|H_A\&A\&Q')}{P(i|H_A\&\overline{A}\&Q')} = \frac{P(i|A)}{P(i|\overline{A})} \tag{2-3}$$

where Q' is any subset of $\{Q-i\}$. This assumption is typically made in the computer information retrieval literature for purposes of tractability.[1]

The first term in Equation 2-2, $P(A|H_A)/P(\overline{A}|H_A)$, is basically a prior odds ratio for the item given its past history. This is the *history factor*. H_A is a record of all the times A has been needed. As such, it reflects (among other things) frequency of use and how recently it was last used. The other quantities, the $P(i|A)/P(i|\overline{A})$, are the odds ratios of the conditional probabilities of the cues given that the structure is relevant versus not relevant. These ratios can be thought of as associative strengths. They constitute the *context factor*.

If one is willing to make a somewhat different assumption:

$$\frac{P(i|H_A\&A\&Q')}{P(i|H_A\&Q')} = \frac{P(i|A)}{P(i)} \tag{2-4}$$

then we can write an equation that is, for some purposes, more useful.

$$P(A|H_A\&Q) = P(A|H_A) * \prod_{i \in Q} \frac{P(i|A)}{P(i)} \tag{2-5}$$

This equation gives us a direct formula for the need probability rather than the odds ratio. Note $P(i|A)/P(i) = P(A|i)/P(A)$. This equation says that the posterior probability that A is needed can be gotten from the prior probability by multiplying it by terms that reflect the association between A and elements in the context.

The basic behavioral assumption is that memory performance will be monotonically related to the conditional need probability, $P(A|H_A \& Q)$. Later, this chapter offers a proposal for how increased need probability maps into higher recall probability and faster reaction times. First, the chapter considers the two components in Equation 2-2 that determine the probability of a trace being needed—the history factor and the context factor. We show that many qualitative phenomena of human memory can be predicted by assuming that human memory is estimating need probability from these factors.

---

[1] Human memory may not be so constrained, and it is interesting to inquire as to which predictions might be upset by non-independence.

THE HISTORY FACTOR

To address the history factor, $P(A|H_A)$, we need to determine how the past history of a structure's usage predicts its current usage. To determine this in the most valid way, we would have to follow people about in their daily lives, keeping a complete record of when they use various facts. Such an objective study of human information use is close to impossible.[2] What is possible is to look at records from nonhuman information retrieval systems that can be objectively studied. For instance, such studies have been done of borrowing from libraries (Burrell, 1980; Burrell & Cane, 1982) and access to computer files (Satyanarayanan, 1981; Stritter, 1977). Both systems tend to yield rather similar statistics. If we believe that the statistics of human memory information retrieval mirror the statistics of these nonhuman systems, we are in a position to make predictions about how the human should estimate need probabilities given past history.

Should we really believe that information retrieval by humans has the same form as library borrowings and file accesses? The fact that two very different systems (library and file systems) display the same statistics suggests that there are "universals" of information retrieval that transcend device and would generalize to human memory, as well, and that these systems all obey the same form but only differ in parameterization. Also, when we look at Burrell's (1980, 1985) explanation of library borrowings, it seems plausible that it would extend to human memory and other information retrieval systems. Finally, the success of the model in accounting for human memory suggests that it applies.

This section presents a mathematical model of information use for the human system assuming that it is analogous to these objectively observable information retrieval systems. Predictions for human memory are derived from this by an optimization analysis. In case the basic point gets lost in the mathematics that follow, I want to state it up front: A system that is faced with the same statistics of information usage as a library or a file system and that is optimized in the sense already defined will produce the basic human memory functions. *No additional assumptions are required.*[3]

---

[2]On the other hand, it is possible to perform less ambitious studies. Lael Schooler and I are currently doing a study of work usage in *The New York Times* headlines. Another possibility would be to look at addressees in electronic mail messages. Our research is consistent with the proposals in this chapter.

[3]For instance, Simon (in press), in commenting on this model, argues that "auxiliary assumptions" are doing all the work. In fact, all the "assumptions" are characterizations of observed properties of information retrieval systems and the most important characterizations are taken whole cloth from Burrell.

Burrell's Model of Usage

Burrell (1980, 1985) has developed a mathematical theory of usage for information retrieval systems such as libraries (a similar model appears in Stritter, 1977, for file usage). His theory involves two layers of assumptions. First, Burrell assumed that the items (books, files, memory structures) in an information retrieval system vary in terms of their desirability. He assumed that they vary as a gamma distribution with parameter b and index v. Such a distribution will produce mean desirability values of v/b and variances v/b^2. Desirabilities can be interpreted as mean rates of use (in Burrell's case, usage is borrowing). Burrell's second assumption is that uses are described by a Poisson process. This means that, given an item with desirability λ, the time to the next use is an exponential process with mean $1/\lambda$.

Anderson (1989) has developed an analysis of human memory, using this model of Burrell's. This chapter presents a sophistication of this model based on some ideas in Burrell (1985). Burrell noted that there are problems with the ahistorical character of the exponential distribution of times until next borrowing. The problem he was concerned with in library systems is that there is an aging phenomenon — books become less used with time. He chose to model the aging process by assuming that borrowings are a nonhomogeneous Poisson process whose rate varies as $r(t)\lambda$ as a function of time. In the simple homogeneous case, $r(t) = 1$. In his model for aging, Burrell assumed $r(t) = e^{-at}$. The initial derivations will generate some general equations that are independent of the form of $r(t)$. Then, I consider in more detail the form of $r(t)$.

Table 2-2 contains an analysis of the implications of Burrell's model for the estimation of $P(A|H_A)$, the probability that it is needed given its history, H_A. That analysis only considers two pieces of information from H_A — the total amount of time, $t,$ that A has been in the system and the total number of times, $n,$ that A has been used. Basically, what is happening there is a Bayesian estimation process. Burrell's model gives us a prior distribution $\pi(\lambda)$ of desirabilities and a conditional probability of $p(n,t|\lambda)$ of n uses in time t given a desirability λ. From these we infer a posterior distribution $\pi(\lambda|n,t)$ of desirabilities given n uses have been observed in time t. This turns out to be a gamma distribution with parameters $v + n$. and $b + M(t)$, where $M(t)$ grows with time according to the function $r(t)$ — see Equation 2-8 in Table 2-2.

The mean of this distribution is $(v + n)/(M(t) + b)$. Because this is a rate, it could potentially be greater than one. However, if we set our time scale so that we are looking at a rate for a small enough interval, this quantity effectively becomes a probability of a use in that interval — that is, a quantity that will vary from zero to one. For instance, if we measured time in seconds, this would give us probability of use in a second. Because there

TABLE 2-2
Bayesian Estimation of Desirabilities

Formally (see Berger, 1985, for discussion of conjugate Bayesian families), what the Burrell model gives us is a prior distribution for the desirability, λ, of an item. We can specify this as the gamma distribution:

$$\pi(\lambda) = \frac{b^v \lambda^{v-1} e^{-b\lambda}}{(v-1)!} \tag{2-6}$$

What we observe of a particular item is that it was used n times in the first t time units since its creation. What Burrell's model tells us is the probability that we would see such a history given a book with desirability λ is described by the equation for a nonhomogeneous Poisson process:

$$p(n,t|\lambda) = \frac{e^{-\lambda M(t)}[\lambda M(t)]^n}{n!} \tag{2-7}$$

where

$$M(t) = \int_0^t r(s)ds. \tag{2-8}$$

What we are interested in is the posterior distribution of λ given n and t. A Bayesian estimate of λ be derived as:

$$\pi(\lambda|n,t) = \frac{\pi(\lambda)p(n,t|\lambda)}{\int_0^\infty \pi(x)p(n,t|x)dx} \tag{2-9}$$

which has the solution:

$$\pi(\lambda|n,t) = \frac{(M(t)+b)^{v+n}\lambda^{v+n-1}e^{-\lambda(M(t)+b)}}{(v+n-1)!} \tag{2-10}$$

which is itself a gamma distribution with parameters $M(t)+b$ and $v+n$.

---

is a decay process, we can take our estimate of $P(A|H_A)$ to be this quantity times $r(t)$ for decay. Thus:

$$P(A|H_A) = \frac{v+n}{M(t)+b}r(t) \tag{2-11}$$

In the case where $r(t) = 1$ (i.e., no aging or loss of desirability), this becomes:

$$P(A|H_A) = \frac{v+n}{t+b} \tag{2-12}$$

Burrell tends to get best fits for library borrowing by estimating b to be about a year and v to be about one. This yields the average borrowing rates for a book of about $v/b = 1$ time per year. The low value of v produces a distribution of desirabilities such that most books have very low borrowing rates and a few have high. In the applications in this chapter, I have set $v = 2$ to give a somewhat more normal distribution of desirabilities for human memory. (Unlike Burrell, there is not a data base from which to directly estimate v.) The b parameter defines the time scale. I have set it arbitrarily at 100 and tried to scale the results of experiments to fit the time scale of the model. It remains a future goal to try to get systematic estimates of b and v for the human case. Many of the analyses are sensitive only to the general function and not to the exact values of b and v.

$P(A|H_A)$ is not the same thing as need probability, because it is only conditioned on the history and not the context factor. Equation 2-2 is needed to integrate the two together. Nonetheless, in many situations, the context is the same for a set of items and only their experimental history varies. For such situations, it is reasonable to treat $P(A|H_A)$ as the need probability, because it is directly related to the actual need probability. We do this in discussing recency, frequency, and spacing effects.

Frequency and Recency

There are some further developments that potentially might complicate Equation 2-11, but it is of interest to inquire how its current form relates to the basic variables of presentation frequency and recency. Let us consider the retention function, where we wait t seconds after an item was studied and first test it. In this case, $n = 0$ and Equation 2-11 takes the form $vr(t)/(M(t) + b)$. Thus, depending on the form of $r(t)$, the function in Equation 2-11 could give a very good mimicry of human retention functions that are typically characterized as rapidly negatively accelerated. I specify $r(t)$ in the subsection titled "The Augmented Burrell Model" after considering the spacing effect.

The function in Equation 2-12 can also be analyzed to predict the relationship between frequency of exposure and memory performance. In this case, n is our independent variable. Let us assume that t is constant—that is, we are manipulating number of exposures in a fixed interval. The form of the Equation 2-10 is $l + sn$ where $s = r(t)/(M(t) + b)$ and $l = v *s$. Such a linear growth model is the strengthening model in ACT* that has been shown to yield a good approximation to human learning data.[4] Again, we develop a more precise mapping in subsequent sections.

---

[4]Here and elsewhere the assumption is that every time an item is presented for study there is another need for the memory trace of the item.

Spacing Effects

According to Burrell's model, it does not matter what is the spacing of these n presentations. All that matters in Burrell's model is the total number of uses (n) and the total elapsed time (t). This is a consequence of the fact that the rate of a Poisson process depends only on the time (according to the function $r(t)$) and not on the history of past events. The question arises whether Burrell's model correctly describes the likelihood function. Is it the case that in information retrieval systems that there is no massing of need? Burrell's model implies that the probability of next use of an item used n times should depend only on the elapsed time since the item was introduced and not the time since the last use of the item. In fact, Burrell's model is not descriptively accurate here, as one might expect.[5] For instance, in Carnegie-Mellon's library system, there are definite clusterings of borrowings and one can reject the hypothesis that the n borrowings of a book in a fixed time interval are independent samples from a monotonically decreasing probability density. There are lots of reasons for such massings, such as a book being relevant to a course taught only one semester. Stritter (1977) noted such deviations from independence of file accesses, but also chose to ignore them in developing his model of file system access. It is fairly intuitive that the same is true of human memory, although it is hard to objectively verify what the human likelihood function is.

  If some use is massed and some is not, then the intervals between successive uses should predict the probability of the item being needed now. For example, compare one item that has been used fairly uniformly n times over the year and another item whose n uses all occurred in a 3-month period, 6 months ago. Intuitively, the first is more likely to be needed now. Thus, we would predict better memory for spaced items, as long as we are not comparing it to a massing of study that has just occurred.

The Augmented Burrell Model

The question arises as to what kind of formal model might underlie the observed clustering behavior in libraries and file systems. Burrell's model provides us with two assumptions that he is able to justify in the library domain:

  1. There is a distribution of desirability of items, where the desirability of an item controls the rate at which it is accessed.

---

[5]Burrell (personal communication) in fact acknowledges that there are massings of borrowings but points out that this was not relevant to his applications.

2. There is an aging process for items, and their effective rate of use decays with time.

By adding the following two plausible assumptions, one can account for spacing phenomena:

3. There is also variation in the rate of decay across items. For simplicity, I assume that the decay rates are exponentially distributed. This means that the probability of a decay rate, δ, is $\alpha e^{-\alpha\delta}$. Thus, according to this augmented model, memories that we form vary in two independent dimensions. They can vary in their initial desirability and in the rate at which desirability decays. It is possible to imagine a 2×2 matrix formed from extremes of these two dimensions and memories occupying all cells. Memory for facts such as our children's names presumably are facts that start out very useful and whose usefulness does not decay with time. Memories for partial products in a problem start out very useful but lose their value rapidly. Memories for where we put the first-aid supplies hopefully are not used very often but do not lose what usefulness they have with time. Finally, memories for where the lockers were seen at a novel airport are unlikely to be useful (at least for me) and rapidly lose what use they have.

4. Items in the set undergo random revivals of interest in which they return to their original level of desirability. The probability of a revival at time t is an exponential process with probability $\beta e^{-\beta t}$. In a library system, this gives us the effect of current events (e.g., a course) suddenly making a book relevant again. It is these revivals that will give us the massing that we observe in library systems and file systems. Assumption 4, by itself, will introduce the phenomenon of clustering in use. However, without assumption 3, we will not get the effect of a relationship between massed use and lower need probability at a delay. With both assumptions in place, the Bayesian estimation procedure tends to interpret massed use of an item in the past as a revival of an item with high desirability but high decay. Because that item has not been subsequently used, the estimation procedure infers that it has decayed away into oblivion.

If Assumptions 3 and 4 from the preceding list do describe features of the environment, then the system will have to adapt to them just as it does to the features in the original Burrell model. I derived predictions from the augmented Burrell model by estimating mean need probabilities by Bayesian means assuming the environment is as described in Assumptions 1 through 4. In deriving predictions from the augmented Burrell model, the following settings were used for the environmental parameters: $v = 2$, $b =$

100 (which establishes our time scale) $\alpha = 2.5$, and $\beta = .04$. The last two are arbitrary and can be questioned. They are set such that the mean rate of decay $(1/\alpha)$ is 10 times the revival rate.

The augmented model poses serious complications. Because of the revival process, we no longer have independence of rate from past history, which violates an assumption in the derivation of Equations 2-10 and 2-11. Thus, it is necessary to estimate need probabilities by Monte Carlo means. It takes on the order of 100,000 runs to get stable estimates for 100 time units given the parameters in the preceding paragraph. Each run involves choosing a random revival pattern and decay rate and calculating the expected need probability under that revival pattern and decay rate. The more time units, the more runs to get stable estimates, and the longer each run takes. The actual algorithm that performs these calculations is described in Anderson & Milson (1989).

Simulation of Recency and Frequency Effects

Figure 2-1 examines the relationship between delay and the need probability—that is, the retention function.[6] It plots on a log–log scale the relationship between need probability and delay. The assumption is that the item was introduced t time units ago and has not been used in the intervening interval. The reader can confirm the linear relationship that exists, implying that retention is a power function of delay. Such power functions are typically found in the experimental literature (e.g., Wickelgren, 1976). One might have thought that the rate of decay would be a more rapid exponential to reflect the aging process; however, the revival process slows down this decay process. In the long term, the retention function is dominated by the fact that the Bayesian estimation becomes more and more biased to low desirabilities if the item has not been used. If we think of Equation 2-11 as providing the retention function, this amounts to saying that $r(t)$ reaches a nonzero asymptote because of the revival process, but $M(t)$ continues to grow and dominates the retention function in the long run.

When it comes to looking at practice effects on memory, one is forced to try to deal with conflicting variables—the number of exposures to the item, the spacing of exposures, the total interval, and the time from last exposure to test. One cannot hold all these variables constant and only have number of exposures vary. Typically, time from last exposure is held constant because of the large retention effects. One either holds spacing constant and

---

[6]Note in this section that the assumption is that the contextual factor is constant and we are just looking at the history factor.

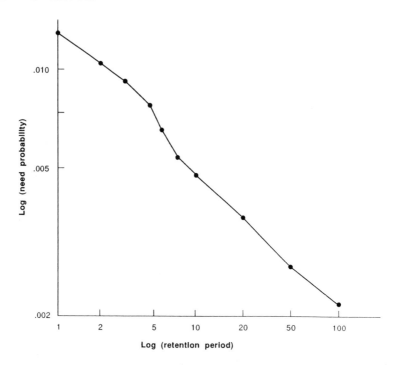

FIG. 2-1. The relationship between need probability and delay since an item has been studied.

lets total time vary or holds total time constant and lets spacing vary. Thus, we have graphed both functions in Figs. 2-2 and 2-3. In Fig. 2-2, an exposure was given every 10 time units, and the test was 10 time units after the last exposure—thus, total time is $10n$, where n is the number of exposures. In Fig. 2-3, the total exposure was held constant at 100, and the last study was at 80, and the remaining studies were placed from 0 to 80 at intervals of $80/(n - 1)$, where n was the number of exposures. (In this case, the minimum number of trials is two—one at time 0, one at 80, and then the test at 100). The functions are plotted on a log–log plot and, again, they are linear, implying that *need* is a power function of *use*. Such power functions are typically found (Newell & Rosenbloom, 1981). The linear functions in Figs. 2-2 and 2-3 have slopes close to 1, which is what we would have predicted from Equation 2-12. Thus, the complications introduced after deriving Equation 2-12 have not changed its basic prediction about the practice function.

It should be emphasized that fitting the retention and practice functions as power functions is not a trivial feat. Psychology has had a long history of mechanistic models in which predicted these functions should be exponential in character, but these functions are better characterized as

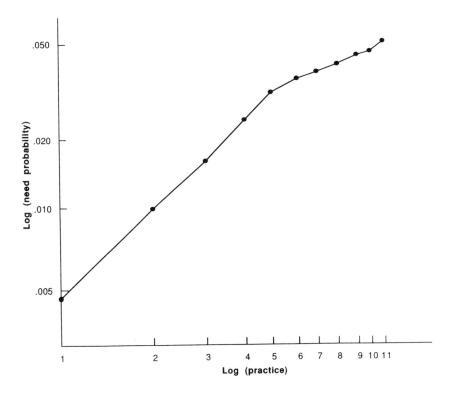

FIG. 2-2. The relationship between practice and need probability. In this figure, spacing between studies are held constant.

power functions. (Newell & Rosenbloom, 1981). So, it seems that the natural mechanistic models lead to exponential functions. It is interesting that the natural environmental models lead to power functions. The insight for why the environmental model predicts these effects basically can be obtained from Equation 2-12. (As we noted, it is not really valid, but it serves as a basis for insight.) This equation gives the Bayesian estimate of the expected desirability of an item with n uses in a time period t. The estimate of its desirability increases as a linear function of n and as an inverse linear function of t. Linear functions are special cases of power functions with exponents of 1 and slopes of 1 when plotted on log-log graphs. Figures 2-2 and 2-3 basically show slopes of 1 but the slope in Fig. 2-1 is slightly less than .5. Thus, the complications have not really changed the effect of n in Equation 2-12 but have changed the effect of t from inverse linear to something close to the inverse of the square root of t.

One might wonder about the match of the theoretical functions for need probability to empirical power functions for speed and accuracy. There has to be some transformation from need probability to these dependent

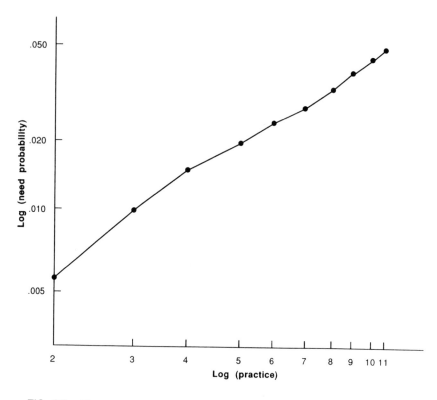

FIG. 2-3. The relationship between practice and need probability. In this figure, time since initial study and time since last study are held constant.

variables. When we examine plausible transformations in later sections we can see that they basically raise need probabilities to some power (typically, less than one). Such transformations would preserve the power relationship between the measure and the independent variables of delay and practice. It is also the case that the empirical functions typically have shallower slopes than those in Figures 2-1 through 2-3.

Although mechanistic models more naturally seem to predict exponential learning, finally there has been a flurry of theories that are able to predict power-law learning. Newell and Rosenbloom (1981), expanding on ideas in Lewis (1978), attributed power-law learning to chunking macro-operators in exponentially complex problem spaces. MacKay (1982) attributed it to a strengthening process. Anderson (1982) derived it from the power-law form of strength decay. Shrager, Hogg, and Huberman (1988) produced power-law learning by a procedure that learns new operators and optimizes the decision procedure. Logan (1988) attributed it to a race among retrieval of previous experiences. The rational analysis given here does not necessarily contradict any of these models. They could be interpreted as simply proposing mechanisms to achieve the prescriptions of a rational analysis. The wide variety of mechanisms proposed should convince us that there is not a unique mechanism to get power-law learning. There is one critical feature that these models lack, however. They focus only on the effect of practice and do not take into account its relationship with spacing and forgetting effects (Anderson does deal with forgetting but not with spacing). A theory that fails to deal with such fundamental variables of practice cannot really claim to explain practice effects. Indeed, if one tried to integrate directly into these models facts such as the power-law decay with delay or the nearly total ineffectiveness of highly massed training, the models might fail to predict power-law learning.

Simulation of Spacing Effects

So, let us turn to whether the rational model can predict the spacing effect. This is where Burrell's model is not descriptively accurate of information usage. Although usages are not independent in the rational model, it remains a question whether this model of the environment will produce need probabilities that match the human spacing functions. Some of the richest data on human spacing functions comes from Glenberg (1976), who looked at the interaction between the spacing effect and the retention function. That is, he orthogonally manipulated the delay between the two study presentations of an item and the delay between the second study and test. Figure 2-4a plots his data, and Fig. 2-4b plots estimated need probability. The unit of time in Glenberg's study was a 3-second presentation of an item. The unit of time on the simulation was .33 time units. Thus, one of its time units equals 9 seconds.

Glenberg's basic result is that, at short testing lags, recall decreases with spacing between studies, whereas at long lags it increases. The one exception is that, at very short lags (zero and one item), there is universally poor performance. This poor performance is typically attributed to inattention (e.g., Crowder, 1976) — something not modeled in the current approach. However, except for this, the model does a remarkably good job of reproducing the data of Glenberg. The correlation between his recall probabilities and the need probabilities is .86, which is quite good, considering the peculiarities at 0 and 1 lags and the fact that the two measures are only monotonically related and not linearly related (the rank order correlation without the 0 and 1 points is .99).

Bahrick (1979) did an interesting experiment that studied the interaction between spacing and repetition. He presented subjects with a number of memory trials for 50 English–Spanish vocabulary pairs. The first trial was a study, and the remainder were test followed by study. There was either no delay between trials, 1 day, or 30 days. This was followed with a final test

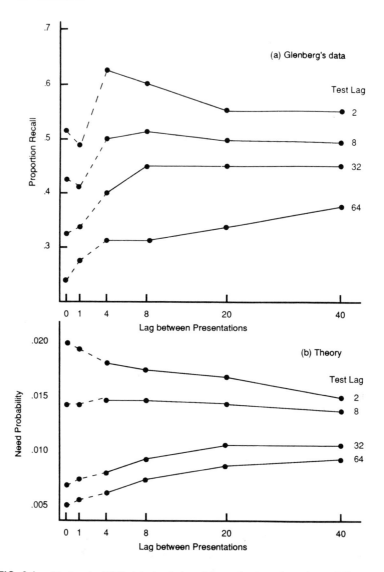

FIG. 2-4.   Glenberg's (1976) data (part a) and the estimates of need probability (part b). Glenberg studied the effect of spacing between two studies (the abscissa) as a function of the spacing from second study to test (the different curves). The curves, from top to bottom, reflect 2, 8, 32, and 64 events intervening between second study and recall.

after a 30-day interval. For the subjects who had been studying with 30-day intersession intervals, this is like another test. He ran two groups of subjects — one who had an initial study session, two test–study sessions, and a final test session and another group who had a study, five intermediate test–study sessions, and a final test. The results are shown in Table 2-3, both for performance on the test–study trials after the first and for performance on the final test. Bahrick's basic point is that there is an advantage if the retraining interval matches the retention interval.

Bahrick's experiment was simulated with the model, using .01 time unit intervals to simulate Bahrick's massed condition, 1 time unit intervals to simulate his 1-day delay condition, and 30 time unit intervals to simulate his 30-days conditions. The results are shown in Table 2-3 also. Certain of Bahrick's six-session data points are replications of the three-session data points. Altogether, there are 20 distinct conditions in the table. There is a rank-order correlation of .95 between the need probabilities and his percent recall (averages of two percentages in the case of replicates). In short, the rational analysis of the historical factor does a good job of accounting for the effects of frequency and recency of presentation.

THE CONTEXT FACTOR

The preceding analysis has been concerned with analyzing the history factor, which was the first term in Equation 2-2. Now we turn to estimating

TABLE 2-3
Mean Percentage Recall and Need Probabilites (in Parentheses) for Bahrick
(1979)

(a) Final 30-day test after 3 training sessions

Intercession Interval (Days)	Session					
	2	3	4	5	6	7
0	77 (.0201)	89 (.0298)	33 (.0057)			
1	60 (.0144)	87 (.0192)	64 (.0087)			
30	21 (.0032)	51 (.0069)	72 (.0108)			

(b) Final 30-day test after 6 training sessions

Intercession Interval (Days)	Session					
	2	3	4	5	6	7
0	82 (.0201)	92 (.0298)	96 (.0394)	96 (.0488)	98 (.0576)	68 (.0075)
1	53 (.0144)	86 (.0192)	94 (.0256)	96 (.0329)	98 (.0424)	86 (.0214)
30	21 (.0032)	51 (.0069)	72 (.0108)	79 (.0144)	82 (.0167)	95 (.0183)

the remaining quantities—the $P(i|A)/P(i|\overline{A})$, which are the cue strengths. It is almost certainly the case that $P(i)$ and $P(i|\overline{A})$ are going to be nearly identical, because conditionalizing on the nonrelevance of one memory structure out of millions cannot much change the probability of any cue. Thus, this discussion of cue strength focuses on the simpler form of $P(i|A)/P(i)$. As noted earlier, $P(i|A)/P(i) = P(A|i)/P(A)$. The cue strength (the ratio) thus reflects either the degree to which the context element is more or less probable when a trace (A) is needed or equivalently, the degree to which it is more or less probable that a trace (A) is needed when a context element (i) is present. Intuitively, these cue strengths reflect the degree of association between the terms i and the memory structures A. The critical issue becomes how to estimate these cue strengths. One idea is incorporated in the SAM model (Gillund & Shiffrin, 1984). This is to make these cue strengths reflect the frequency with which i and A have co-occurred in the past. This is a sensible proposal, but it does have two related difficulties:

1. When a memory structure is just created, there is a poor data base for estimating such strengths and estimates will fluctuate wildly.
2. This scheme loses information by only looking at direct co-occurences. If *school* has occurred in the context when other memories about *teacher* are needed, then there is reason to expect it will occur in the context when a new memory about *teacher* is needed—even if we have not yet experienced that particular co-occurrence.

In Anderson (1989), I proposed a scheme for estimating these conditional ratios based on work from information retrieval (Salton & McGill, 1983). This work avoids the objections just listed, although I have never read a deep explanation of why this approach works in information retrieval.

The analysis here is similar to the analysis in Anderson (1989), but I believe it is conceptually clearer: A memory structure A consists of a set of terms $a, b, \ldots, m$. (For instance, memory for "The hippie touched the debutante" would include the terms *hippie, touch,* and *debutante* among possible others.) The assumption is that $P(i|A)$, the probability of cue i given that A is a target, can be thought of as the probability that i is present given that a structure with elements $a, b, \ldots, m$ is needed. Thus, our expression for cue strength may be written:

$$\frac{P(i|A)}{P(i)} = \frac{P(i|a,b,\ldots,m)}{P(i)} \qquad (2\text{-}13)$$

The key idea is that the relationship between A and i can be decomposed into a set of relationships between the elements of A and i. Let $n(x)$ denote the probability that a trace with element x is needed, to distinguish it from $c(i)$, which is the probability that the context contains element i. Similarly,

$n(x|i)$ is the probability that a trace with x is needed given that i is in the context, whereas $c(i|x)$ is the probability that i is in the context given that a trace with x is needed. Then, under fairly strong independence assumptions, we may write:

$$\frac{P(i|A)}{P(i)} = \frac{P(A|i)}{P(A)} = \prod_{x \in A} \frac{c(i|x)}{c(i)} = \prod_{x \in A} \frac{n(x|i)}{n(x)} \tag{2-14}$$

One requisite independence assumption is:

$$P(A) = \prod_{x \in A} n(x) \tag{2-15}$$

or that the probability that structure A is needed is the product of the probabilities that structures involving the individual components are needed. The other requisite independence assumption is:

$$P(x|i \ \& \ A') = n(x|i) \tag{2-16}$$

or that the probability that x is needed, given that i is in the context, does not depend on any subset, A', of the other elements, $\{A\text{-}x\}$. These are strong assumptions, but they are required to make the standard move in the information-retrieval literature of decomposing the connection between a trace (or file) and a cue (or query element) to the connections between the components of the trace (or file) and the cue (or query element).

It is worthwhile to take an overview of what has happened in developing Equation 2-14. We started out interested in how the set of elements in the context predicted a particular memory trace. The system has little or no experience with this exact pairing and so has no direct basis for making this estimation. Thus, we earlier decomposed (Equation 2-2) the set of contextual elements into individual elements, and, in Equation 2-14, we have decomposed the trace into its elements. We now are looking at the degree to which a specific element in the context predicts a specific element in the trace. The advantage we get out of these moves is that we have much more experience with the pairings of the individual elements than we have with whole contexts and whole traces.

The decomposition in Equation 2-14 is not always the best way to estimate the contextual factor. In some cases, the independence assumptions might be seriously violated, and in some cases we might have enough experience to derive more direct estimates of context-to-trace predictability. Equation 2-14 is being advanced as an analytical convenience to determine what the rational analysis might predict. It remains an open issue just how to best estimate the context factor.

Assuming that we do want to compose estimates of the $n(x|i)/n(x)$ to estimate the context factor, the question arises of how to estimate the individual $n(x|i)$ and $n(x)$. A simple idea is to base them on frequency in experience. That is, define $n(x|i)$ to be the proportion of times that a trace with x is needed when i is present in the context, and define $n(x)$ to be the unconditional proportion of times that a trace with x is needed. This is a reasonable solution in cases of large samples. If x is an established concept, experience would give a good basis for estimating $n(x)$. If, in addition, i is a frequently occurring contextual element, one can accurately estimate $n(x|i)$. However, such estimates would still fluctuate radically in a case of infrequent elements.

Consider the predicament of moving to a new psychology department and meeting Professor c and Professor b. How does one set $n(c|b)/n(c)$ where $n(c|b)$ is the probability that a memory about c will be needed if b is mentioned and $n(c)$ is the base probability that a memory about c will be needed? One should set these probabilities at some default value and adjust with experience. The initial default value should be influenced by one's knowledge. Thus, if c and b are both professors of social psychology, $n(c|b)$ should be set initially higher than if one is a professor of social psychology and one is a professor of cognitive psychology. Eventually, with enough experience, one would adjust from these initial estimates to estimates that reflect proportions in experience. I am not in possession of a precise model of how to set initial values based on knowledge and how to adjust with experience; so this analysis will have to remain at the informal level.

Word Frequency Effects

The probabilities $c(x)$ and $n(x)$ should be related to frequency norms, although there is no reason to believe that the relationship will be perfect. Similarly, $n(x|i)$ should be related to free association norms (associations of x to i), but, again, there is no reason to believe that the relationship will be perfect. It is interesting to inquire whether empirical results relating memory to such norms can be predicted within this framework. Consider word frequency effects in recognition memory. In this case, the cue is the word, and the target is a trace involving the same word. The ratio from Equation 2-14 varies with[7]:

$$\frac{n(word|word\ in\ context)}{n(word)}$$

The numerator is to be read as the probability that a memory trace involving the word is needed given that the word is present. Presumably, this conditional probability is relatively high, although it is not 1. It is

---

[7] This and subsequent analyses in this section examine single terms of the product from Equation 2-14, assuming that the other terms do not vary in the particular experiment in question.

probably fairly constant for all words. In contrast, the denominator will vary with the frequency of the word. Thus, low-frequency words are predicted to be better recognized, a well-documented result (e.g., Kintsch, 1970a). The basic point is that low-frequency words are statistically better predictors of traces involving themselves than are high-frequency words.

Second, consider the case of paired associates where we present a pair, word1–word2, for study and test with word1 for the recall of word2. The ratio in this case is:

$$\frac{n(word1 \mid word1 \ in \ context)}{n(word1)} \times \frac{n(word2 \mid word1 \ in \ context)}{n(word2)}$$

If the words are of equal frequency, the relevant variable becomes $n(word2 \mid word1$ in context), which will vary with the associative strength of the words. This predicts the result (Eich, 1982) that it is easier to learn experimental associations between words with strong prior associations. It is worth noting the rational basis for this effect. It is based on the assumption that new knowledge involving highly interassociated terms is, in fact, more likely to be needed. Thus, for instance, if we are told that George Bush believes that Howard Baker is dishonest and that George Bush believes that Wayne Gretzky is dishonest, the prediction is that it is more likely that we need to reuse the Howard Baker fact when we hear George Bush because of the greater interassociation between Bush and Baker.

An interesting feature of the ratio just displayed for paired-associate learning is that it does not predict any effect of the word frequency of the response in paired-associate learning—a result that is approximately correct. In a typical experiment looking for word frequency effects, nouns of different frequency are basically paired randomly. This means that as we increase the frequency of a word and so $n(word2)$, its prior probability of association, $n(word2 \mid word1$ in context), will, on average, grow proportionately. Thus, the numerators and denominators in these ratios should tend to cancel themselves out.

Because of $n(word1)$ in the denominator, the analysis does predict a negative effect of stimulus frequency, a result that is supported in Paivio (1971). Gillund & Shiffrin (1984) failed to find any significant effects in recall, but they did find considerable advantage for low-frequency words in paired-associate recognition.

Finally, let us consider a free-recall situation where the subject is given no cues except the random elements in the environment, which I denote as *context*. Then, the probability of recall is governed by:

$$\frac{n(word \mid context)}{n(word)}$$

In this case, we might assume that the frequency of the word given the context matches its base frequency and so we have a ratio of 1 for all words independent of their frequency. However, it is known that high-frequency words are better recalled in free-recall tests (Kintsch, 1970a).

One possible explanation of this discrepancy is to relate it to an organizational strategy by which a subject tries to interrelate items in the list. High-frequency words, having more traces involving them, will be more easy to interrelate. In fact, there is considerable evidence that the frequency effect is due to organizational strategy. First, if one designs high-frequency lists without strong inter-item associations, the word-frequency effect disappears (Deese, 1960). Second, recall of high-frequency lists shows more subjective organization (Postman, 1970). Third, and most critically, when subjects are given distractor activity during study to prevent them from engaging in an organizational strategy, the word-frequency effect disappears (Gregg, Montgomery, & Caslano, 1980). Thus, it seems that the word-frequency effect for free recall is a strategy effect. In contrast, the word-frequency effect for recognition is more robust across the manipulations that influence the effect for recall.

This explanation of the word-frequency effect in free recall places it outside of the rational model, which, by itself, clearly fails to predict the phenomenon. The fact that it fails to predict the phenomenon should help allay doubts that rational models do not have clear predictions. However, there have to be such things as memory strategies that will affect the behavior of a subject over and above the basic tendencies of human memory. At the end of this chapter, I discuss how this rational analysis can be related to the effects of memory strategies in free recall.

As a final comment, it should be noted that the predictions of the rational model for word-frequency effects are quite similar to those developed by Gillund & Shiffrin (1984). Indeed, one might look to their model as a reasonable proposal for how such word-frequency effects might be implemented.

Priming Effects

We can relate this analysis of the contextual factor fairly directly to the priming literature. Consider a typical experiment where the subject is asked to judge whether a string of letters like "cat" is a word. This judgment can be more rapidly made when that word is preceded by an associated word, like "dog." To explain this result, it is necessary to recognize that, to judge the word "cat," we have to access memory of its spelling. A priming experiment looks at this access as a function of context. In this example, the relevant context is the cue term *dog*. The ratio in a rational analysis would be P(cat's spelling is needed|dog in context)/P(cat's spelling is needed). The assumption is that this ratio is greater than 1 in this case because of the inter-item association between dog and cat. Said in other words, the Bayesian estimation procedure increases the probability that the spelling of cat will be relevant in the presence of the word dog.

In explaining such priming effects, the Bayesian analysis, as currently developed, offers no more predictive power than any of the many competing analyses. However, it adds some explanatory power. It embodies the claim that we can recognize the spelling of *cat* faster in the presence of *dog* because, in actual fact, there is a higher-than-average probability that we will have to recognize the spelling of cat when dog is present.

An interesting feature of this Bayesian analysis is that it predicts the inhibitory priming effects that occur. That is, recognition of cat is worse in the presence of an unrelated stimulus (like lip) than it is in the presence of a neutral cue (like XXX). These conditional likelihood ratios have to average out to 1 (in a probability definition of average). Thus, because related terms have greater-than-1 ratios, unrelated terms will have less-than-1 ratios. Moreover, it again makes rational sense. In fact, the odds are lower than chance that we will have to recognize the word *cat* in the presence of an unrelated word like *lip*.

It has been argued that the mechanisms underlying the inhibition effect are different than the mechanisms underlying the facilitation effect (Lorch, Balota, & Stamm, 1986; Neely, 1977). Part of this argument involves the claim that, early on, there is only an automatic facilitation that gives way to a strategic process, which can produce both inhibition and facilitation. The principal evidence for this is the observation that inhibitory effects appear later than do facilitatory effects. This rational analysis does not really take a position on mechanisms and certainly does not deny the possibility that different mechanisms may implement different aspects of rational prescriptions. There is neural evidence that inhibitory processes are slower because their paths involve more synapses (Shepherd, 1979). This may be a case where the constraints of the brain impact on rational derivations. The differences are not huge—facilitatory effects make themselves known in 100 msec., and inhibitory effects take 500 msec. The ideal would be instantaneous, which is not possible in any physical system.

Finally, this analysis can predict a result that ACT* failed to handle. This is the observation that one cannot seem to get second-order priming. DeGroot (1983—see also Balota & Lorch, 1986; Ratcliff & McKoon, 1988) used triplets of words, like bull–cow–milk where there is a strong association between the first and second and between the second and third but not between the first and third. The first did not prime the third, in contrast to what would be predicted by a spreading activation model, where activation would spread from the first to the second and, hence, to the third. However, on the preceding analysis, the first and third terms would have low relatedness. This is, in fact, the rational thing to do: If *milk* is never processed in the presence of *bull,* then one should not prime structures involving *milk* when *bull* appears.

The exact status of this result is somewhat in debate. Balota & Lorch (1986) did find second-order priming in a word-naming task but not in a lexical decision task. Even more recently, McNamara & Altarriba (1988) found evidence for weak, second-order priming more generally. One could argue that, for low-frequency words, second-order priming might reflect a rational estimation procedure. That is, if one has seldom seen *A, B,* or *C* but has seen *A* and *B* together and *B* and *C* together, it might be reasonable to guess that *A* and *C* will occur together. However, the words in these experiments were not low-frequency. The relative frequency in experience of *B* given *A* should have been an adequate basis for estimating the conditional need probability.[8]

If there are second-order priming effects, I suspect they reflect problems with the definition of second-order associates. Just because subjects do not give *milk* to *bull* does not mean that *bull* and *milk* are never encountered together. Indeed, Balota & Lorch (1986) reported that subjects rate these as more related than random pairs. Looking over the second-order associates of Balota and Lorch and of McNamara & Altarriba, it seems to me that the probability of the second-order associate is raised by the stimulus − that is, $n(\text{milk}|\text{bull}) > n(\text{milk})$. The basic problem is that free-association norms are only imperfect reflectors of the underlying probabilities.

Fan Effects

This analysis also relates fairly directly to fan effects (Anderson, 1983). The *fan effect* involves manipulating the number of facts in which a particular concept appears (the fan of the concept). The basic fan result is that a particular fact is more slowly retrieved when the concepts that compose it occur in more other facts. The result can be seen as directly arising from the conditional probability ratio $P(A|i)/P(A)$. The denominator, the probability of the trace, will be constant for the traces in a particular experiment, whereas the numerator should decrease with the fan of i. As the fan of i increases, it is associated with more traces and so the

---

[8]It is worth contrasting this discussion with the one on p.62. There, the argument was that first-order associates between elements such as milk and cow were useful estimates of the predictive relationship between milk and a *specific trace* involving cow. This is because we have a poor base for estimating the element-to-trace strength relative to the element-to-element strength (i.e., $P(A|i)$ versus $n(x|i)$). Here, the argument is that there ought to be enough information in first-order-associates to make second-order associates noninformative.

probability of any particular trace goes down. This analysis predicts that it is probability of the association, and not fan, that is the critical variable. It is just that as we increase fan, we decrease probability on the average. Anderson (1976) reported an experiment where fan was decorrelated from probability by studying different facts about a concept with different frequency: It was probability, and not fan, that was the controlling variable.

This analysis also predicts fan effects for foils. The more sentences that are studied about the concepts in the foil, the longer it takes to reject a foil. This is because the more facts there are about a concept, the more facts will have probabilities above the threshold for consideration (Equation 2-1). Considering these will slow down the rejection of the foil.

I have done a number of fan experiments (see Anderson, 1983) looking at the effect of the number of cues or terms in the sentence to be recognized. It turns out that it is easy to confound number of cues with the complexity of the memory task. However, when this is avoided, recall increases with number of cues. Each relevant term should increase the odds ratio for the target trace in Equation 2-2. The current analysis would also predict that retrieval time would be a function of the product of the fans of the individual cues, a prediction that is also generally confirmed (Anderson, 1976). A final prediction is that the fan of existing cues will be attentuated if an additional relevant cue is added. This prediction also has been confirmed (Anderson, 1983).

Another interesting wrinkle in the fan effect is what is known as the *negative fan effect* (Reder & Ross, 1983). In the Reder and Ross experiment, subjects are asked to study a number of thematically related facts about a person, such as:

Alan bought a ticket on the 10:00am trip.
Alan heard the conductor call "All aboard."
Alan read a newspaper on the train.
Alan arrived at Grand Central Station.

After memorizing such facts, subjects are asked to judge a query that tests the theme, such as:

Alan took a train trip.

The more such facts the subject has studied, the faster he or she is to judge such a probe. Thus, when any of a number of facts can be used to yield the same answer, we get a reverse of the fan effect.

This can be explained if we observe that the probability of some fact being relevant to answering this probe goes up with fan. Let A denote the event that any of the preceding facts associated with Alan are relevant. Then, the critical quantity from Equation 2-2 becomes:

$$\frac{P(A|H_A)}{P(\overline{A}|H_A)} \cdot \frac{P(A|Alan)}{P(A)} \cdot C$$

where C reflects other quantities that are constant across the fan manipulation. (Note that A denotes any of a set of facts, in contrast to previous discussion where we were interested in a single fact.) To an approximation, $P(A) = P(A|H_A)$, because they are both estimates of the base probability of a relevant fact, and H_A is not being manipulated. Similarly, to an approximation, $P(\overline{A}|H_A) = 1$, because the probability of any small set of facts is near zero because there are so many facts. Thus, the preceding ratio approximates $P(A|Alan)$ • C, which isolates $P(A|Alan)$ as the critical variable. The more relevant facts we study about Alan, the greater the probability of one of the facts in the presence of Alan, even though the probability of any particular fact goes down.

Again, this analysis exposes the basic rationality of the negative fan effect. In the presence of probes like "Alan took a train trip," the combined probability of the relevant knowledge can be high. This requires that we have a system that can aggregate probabilities when multiple memories agree on the answer. This is a common property of distributed processing models, so such a mechanism is not magical. It was also a property of the ACT* spreading activation (Anderson, 1983). The data indicate that it is apparently what the human mind does.

The Paradox of the Expert

One of the standard issues about the fan effect has been its implications for the nature of expertise (e.g., Smith, Adams, & Schorr, 1978). We assume experts to be people who know a lot about concepts in the domains of their expertise; thus, concepts in their field of expertise are high fan concepts. Or, said differently, the conditional probability of a fact given a domain concept must be low, because experts know so many facts about domain concepts. This seems to imply that they should be slowest to retrieve facts in the area of their expertise. However, this does not appear to be especially true. We are often faster to retrieve facts about familiar concepts. For instance, we can retrieve the fact that Ted Kennedy is a senator faster than we can retrieve the fact that Arlen Spector is a senator (Anderson, 1976).

It turns out that this result is predicted from our rational analyses. Recall that our need function depended on a history of that item and the fan of the cues. If the target memory has occurred frequently enough, its history component can overwhelm its fan component. Thus, provided that we have encountered the fact that *Ted Kennedy is a senator* much more often than *Arlen Spector is a senator,* we would be faster to retrieve the former, despite the fact that we know more things about Ted Kennedy. The saving grace for facts in our area of expertise, then, is that we encounter them more often.

The following algebraic analysis shows how frequency and fan relate in a rational model. Let *A* be *Ted Kennedy is a senator* and *B* be *Arlen Spector is a senator.* Then, adapting Equation 2-2, we have:

$$\frac{P(A|H_A+Q_A)}{P(\overline{A}|H_A+Q_A)} = \frac{P(A|H_A)}{P(\overline{A}|H_A)} \bullet \frac{P(A|Kennedy)}{P(A)} \bullet \frac{P(A|senator)}{P(A)} \tag{2-17}$$

$$\frac{P(B|H_B+Q_B)}{P(\overline{B}|H_B+Q_B)} = \frac{P(B|H_B)}{P(\overline{B}|H_B)} \bullet \frac{P(B|Spector)}{P(B)} \bullet \frac{P(B|senator)}{P(B)} \tag{2-18}$$

where Q_A refers to the cues in a probe for *A* and Q_B refers to the cues in a probe for *B*. As argued with respect to the negative fan effect (p.70), we can assume to an approximation that $P(A|H_A)/P(A) = P(B|H_B) / P(B) = 1$, $P(\overline{A}|H_A) = P(\overline{B}|H_B) = 1$. If we further assume that $P(A|senator)/P(A) = P(B|senator)/P(B)$, then the relevant terms to compare are $P(A|Kennedy)$ and $P(B|Spector)$. The point of setting up Equations 2-17 and 2-18 is to show that only one term is relevant to the comparison.

Now that we have identified it as the relevant term, let us analyze how $P(X|i)$ will vary with the frequency of *X,* which will be denoted *F,* the fan of *i,* which will be denoted *f.* This turns out to depend on *N,* the number of times *i* appears in the context, but no fact involving it is relevant. If we assume that each of the *f* facts is equally frequent:

$$P(X|i) = \frac{F}{f\bullet F + N} = \frac{1}{f + N/F} \tag{2-19}$$

Thus, the value of this probability both decreases with fan *(f)* and increases with frequency *(F)*. Which dominates depends on the exact values of *f, N,* and *F.* In particular, in a noisy environment (large *N*), *F* can dominate, creating an advantage for high frequency, high fan facts over low frequency, low fan facts.

I have done experiments (Anderson, 1983) where I had subjects learn experimental facts about either well-known people or unknown people and controlled the frequency of these facts. I found that, even though frequency is controlled, one can retrieve the experimental facts more rapidly about the well-known people. This is a result that cannot be predicted by the formal analysis here. However, it is more a fault of the analysis here than the rationality of memory. Although you do not know what the asymptotic frequency of a fact will be when you first encounter it, you can make an estimate based on frequency of other facts associated with the concept. By analogy, a library retrieval system can predict that a new book by a well-liked author will be borrowed frequently. Thus, the problem with our formal analysis is that the estimation of the history factor for a fact does not consider the content in the fact.

This predicts that as one gains experience with the frequency of experimental facts about familiar and unfamiliar people, and the frequencies of occurrence remain identical, the familiarity effect will disappear. That is to say, with enough experience, experimental frequency of facts can override prior frequency of the concepts that compose these facts. This result was obtained in Anderson (1983).

A further elaboration on the idea that subjects should use concept frequency to estimate need probability is that they can use the actual content of the memories to estimate need probability.[9] Thus, one might expect that memories involving oneself are more likely to be needed than memories concerning others, and there is evidence that autobiographical memories do enjoy an advantage, holding other factors constant (Keenan & Baillet, 1980). This may also be part of the resolution of the paradox of the expert. People's memories may assign higher need probabilities, rationally, to facts from their domain of expertise. There is evidence that memory retrieval does get better with practice in a particular domain (Chase & Ericsson, 1982).

RELATIONSHIP OF NEED PROBABILITY TO PROBABILITY AND LATENCY OF RECALL

The analysis to date has been really concerned with need probability. That is, the theory is about how the probability that an item will be needed varies as a function of its history and the cues presented. I have only assumed that it will be related monotonically to the two principal behavioral measures of memory, namely probability of recall and latency in recall. The basic assumption was that a subject would consider items in memory in the order of their need probability until the need probability fell below some threshold. This produces a monotonic relationship between need probability and recall latency.

The scheme of stopping when need probability falls below a threshold might seem to make probability of recall a step function of need probability. Indeed, as much of the research on all-or-none recall has demonstrated, there is a step-function-like quality to probability of recall such that if an item can be recalled on one occasion there is a high probability (often near 1) of its being recalled on later occasions, whereas if an item cannot be

---

[9]It turns out that in file systems one can use the type of file (e.g., program versus document) to help predict the probability of access (Satyanarayanan, 1981).

recalled on one occasion there is low probability (often near 0) of its being recalled on later occasions (for reviews, see Battig, 1968; Restle & Greeno, 1970). Latency has been shown (Anderson, 1981c) to be much more sensitive to presentation variables.

This does not imply, however, that all items with the same experimental history will be recalled or that all will not. There are at least two reasons why we cannot predict a particular item's recall from its history. The first is that we do not know its pre-experimental history. The second is that we are not sure of its experimental history. The subject may not have attended to it during some presentations, and the subject may have rehearsed it covertly during other time periods. There is evidence that we can improve our ability to predict subject's recall if we try to track attention (Loftus, 1972) or if we try to monitor rehearsals (Rundus, 1971).

This section considers some possible transformations from need probability to recall probability and latency. What would be desirable are transformations that are both very plausible and do not depend on much specific memory mechanisms. I was surprised to find out that there exist transformations that depend only on very general statistical properties that are true in a great variety of situations.

Analysis of Latency of Recall

We need some theory to relate the probability that an item is needed (which is the quantity we have analyzed to this point) to the time it will take to retrieve it. In the current analysis, need probability determines the order in which knowledge is examined which in turn determines latency. Given a particular item with need probability p we do not necessarily know the exact ordinal position in which it will be examined. This will depend on how many higher probability items there are in the situation. However, as an approximation we can assume probabilities are distributed according to Zipf's law. This law has been found to describe such things as distributions of words in prose samples by their frequency of occurrence, distribution of scientists by numbers of papers published, distribution of cities by population, distribution of names by size, and distribution of biological genera by number of species (Ijiri & Simon, 1977). The proposal here is that it describes the distribution of memories by their need probability.

A close approximate form for Zipf's law is $f(i) = ri^{-d}$, where i is the ordinal position of the item, f is the measure (count, income, need probability, etc.), d is a constant often estimated to be 2, and r is a scale factor (Ijiri & Simon, 1977). In the case of need probabilities of memories, we can use the following form:

$$p = rt^{-d} \qquad (2\text{-}20)$$

where p is the need probability of a fact and t is the time for its retrieval. Inverting this, we get the relationship between time and need probability:

$$t = [r/p]^{1/d}$$

Adding an intercept to t gives us a formula for reaction time, T:

$$T = l + [r/p]^{1/d} \qquad (2\text{-}21)$$

Earlier, Figs. 2-1 and 2-2 related need probability to frequency and recency of presentation. Figure 2-5 shows these functions transformed to give times setting $l = .3$, $r = .02$, and $d = 2$. As can be observed, we get typical practice effects and retention effects when measured by latency. That is to say, the transformation based on Zipf's law preserves the power–function relationship. It should be noted that the relationship between the slopes of the functions in Figs. 2-1 and 2-2 and the slopes of the functions in Fig. 2-5 is basically $1/d$.

Analysis of Probability of Recall

In the current theory, memory fails to recall an experience because the need probability for that memory is below the threshold that the system is willing to consider. As mentioned earlier, one might expect a perfect step function from a probability of 0 to 1 as the threshold is crossed. However, it is quite possible that the threshold will vary, depending on the situation. It is also possible that the actual evidence will vary from our estimate, depending on past history, lapses of attention, hidden rehearsals, and so forth that we cannot observe. It is also possible, all consideration of rationality aside, that there is some noise in the system. For all these reasons, there is some variance in our estimate of the distance between the evidence and the threshold and the actual distance. The natural distribution for this variance would be a normal distribution but, for purposes of analytic tractability, I replace it by the similar logistic distribution. Formally, the assumption is that the distance between the log need odds estimated, h, and the threshold θ, is distributed as a logistic function with parameter s. (The parameter s is related to the variance, which is $\pi^2 s^2/3$.) Then, the probability that a memory with log need, h, will be recalled is:

$$P = \frac{1}{1 + e^{(\theta - h)/s}} \qquad (2\text{-}22)$$

This implies that the relationship between the log odds of recalling an item, H, and the log need odds, h, is:

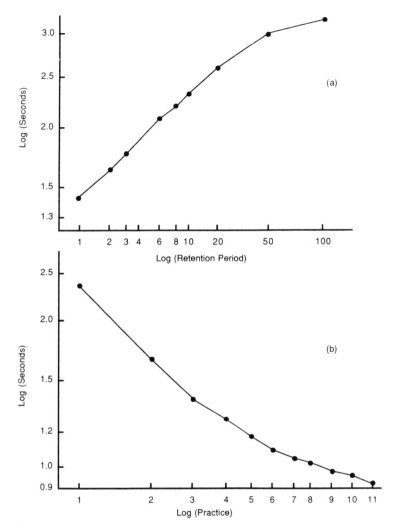

FIG. 2-5.   Transformations of Figs. 2-1 and 2-2 to introduce the dependent measure of response latency.

$$H = (h - \theta)/s \qquad\qquad (2\text{-}23)$$

Figure 2-6 shows transformations of the retention and practice functions (Figs. 2-1 & 2-2), setting $\theta = -5.0$ and $s = .5$. This plots probability of recall, untransformed, as functions of delay and practice, also untransformed. However, if we were to take log transforms and plot odds recall, rather than probability of recall, we would get linear functions with slopes $1/s$ of what they are in Figs. 2-1 and 2-2.

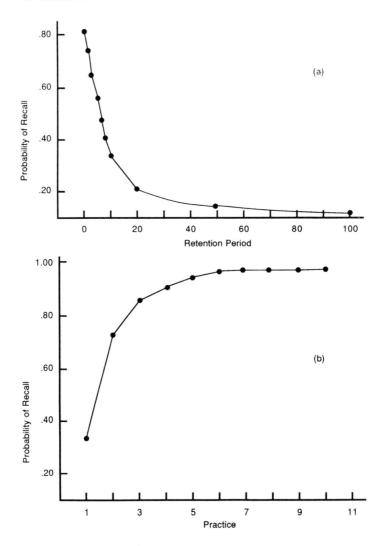

FIG. 2-6 Transformation of Figs. 2-1 and 2-2 to introduce the dependent measure of probability of recall.

This section has shown how need probability, which is a statistic derived from the environment, might plausibly be related to probability of recall and latency, which are statistics derived from the subject's behavior. These transformations preserve ordinal relationships in the need probabilities. Moreover, one important parametric property of need probability, the power function, is mirrored in the dependent measures. Subsequent sections examine how these transformations of need probability fare in terms of reproducing other parametric properties of memory data.

COMBINING INFORMATION FROM CUES

There has been a history of interest in how multiple cues combine to access a memory. The analysis we have sketched out earlier certainly has some predictions to make about this matter. I briefly develop the predictions of this analysis for reaction time, where there has been some research, and then go into a more extensive analysis of probability correct, where there is a correspondingly more extensive literature.

In this section, I use the following conventions: p to refer to need probability, o to refer to need odds $(o = p/(1-p))$, P to refer to recall probabilities, O to recall odds $(O = P/(1-P))$, and T to refer to recall times. The subscript Σi is used to refer to a set of cues, i. A single cue is denoted by just the subscript i. In this notation, Equation 2-2 may be rendered:

$$o_{\Sigma i} = \prod_{i=0}^{n} o_i \qquad (2\text{-}24)$$

where

$o_{\Sigma i} = P(A|H_A \& Q)/P(\overline{A}|H_A \& Q)$ is the need probability

$o_0 = P(A|H_A)/P(\overline{A}|H_A)$ is the history factor, and

$o_i = P(A|i)/P(\overline{A}|i)$ is the contextual effect of element i.

Analysis of Latency

The following equation, derived from Equations 2-21 and 2-24 relates the time to retrieve a memory trace given a set of cues, Σi, to the individual odds ratios:

$$T_{\Sigma i} = \left[r \, \frac{1 + \prod_{i=0}^{} o_i}{\prod_{i=0}^{} o_i} \right]^{1/d} \qquad (2\text{-}25)$$

where we ignore intercept.

It is also of interest to compare the predictions from this rational analysis with predictions from ACT* with respect to how time to retrieve a memory from multiple sources relates to time for retrieval from a single source. In ACT*, ignoring intercept, the basic equation took the simple form:

$$T_{\Sigma i} = \frac{\prod\limits_{i=1} T_i}{\sum\limits_{i=1} \prod\limits_{j \neq i} T_j} \qquad (2\text{-}26)$$

where the T_i are the times to retrieve the memory in response to single cues i.

We can convert Equation 2-25, for the current analysis, into an equation that relates retrieval time in response to a multiple-cue probe to times in response to single-cue probes:

$$T_{\Sigma i} = r^{1/d}[1 + o_0^{n-1}\prod_{i=1} (T_i^d/r - 1)]^{1/d} \qquad (2\text{-}27)$$

where T_i is the time in response to a probe consisting of just cue i. Again, o_0 is the odds associated with the history factor, and n is the number of cues. Despite their visible differences, it turns out that the quantities are quite similar in their predictions. For instance, both are dominated by the product ΠT_i, which means that both predict what has been called the min effect (Anderson, 1976) — which is that the more potent is a cue i, (i.e., the smaller T_i), the less of an effect there is of other cues.

In general, although the current equations are different superficially from the ACT* equations, they are highly correlated. For instance, Anderson (1974a) reported an experiment that orthogonally manipulated the fan of two cues from 1 to 3 to create nine conditions in total. The predictions of ACT* and this rational analysis correlate .99 for this experiment. This is closer than either correlate with the data (because of noise in the data). This is an example of a mechanistic model induced from data that coincides nearly perfectly with the outcome of a rational analysis.

Analysis of Accuracy

Similarly, we can relate probabilities of recall as a combination of need odds associated with each element in the probe. Combining Equations 2-22 and 2-24, we get:

$$P_{\Sigma i} = \frac{\prod\limits_{i=1} P_i}{(Bo_0^{1/s})^{n-1}\prod\limits_{i=1}(1 - P_i) + \prod\limits_{i=1} P_i} \qquad (2\text{-}28)$$

where $P_{\Sigma i}$ is probability of recall to a set of cues Σi, P_i is the probability of recall to cue i, n is the number of cues, and $B = e^{-\theta/s}$ is from Equation

2-22. This contrasts with a much simpler relationship in the ACT* model, which is:

$$P_{\Sigma i} = 1 - \prod_{i=1} (1 - P_i) \qquad (2\text{-}29)$$

As is discussed in more detail shortly hereafter, the ACT* analysis assumes that each cue contributes independently to recall, and the probability of failure of recall to a multiple cue is simply the product of the failures to the individual cues. In the rational analysis, it can be shown that, provided

$$(Bo_0^{1/s})^{n-1} = \frac{\prod\limits_{i=1} P_i}{1 - \prod\limits_{i=1}(1 - P_i)} \qquad (2\text{-}30)$$

the ACT* prediction will hold. If the left-hand side is smaller, recall will be larger than the ACT* bound, and if the left-hand side is larger it will be less than the ACT* bound.

There has been a considerable history of research concerned with how two cues combine to impact on probability of recall (Anderson & Bower, 1972; Bruce, 1980; Foss & Harwood, 1975; Jones, 1980; Le Voi, Ayton, Jonckheere, McClelland, & Rawles, 1983; Rubin & Wallace, 1989; Tulving & Watkins, 1975). This research has played an important role in the development of HAM and ACT.

One line of research concerned how well the verb and subject of a sentence combine to produce recall of the object. If we let P_s be the probability that a subject cue will lead to recall of the object, P_v be the probability that the verb cue will lead to recall of the object, and P_{sv} be the probability that a combined cue will lead to the recall of the object, ACT and HAM predicted:

$$P_{sv} = P_s + P_v - P_s P_v \qquad (2\text{-}31)$$

These models assumed that recall to a combined cue was an independent recall from each cue. Jones' (1980) fragment model made another prediction. It assumed that the trace of a subject-verb-object could be fragmented into a trace consisting of a subset of the subject, verb, and object. The SV probe would cue the object if there were SVO or SO or VO fragments. The S probe would cue recall if there was either a SVO trace or a SO trace. The V probe would cue recall if there was either a SVO or VO trace. Since Jones did not commit himself to the probabilities of the various fragments, he was left with the prediction

$$P_{sv} \leq P_s + P_v \qquad (2\text{-}32)$$

The problem with both of these predictions is that there are reliable circumstances where probability of recall to a combined cue exceeds the sum of probability of recall to individual cues (Anderson & Bower, 1972; Foss & Harwood, 1975; Rubin & Wallace, 1989).

The current view can accommodate and explain this variation of results. As noted earlier, the ACT* prediction will fail unless Equation 2-30 holds. In the case of the subject–verb–object cues, we can restate this equality as:

$$Bo_0^{1/s} = \frac{P_s P_v}{1 - (1 - P_s)(1 - P_v)} \qquad (2\text{-}33)$$

The ACT* prediction will hold only if this equality does. If the left-hand side is smaller, we get the higher-than-predicted recall to the combined cue. If it is sufficiently smaller, we will exceed the bound based on Jones' model (Equation 2-32) as well as the bound of the ACT* model. This inequality will obtain when the values of o_0 are small or the values of P_s and P_v are large. P_s increases with o_0 and o_1, and P_v increases with o_0 and o_2. Therefore, the only way to decrease o_0 and increase or maintain P_s and P_v is if o_1 and o_2 increase. Thus, we expect the bound to be exceeded in cases where the underlying o_0 is low and o_1 and o_2 are high—that is to say, when the strength of the trace is low but the strength of associations from subject and verb are high.

In a series of experiments, Anderson and Bower (1972) obtained such super recall by having the subject engage in elaborative processes. Presumably, these elaborative processes decrease the prior probability of the target item (o_0) by increasing the number of alternative structures in the data base. However, they should increase the strength of connection from the subject and verb to the target structure (o_1 and o_2) by increasing the co-occurrence of subject, verb, and object (and so increase $n(x|i)$). Thus, the elaboration manipulation should decrease o_0 in the preceding relationship but increase o_1 and o_2. Thus, we predict that elaborative processing could produce super recall.

Jones Experiment

The experiment by Jones (1980) is another research effort that was able to manipulate whether super recall was obtained. He created different conditions where the observed probabilities of recall to the subject–verb cue fell below and above the postulated bounds. His conditions were defined by the likelihood of the sentences subjects had to study. *Unlikely* sentences were sentences like *"The archer painted the dust"; possible* sentences were sentences like *"The judge jerked the boat"; and likely* sentences were sentences like *"The artist raised the pencil."* Table 2-4 shows recall to subject, verb, and object in these three conditions as well as the postulated bound based on the ACT* theory.

Let O_s be the observed odds of recall to the subject cue, and let O_v and O_{sv} be similarly defined. Let o_0 be the estimated odds in the history factor, o_1 the estimated ratio of conditional probabilities for the subject cue, and o_2 be the ratio of conditional probabilities for the verb cue. Then, there are the following relationships between the observed odds and the theoretical odds:

$$O_s = B(o_0 o_1)^{1/s} \tag{2-34}$$

$$O_v = B(o_0 o_2)^{1/s} \tag{2-35}$$

$$O_{sv} = B(o_0 o_1 o_2)^{1/s} \tag{2-36}$$

There are only three observed probabilities above but there are five parameters. We can define from these observed probabilities three composite numbers that allow us to detect changes in o_0, o_1, and o_2, even if they do not allow us to estimate them:

$$Bo_0^{1/s} = O_s O_v / O_{sv} \tag{2-37}$$

$$o_1^{1/s} = [O_{sv}/O_v] \tag{2-38}$$

$$o_2^{1/s} = [O_{sv}/O_s] \tag{2-39}$$

Table 2-4 reports these three measures for the three conditions. What is apparent from Table 2-4 is that the prior odds for the sentence have gone down in the likely condition, whereas the conditional odds for the subject

TABLE 2-4
Data from Jones Experiment and Parameter Estimates

		Sentence Type		
		Unlikely	Possible	Likely
ACT* bound	P_S	.361	.421	.396
	P_V	.293	.332	.386
	P_{SV}	.443	.500	.687
	$1-(1-P_S)(1-P_v)$	.548	.613	.629
	$Bo_0^{1/s}$	.294	.361	.188
	$o_1^{1/s}$	1.92	2.01	3.49
	$o_2^{1/s}$	1.41	1.38	3.36

and verb cues have gone up. This is the pattern we would predict. The subject is spending less time studying the sentence *per se* and more time strengthening the associative links. An extreme version of this would be cuing the subject for some well-known fact that he or she has not studied. Presumably, given *Reagan* or *defeated* alone, the probability of recall of *Carter* would be low, but in combination the probability of recalling *Carter* would be high. This is because the prior probability of this fact out of the blue is low, but it has strong associations to the combination of *Reagan* and *defeated*.

We see that the predictions of the rational model are basically much less constrained than those derived from the HAM or ACT models. Depending on the need odds, we can predict probabilities equal to, less than, or greater than the proposed bounds. Because the data show all directions of effects, such flexibility is required. All we can do is ask, as we have with respect to Table 2-4, whether the parameter values behave sensibly.

IMPLEMENTATION IN THE ACT FRAMEWORK

An interesting question is how we might implement the rational analysis sketched herein in the ACT framework. Recall that ACT* is a special theory within the ACT framework and it is possible to have other theories in that framework. Indeed, ACT* had a long line of predecessors. It appears that although this rational analysis is not consistent with ACT*, it can be implemented by a theory within the ACT framework.

It is useful to return to our earlier Equation 2-24:

$$o_{\Sigma i} = \prod_{i=0}^{n} o_i \qquad (2\text{-}24)$$

where the left-hand side denotes the odds that a memory trace is relevant in the presence of a set of cues, i; o_i reflects the odds associated with cue i [that is, $P(i|A)/P(i|\overline{A})$]; and o_o is the odds associated with prior history—that is, $P(A|H_A)/P(\overline{A}|H_A)$. One can take logarithms of Equation 2-24 and get:

$$h_{\Sigma i} = \sum_{i=0} h_i \qquad (2\text{-}40)$$

where $h_i = \log o_i$. The h_i can be interpreted as activation quantities that are computed in an activation model. The motivation in going from Equation 2-24 to Equation 2-40 is that we get a summation of quantities, and neural processes are typically thought of as summing activations rather than multiplying them. The summation of activation implied by Equation 2-40 is like that proposed in ACT*, with two important differences:

1. Each item starts out with its own activation level, h_0. Thus, items can be retrieved in the absence of relevant cues.

2. It is quite possible for the odds associated with a cue to be less than 1 and log-odds to be negative. This means that a cue can inhibit or make less likely a memory item. Although there was some controversy about whether cues could inhibit in 1983, when ACT* was published, by now such inhibitory effects are well established. Such inhibitory effects were discussed in the earlier section on priming.

Neither of the preceding two ideas is really possible in the ACT* formulation.

The major concepts of the ACT* theory are activation, node strength, and link strength. Activation controls the rate of processing of information in the production system. Thus, activation is the analogue of need probability that determines order of consideration in the current theory. Node strength is a function of a node frequency, and it determines how much activation can spread from a node. This is the analogue of the history factor in the rational theory. Link strength determines how activation spreading from a node is divided up among associated nodes. This is the analog of the contextual factor in the rational analysis—that is, the ratio of conditional probabilities. Thus, we can think of the activation in ACT* as a rough approximation to need probability—and indeed, this is how I thought of it, calling it a relevancy heuristic.

The one major discrepancy between this need analysis and the spreading activation analysis concerns the spreading process itself. In ACT*, activation starts at a node, spreads to its associates, and to their associates, and so on until it dampens away. In contrast, this need analysis, as discussed with respect to the issue of second-order priming, implies that we should only consider the first-order associates of an item. Curiously, few of the predictions in the ACT* book depended on its more extensive spread of activation.

In ACT*, there is more to retrieval than just spreading activation. The activated structures have to be matched against production patterns. Retrieval time in ACT* is really a function of the time for this pattern matching to complete, which, in turn, is a function of the level of activation of the data structures to be matched. The factor corresponding to pattern matching in this rational analysis is the time that it takes to test whether a particular memory trace is needed in the current situation. The ACT* pattern-matching theory might be a reasonable model of how this is done. However, it is at a level of detail too far removed from behavioral data to be of relevance to a rational analysis.

There are a few points that can be made by way of a rational analysis of this relevance testing that are critical to prediction, however. The central one is that the system can vary the depth with which it tests a candidate structure. Clearly, the fewer tests, the less time to process a memory trace, but the more errors there will be. Thus, in manipulating the number of tests, we get the basic prediction of a speed–accuracy trade-off. This is something that is not naturally part of the ACT* theory. The basic claim here is that the memory system sets up a level for testing that optimizes the outcome in terms of trading off reduced cost of testing against increased probability of false alarming.

One of the important empirical observations in motivating ACT* over its predecessors in the ACT line of theories is that the fan of data structures and the complexity of the tests being performed on the data in production matching interact multiplicatively. That is, the difference between complex and simple tests are greater when these tests are performed on high-fan items. In Anderson (1976), while concluding my evaluation of ACTE (a predecessor of ACT*), I noted that the empirically observed interaction between fan and test complexity was one of the major problems for that theory. Earlier ACT theories had claimed that relevant knowledge was first activated and then tested. This implied that fan (affecting retrieval) and complexity of test should have additive effects. In the ACT* model, however, activation (and hence fan) determined how fast the pattern would match, producing a multiplicative effect.

It should be clear that the current analyses, although not as detailed as the ACT* analyses, predict the same multiplicative relationship. The more complex the test, the more time that will be spent to reject an item. The larger the fan, the more items that will be tested and rejected before the target. Thus, the extra cost of a complex test will be expanded in the case of a high-fan item.

EFFECTS OF SUBJECT STRATEGY

The discussion, so far, has ignored any systematic analysis of possible effects of subject strategy on memory performance. However, it is well documented that subjects engage in numerous strategies for processing to-be-learned material and that these strategies can substantially affect their memory performance. Moreover, the evidence is that such strategies are acquired, and younger children's different memory performance may simply be a function of their different memory strategies (e.g., Flavell, 1977).

The question naturally arises as to how one is to conceive of memory strategy in a rational analysis. One attitude would be to ignore its role and assume that memory strategy is just part of the black box that is being optimized for memory performance. However, the radically different behavior that can occur as a consequence of strategy choice causes fundamental problems for this approach. For instance, in the same experiment, one subject will choose to repeat the items over and over again in a rote fashion, whereas another subject will engage in an elaboration strategy and enjoy a much better memory performance as a consequence. How can one argue that both subjects are engaging in behavior that will optimize their memory performance in the same environment?

A better way to conceive of this is that subjects are manipulating the information that is presented to human memory by their choice of strategy. Given different strategy-determined experiences, memory is behaving optimally in response to those experiences. Thus, for instance, given multiple redundant traces created by an elaboration strategy, memory has more traces to call upon and more interassociated traces. Thus, the advantage of elaborations is to be understood in terms of the same redundancy analysis that has been given for the ACT* theory (Anderson, 1983).

Thus, subjects can essentially manipulate the input to their memories. Their memories, blind to the intentions of the subjects and the fact of a deliberate manipulation, behave as rationally as they can given the statistics of the input they receive. This view leaves open the question of the rationality of subjects' strategy choice—that is, whether their manipulations are optimal by some criteria.[10] This question is not addressed in this book.

A consequence of this analysis is that understanding the details of human memory performance in many circumstances will require specifying the subjects' memory strategy; one cannot simply derive their behavior from an analysis of the information that the experimenter is presenting them.[11] This is because these strategies are intervening between the experimenter and their memories and transforming the information presentation. Indeed, in some situations, the subjects' memory performance will be more a function of strategy choice than any direct properties of the experimental manipulation. The next subsection provides one example of this in simulating the traditional free-recall experiment.

Simulation of Free Recall[12]

A basic observation about subjects in a free-recall experiment is that they often covertly rehearse items in addition to the item currently being presented. Modeling this particular phenomena has been part of a good

---

[10]Indeed, Reder (1987) has shown that memory strategies can have a highly adaptive character.
[11]In a way, this is just making the old point that the stimulus from the point of view of the subject may be different than the stimulus from the point of view of the experimenter.
[12]I would like to acknowledge the contribution of Bob Milson in developing this simulation.

many models of memory, including the original Atkinson & Shiffrin (1968) model, and was incorporated into the FRAN model of free recall (Anderson, 1972). It is also part of the more recent SAM model of free recall (Gillund & Shiffrin, 1984; Raaijmakers & Shiffrin, 1981).

It would be interesting to see what would happen if one placed on top of this rational model a simple version of this rehearsal process like the one in the SAM model. I assumed that subjects could maintain a buffer of four items for rehearsal. Each time an item was presented, it entered the buffer and, if the buffer was full, an existing item from the buffer was thrown out. The choice of which item to throw out was made randomly, with each item equally likely. When an item was first presented to the subject, it was encoded by memory. Every second it was in the buffer it had a .2 chance of being encoded anew. The benefit of residing in the buffer was these opportunities for further encodings.

Another assumption was that the memory system responded to each encoding of the item as a new use, whether that encoding came from experimenter presentation or buffer residence. Upon completion of the study, it was assumed that the subject would recall items with need probabilities above a certain threshold. The need probability of each item was a function of its rehearsal history, which reflected the factors of recency, number of repetitions, and the spacing of repetitions.

To completely specify the recall procedure also requires a description of the role that noise plays in converting from estimated need probabilities to probabilities of recall. An earlier section ("Analysis of Probability of Recall") provided the theoretical discussion of a noise factor, and the actual transformation from need probabilities to probabilities of recall was given by Equation 2-22.

The parameters for our simulations were:

- Rational model: $b = 100$, $v = 2$, $\alpha = 2.5$, $\beta = .04$
- Buffer rehearsal model: buffer size $= 4$, probability of rehearsal when in buffer $= .2$
- Noise model: $\theta = -4.7$, standard deviation $= .1$ and hence $s = .055$

A more detailed description of this simulation can be found in the appendix of Anderson & Milson (1989).

This undoubtedly underestimates the complexity of the memory strategies that are actually occurring in a free-recall experiment. The reader is invited to read the Appendix to Anderson (1972) to see how rich free-recall strategies can really be. However, this gives us a first-order approximation from which we can try to predict some of the basic statistics of recall.

Serial Position Effects

A classic datum from free recall concerns the serial position function — how probability of recall varies as a function of serial position in the study list. Murdock's (1962) data are shown in Fig. 2-7a, and the simulation of them is shown in Fig. 2-7b. The correspondence is quite good. The basic character of these data is the strong recency effect such that the recall drops off from the end, the lesser primacy effect where recall drops off from the beginning, and the flat region between. The recency effect is produced by the decay in need probability, and the primacy effect is produced because the first items in the buffer have an advantage in terms of number of rehearsals. It is not obvious that we would get the right orders of magnitude among these three regions of the serial position curve.

The primacy effect deserves a little comment. It is produced directly by the assumption of a buffer model and the fact that it takes a few items for the buffer to fill up and, so, the first items are not pushed out right away. Thus, in contrast to the recency effect, which is a result of the rational model, the primacy effect is a consequence of strategy choice. One might wonder whether this attribution of the primacy effect is correct. Perhaps, the first things in a new context tend to repeat more often or are more important (i.e., perhaps there is a rational explanation of the primacy effect). Certainly, prose (especially newspaper stories) tends to be structured with the important things first, but one can view this as writing adapting to the primacy effect rather than the cause of the primacy effect. Outside of human communication it is unclear whether there is any validity to the idea that first things are more important. The analogy in the library system would be something like the first borrowings of the day identifying the more often borrowed books. In a file system, it would be the first files accessed in the day being more important. It is unknown whether these effects exist in such systems, and even if they do they might exist for reasons that do not apply for the human system. For instance, borrowers might be lining up the door outside of the library to get the book that that night's newscast made critical.

On the other hand, recent evidence (Baddeley, 1986; Glenberg et al., 1980) suggests that the primacy effect in free recall may be due largely to the strategy of rehearsal. Manipulations that discourage rehearsal largely eliminate the primacy effect while they leave the recency effect unaffected. Thus, the current analysis may be correct in its attribution of primacy effect to rehearsal-strategy factors and the recency effect to rational factors.

Inspection of the simulation in Fig. 2-7b reveals that the curves do not really flatten, in contrast to the appearance of the empirical curves in Fig. 2-7a. This is because there is a retention effect throughout the serial positions, and earlier positions suffer because of their greater lag from test.

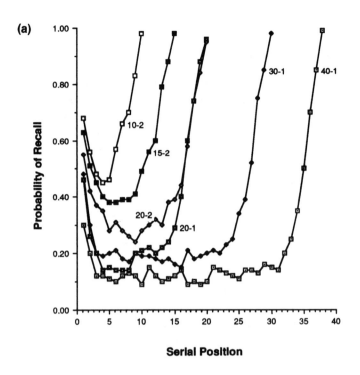

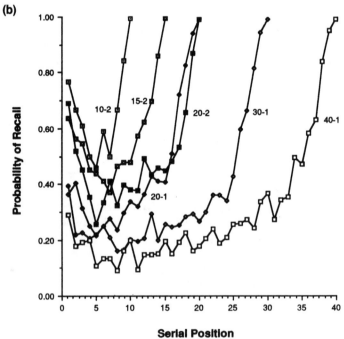

FIG. 2-7. Serial position effects for lists of various lengths and rates of presentation (seconds per minute). Part (a) is Murdock's (1962) data, and Part (b) is the simulation.

I suspect that I could make these curves indistinguishable from the data by suitably playing with the parameters. Nonetheless, Fig. 2-7b is more informative, because it reveals the prediction of a continually decaying serial position curve until the primacy portion. I predict that if the empirical serial position curve were long enough (i.e., stretched out over enough time) the decay would be apparent also.

Effects of Presentation Time and List Length

Roberts (1972) reported an experiment that systematically manipulated list length and study time per item. Figure 2-8a reports his data for list lengths of 10, 20, 30, and 40 items and for presentation rates of 1, 2, 4, or 8 seconds per item. Figure 2-8b reports the predictions derived from the theory. Both figures plot recall as a function of total study time, and the simulation provides a good fit. It is interesting to note that both Roberts' and simulation data display the phenomenon that, for the same total presentation time, recall increases as list length becomes larger (and presentation time per item decreases). This is not an obvious prediction of the theory. On the one hand, the longer the list of presented items, the more things there will be to choose from, but, on the other hand, the lower will be their mean need probability (presentation time decreases for each item). Apparently, the former factor overwhelms the latter.

We can reproduce Roberts' data, because the variance in need probability of individual items was sufficiently high to produce an advantage for a longer list with lower mean need probability. With high enough variance, a longer list with lower mean need probability will have more items with need probability over the threshold for recall. Variability in need probability is both determined by the parameter s and by the randomness of the rehearsal algorithm. The parameter s (set at .055) determines the variance in the need probability of items with the same rehearsal history. At this value of s there was not much variance in the need probability. Thus, this parameter setting did not produce Roberts' result; rather, it comes from the randomness of the rehearsal patterns. Hence, the Roberts' result is a consequence of the rehearsal strategy and not a parameter setting of the rational model.

CONCLUSIONS

This chapter began with an effort to derive some of the most robust results in human memory from a rational analysis. Many of the results dropped out of an analysis that assumed that subjects were responding to the objective statistics of information presentation. However, the analysis of free recall showed potential effects of subject strategy. This means that any

Mean total words recalled as function of TPT with PT as the parameter (Roberts' data)

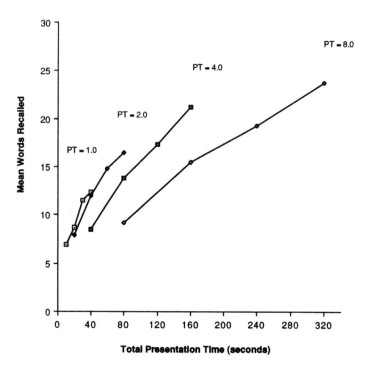

Mean total words recalled as a function of TPT with PT as the parameter (model prediction)

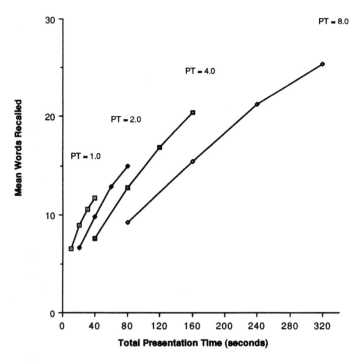

FIG. 2-8. Mean number of words recalled as a function of presentation time (abscissa) and test length (LL). Part (a) is Roberts (1972) data and Part (b) is the simulation.

particular memory phenomenon is going to be a joint
factors—general properties of memory that are rational'
specific strategies adopted by the subject to process the i
situation. In general, the effect of one memory strategy versu⌣
shift the relative need probabilities for different memories, making so⌣⌣
memories more available at the expense of others. A strategy can make
experimental traces more available than extra-experimental, it can make
elaborative traces more available at the the expense of verbatim traces, it
can make items in the beginning of the serial position more available at the
expense of later items, and so on. It makes the prediction that every time a
memory strategy produces a benefit we should be able to show a corresponding deficit. From this point of view, there is no better strategy in
general but just a better strategy for certain purposes. This is a perspective
that is very much like the concept of transfer-appropriate processing
(Bransford, Franks, Morris, & Stein, 1979). As said earlier, this leaves open
the possibility that there may be some framework in which the strategy
choices might be rationally determined. However, the nature of that
framework eludes me.

Short-Term Memory Limitations

As a final point in this chapter, I would like to consider the severe
short-term memory or working-memory limitations that we display. The
concept of short-term memory as a distinct cognitive mechanism is much in
dispute today. Although the mechanism is unclear, it is without dispute that
(a) we can maintain rapid and reliable access to but a few items, and (b)
once unattended, those items rapidly decay. Together, these two limitations
have spelled considerable sorrow for modern man. Telephone numbers just
fit in within these restrictions. Many of our errors in formal problem-
solving domains like mathematics and computer programming derive from
trying to keep too many things in working memory or from forgetting what
we are holding in working memory.

It should be noted that the current analysis of memory predicts these two
results. The rapid initial decay in the need probability means rapid loss to
unattended information. The only way to maintain access is to rehearse the
information, but limits on rehearsal rate bound how much information we
can so maintain. This dual model of rapid decay plus limited maintenance
capacity is the basic modern model (e.g., Baddeley, 1986) of short-term
memory, or, as it is more often now called, working memory. However, in
the current context, one can ask why the human has not developed greater
short-term memory capacity to relieve the sorrows of short-term memory
failure.

My guess is that short-term memory limitations do not have a rational explanation. In the terminology of the previous chapter, they reflect the human trapped on some local optimum of evolution. Just as we cannot move by hill climbing from our current morphology to one with wings, so we cannot evolve a separate short-term buffer for maintaining useful information. Rather, we borrow the recency portion of the retention function to serve this purpose as best as it can. In chapter 5 on problem solving, the short-term memory limitation is taken as a basic parameter of the system within which we do the optimization analysis.

ACKNOWLEDGMENT

This chapter is based on a paper that appeared in *Psychological Review* (Anderson & Milson, 1989).

3 Categorization

Contents
Preliminaries   93
The Goal of Categorization   95
The Structure of the Environment   96
   Theory-Based Versus Similarity-Based Categorization   98
   Hierarchical Structure of Categories   99
   Category Labels   99
Recapitulation of Goals and Environment   100
The Optimal Solution   101
An Iterative Algorithm for Categorization   102
   Prior Probability   103
   Conditional Probability   104
Application of the Algorithm   106
   Medin and Schaffer   106
Survey of the Experimental Literature   111
   Central Tendencies, Specific Instances, and Multiple Modes   111
   Correlated Features: Medin, Altom, Edelson, and Freko   114
   Base Rate Effects: Medin and Edelson   117
   Probability Matching: Gluck and Bower   120
   Basic Level Categories   125
   Order Sensitivity   130
Conclusion   132
   Comparisons to Shepard's Theory of Generalization   132
   Performance on Complex Tasks   133
   Implementation Considerations   134
Appendix: The Ideal Algorithm   138
   Prior Probabilities   138
   Conditional Probabilities   142
   Representing Extremity   144
   Hominids of East Turkana: An Example   145
   Rational Analysis   146

PRELIMINARIES

The previous chapter was concerned with a rational analysis of memory—how it is that we get access to past experiences. This chapter is concerned

93

with categorization—how we are able to go from past experience to make predictions about new objects. Because both deal with use of past experience, it is important to emphasize how they are different. Their differences derive fundamentally from their different goals. A memory analysis is appropriate when we need to retrieve and act on a specific past experience— for instance, when I want to remember where I parked my car at the airport parking lot. A categorization analysis is appropriate when we need to make a prediction about something new—such as whether a particular creature is likely to be dangerous.

Despite the fact that there are different goals, a number of mechanistic theories try to get both phenomena out of one mechanism. For instance, parallel-distributed models overlay memories in one system that is responsible for both retrieval and generalization (McClelland, Rumelhart, & Hinton, 1986). Exemplar-based theories of categorization (Medin & Schaffer, 1978; Nosofsky, 1988) categorize by retrieving specific memories and judging the similarity between the new object and the retrieved memories.

This chapter shows that a rational analysis of categorization can predict the empirical phenomena associated with categorization. I leave it largely an open issue as to what mechanisms are responsible for categorization and whether they are different from the mechanisms that are responsible for memory. Quite different ways of implementing categorization, some retrieval-based and some generalization-based, can be equivalent in their behavior (read Estes, 1986, for an elegant analysis). This is another testimony to the lack of identifiability at the mechanistic level. This chapter focuses mainly on a rational analysis that abstracts above such mechanistic indeterminacies. However, the chapter ends with some discussion of the implications for ACT-like implementations.

In contrast to research on memory, where rational analyses are a rarity, rational analyses are a prominent part of the literature on categorization. Many theories of categorization behavior are promoted in terms of their optimality features. In other cases, rational models are taken as first-order approximations against which to compare "more accurate" mechanistic models. Many of these rational models are even Bayesian in character. Most of the existing rational models do not seem to quite represent the situations that people face,[1] and I propose a rational model that I think provides a better characterization. Hopefully, others will complain about the accuracy of my characterization and produce even better rational models.

With these preliminary remarks out of the way, I turn to developing a rational analysis of categorization. First, I need to attend to the three components of framing the information-processing problem: specifying the

---

[1]But see comments later in this chapter on Shepard's (1987) model of generalization.

goals of the system in categorization, characterizing the relevant structure of the environment, and considering computational costs and possible limitations. The first two can be immediately addressed. The third requires some preliminary work to lay the conceptual framework.

THE GOAL OF CATEGORIZATION

Why do people form categories (assuming that they do)? There are at least three views of the origins of categories:

1. *Linguistic.* Linguistic labels provide us with the cues that a category exists, and we proceed to learn to identify it. This view is implicit, at least, in most experimental research on categorization.

2. *Feature overlap.* We notice that a number of objects overlap substantially and proceed to form a category to include these items. This is essentially the position of Rosch (e.g., Rosch, Mervis, Gray, Johnson, & Boyes-Braem, 1976). There is experimental research to show that people can learn categories in the absence of category labeling. Common experience also tells us that this can happen.

3. *Similar function.* We notice that a number of objects serve similar functions and proceed to form a category to include them. This, for instance, is the position advocated by Nelson (1974). It involves distinguishing the features of an object into those that are functional (e.g., can be used for sitting) and those that are not (e.g., have four legs).

These three views need not be in opposition. They are all special cases of the predictive nature of categories. Categorization is justified by the observation that objects tend to cluster in terms of their attributes — be these physical features, linguistic labels, functions, or whatever. Thus, if one can establish that an object is in a category, one is in a position to predict a lot about that object. From this point of view, the linguistic label associated with the category is just another feature to be predicted. It may be that certain features are more important to predict (i.e., the functional ones and linguistic labels) than others but this is just a second-order wrinkle on the basic goal of prediction. The more we can predict about the environment, the better adapted our behavior will be.

Although it is easy to say that prediction is the goal, it remains to be said precisely what that goal means. This requires first specifying the structure of the environment that we are trying to predict. As in the previous chapter, the development is Bayesian and, at some points, quite mathematical. Again, to help the reader, Table 3-1 summarizes the mathematical notation.

TABLE 3-1
Mathematical Notation Used in Chapter 3

Conventions

x	Indexes partitions.
k	Indexes categories.
i	Indexes dimensions (as well as serving as a general index).
j	Indexes values on dimension.
s	Denotes number of categories.
n	Denotes number of objects.
r	Denotes number of dimensions.
m	Denotes number of values on a dimension.
m_i	Denotes number of values on a dimension i.
n_{ij}	Denotes number of objects displaying value j on dimension i.
n_k	Denotes number of objects in category k.

Probabilites

p_{ij}	Probability of displaying value j on dimension i.
$Pred_{ij}$	Predicted probability of displaying value j on dimension i. See Equations 3-1 and 3-2.
$P(ij\|k)$	Probability of displaying value j on dimension i given the object comes from category k. See Equation 3-7.
$P(ij\|x)$	Probability of displaying value j on dimension i given partition x.
$P(F\|k)$	Probability of displaying feature structure F given the object comes from category k. See Equation 3-6.
$P(F_n\|x)$	Probability of the first n objects displaying feature structure F_n given partition x.
$P(k\|F)$	Probability that an object comes from category k, given it has feature structure F. See Equation 3-3.
P_k	Same as $P(k\|F)$.
P_0	Same as $P(k\|F)$ where k is a new category.
$P(x\|F_n)$	Probability of partition x of the first n objects given they display feature structure F_n.
$P(k)$	Prior probability that an object comes from category k. See Equation 3-4.
$P(0)$	Prior probability that an object comes from a new category. See Equation 3-5.
$P(x)$	Prior probability of partition x.

Parameters

c	The coupling probability that two objects will come from the same category. Set at .3 throughout chapter.
α_i	Measure of sensitivity to dimension i. See Equation 3-7′.

THE STRUCTURE OF THE ENVIRONMENT

The proposed structure of the environment is, in many ways, simple-minded. The proposal has as its virtue that it suffices to account for a good number of experimental results. Undoubtedly, as the domain of application is expanded, it will be necessary to consider issues ignored here.

The assumed formal structure of the world is as follows: At any point in time, a person has experienced a set of n objects that can be partitioned into s disjoint sets. Any object can be classified according to some r dimensions. Each dimension i has m_i values.[2] The values of a dimension are thought of as having a discrete, cardinal structure. Each partition or subset is a category and can be defined extensionally by its members. However, its real significance comes from the fact that it also has an intensional definition: It has a set of probabilities p_{ij} that its members will display value j on dimension i. It is these probabilities that will allow the system to categorize new objects and predict their properties. The induction problem for the system is to simultaneously identify the categories, the objects in each category, and the probabilities associated with the category.

Thus, the basic claim is that there are categories in the human head because there are categories in the world that we are trying to predict. What does it mean for there to be a category in the real world? It means that the objects in the world can be divided up into disjoint sets and that the members of a set are defined by shared probabilities of displaying various features. This is the modern scientific understanding of the plant and animal kingdoms. There exist the phenomena of species that produce a disjoint partitioning of the living objects because of inability to crossbreed. The shared genetic code within a species gives rise to traits with probabilities corresponding to the proportion of the phenotype in the species.

It is unclear whether other types of objects really participate in such disjoint, conjunctive, probabilistic categories or just give a good approximation to this. Human artifacts approximately display such a structure. Hammers and violins are disjoint (or nearly so), display a number of common properties within their categories, but do so only probabilistically. Exactly what causes us to create this nearly perfect disjoint structure on the artifacts is unclear to me. The categorical structure of artifacts cannot be explained by appealing to something so straightforward as genetics, but it is nearly as real as the categorical structure of living things.

To the extent that the formal model of the world is only approximately correct, the predictions derived about human behavior should be only approximately correct. It remains to be determined what approximations there might be in the world and what their consequences might be for human behavior.

There are at least three ways in which this characterization of the world might be controversial given the current literature on categorization. These

---

[2]Thus, one restriction on this analysis is that it only deals with cardinal dimensions. I think it could be extended to continuous dimensions along the lines suggested by Shepard (1987). There are, in fact, well-established Bayesian schemes for induction on continuous dimensions (Berger, 1985).

involve the issues of theory-based categorization, hierarchical structure, and the role of category labels. It is important to acknowledge each of these and discuss them.

Theory-Based Versus Similarity-Based Categorization

There is a rather one-sided controversy in the field between proponents of a *similarity-based* approach and a *theory-based* approach to category structure. Practitioners of the similarity-based approach attempt to understand how the similarity among the features of objects determines category formation. They are criticized by proponents of the theory-based approach, who point out that there are often theoretical reasons why objects are placed in categories that go beyond superficial similarity. Thus, for instance, when we are dealing with natural objects, like dogs, we know that features associated with their constitution are critical to their category membership, whereas features associated with their use (hunting) are not (see Gelman, 1988). In contrast, when dealing with artifacts like cups, features associated with their use (for drinking) are critical, but features associated with their constitution are not.[3] Practitioners of the similarity-based approach seem not to argue with these points but, rather, take the attitude that they will work on the part of the story that is most tractable.

Although this chapter gives some attention to theory-based categorization, the current development is largely in the maligned similarity camp. Therefore, two things need to be said. First, this is just an approximate analysis of the part of the phenomena that is most tractable. A rational analysis would predict that to whatever degree one can improve prediction by appeal to theory, then human categorization would appeal to theory. The development in this chapter establishes some hooks for attaching such theory-based considerations, although it will not develop them.

Second, some of the points made by the theory-based camp confuse categorization and labeling. For instance, Murphy and Medin (1985) noted that such dissimilar creatures as camels, ostriches, crocodiles, mice, and eels were put in the "unclean" category by Jewish dietary law, and gazelles, frogs, most fish, grasshoppers, and some locusts were in the "clean" category. Under the analysis advanced in this chapter, it is extremely unlikely that there would be any categories involved here. Rather, it is just a matter of certain creatures from different categories sharing a label, clean or unclean.

---

[3]See the discussion of extremity in the Appendix for a way this might be incorporated into the current analysis.

Hierarchical Structure of Categories

In formal analyses of categories, it is typical to see objects in hierarchies of categories such that an object can be a coho salmon, a salmon, a fish, an animal, and a physical object. In line with arguments of Rosch (Rosch et al., 1976), the rational analysis in this chapter assumes that a certain level in this hierarchy tends to be special. She has called this the basic level. Below this level of categorization, objects do not acquire many more properties with increasing specialization. Above this level, they lose most of their properties. For most of us, the basic level in the preceding example would be fish. The categorization process should strive for a disjoint partition of the objects in the world into mutually exclusive sets. The partition should maximize what we can predict about the world. The most specific partition would be one that had each object in a separate category. The most general partition would be one that put all objects in the same category. Neither would allow us to predict features with greater accuracy than their base rate in the world. Somewhere in between lies the maximally predictive partition, and the categories that this partition produces are the basic level categories. This chapter focuses on a theory of the identification of these basic-level categories but does not deny the possibility of a hierarchy that extends above or below these basic-level categories.

Under this rational analysis, a hierarchical structure should exist if it improves prediction. This will happen if different dimensions could be differentially predicted at different levels. Thus, one might be able to predict ball chasing from knowledge that an animal is a labrador, barking from knowledge that he is dog, and that he has a spleen from knowledge that he is an animal. The exact formal conditions necessary to enhance prediction by a hierarchy are tricky, which is why I am avoiding the issue here.

Category Labels

A number of researchers (e.g., Kahneman & O'Curry, 1988; Mandler, Bauer, & McDonough, 1988) have recently pointed out that there has been a great deal of confusion engendered because of the focus on prediction of category labels. Category formation is not equivalent to assigning labels, and it is possible to form categories in the absence of any labels (Brooks, 1978; Fried & Holyoak, 1984; Homa & Cultice, 1984). A label is just another feature. As becomes evident, the rational model may form categories that disagree with the experimenter's category labels.

Thus, there is no less reason to sort dolphins into a category that includes fish than there is to sort nonflying creatures into a category that includes birds.[4] There is nothing logically different about the label "is a mammal" than about the feature "can fly." They are both features that one wants to be able to predict, although one feature might be more important to predict than the other. If one can maximize prediction by violating a feature, then one will violate that feature even if it is a category label.

If labels are correlated with other category features, as they often are, they will help promote categorization as would any other correlated feature. The more that can be predicted by category membership, the more advantage there is to creating such a category.

RECAPITULATION OF GOALS AND ENVIRONMENT

With these issues discussed, we can restate what the situation is and what the goals of the system should be. Basically, our system has certain priors about the world that correspond to its assumptions about the structure of the environment; our system has experience with certain objects; and, from this, our system makes predictions about features of new objects. To state this more elaborately:

1. The system has certain priors that the objects it encounters will be divided up into various categories, and the categories will display various probabilities p_{ij} of features. These priors amount to a probability density over various partitions of the objects into categories and probabilities p_{ij} for categories. Presumably, one role of theory is to set these priors to be something other than totally uniform (or in the terminology of Bayesian theory, non-informative priors).

2. The actual observed feature structure of objects has different probabilities under different partitions and p_{ij}. These are the conditional probabilities in a Bayesian analysis.

3. The standard Bayesian formula can be applied to Items 1 and 2 to calculate the posterior density over various partitions and p_{ij}.

4. The typical decision that a person has to make is a prediction about the value of a new object on some dimension. The posterior probabilities calculated in Item 3 are the key to this:

   (a) If the person must commit to a decision, then he should choose the feature that has highest posterior probability (assuming equal cost and gains associated with all hits and misses).

---

[4]This does not deny that we can know that dolphins are mammals, but that knowledge may derive from facts we have memorized rather than natural categorical structures.

(b) Often, subjects are asked to assign a probability or confidence, in which case their response should be some monotonic function of the posterior probabilities.

The behavior in situations like (a) should show much more radical shifts as the posterior probabilities cross various decision thresholds in (b).[5] However, as discussed under probability of recall in the previous chapter, it would be unrealistic to expect pure step functions. Thus, in all cases, we are left with a prediction of a monotonic relationship between posterior probabilities and behavioral measures.

THE OPTIMAL SOLUTION

With all of this said, it is fairly straightforward how to go about calculating the probability that an object should display a particular feature if there were no computational limitations. This optimal solution is briefly described and then its serious computational limitation is noted: Assume that the person has seen n objects, is presented with a $n + 1$st object with some dimensions specified, and wants to estimate the probabilities of various values on other dimensions — for example, we want to predict whether the next object we encounter has a positive value on the "dangerous" dimension. We need to consider all possible ways of breaking the $n + 1$ objects into categories. Let x be a variable that ranges over all such partitions. Let $Pred_{ij}$ be the estimated probability that the $n + 1$st object will display value j on dimension i. Then the correct formula for $Pred_{ij}$ is:

$$Pred_{ij} = \sum_x P\ (x|F_{n+1})P(ij|x) \tag{3-1}$$

where $P(x|F_{n+1})$ is the probability of partition x given F_{n+1}, the observed feature structure of the $n + 1$ objects, and $P(ij|x)$ is the probability that the $n + 1$st object displays value j on dimension i in partition x.

The Appendix to this chapter contains an elaborate mathematical analysis of this ideal solution. However, it is not pursued in the main body of this text because it is computationally infeasible. The problem is that the number of partitions of n objects grows exponentially with n. There is only one way to partition one object, which is that it must be in its own category. These are two ways to partition two objects — either they must be in the same category or in different categories. There are five ways to partition three objects a, b, c — {a b c} or {a}{bc} or {ab}{c} or {ac}{b} or {a}{b}{c}.

---

[5]For example, in a simple two-alternative choice situation with equal costs, we should always respond one way if the probability is .49 but the other way when it is .51.

There are 15 ways to partition four objects and 52 ways to partition five. The number of partitions of n objects is a Bell exponential number (Berge, 1971) and is approximated by the following expression:

$$(n + 2)! / (3 * 2^n)$$

which clearly grows exponentially with n.

This means that it becomes prohibitive to calculate $Pred_{ij}$ with n that are of realistic size—that is, we have experienced millions of objects. Also, the ideal solution has the peculiar feature that we reconsider all of the objects we have seen every time we calculate a prediction. At best, the calculations of the mind must approximate this value in some way.

Another peculiar feature of the ideal solution is that it proposes that we never commit on the category structure of the objects we have seen but rather keep all possibilities in mind. This runs contrary to our everyday experience of seeing objects as members of specific categories. What I propose next is an iterative procedure that is similar to a number of proposals in the artificial intelligence literature on machine learning (e.g., Lebowitz, 1987; Fischer, 1987). It has the virtue of avoiding the exponential explosion and delivering a specific category structure for the objects studied.

The motivation for this algorithm is fundamentally an assumption about computational constraints. This is the one place where issues of computational limits, step 3 in a rational analysis, play a role in this theory of categorization. Specifically, the assumption is that an algorithm for categorization must commit to a category structure for the objects seen so far and cannot later consider alternative structures. This prevents the exponential explosion and, as a side effect, produces the phenomenon of a definite category structure. Within the constraint of this assumption, we want to get the most accurate approximation to the ideal $Pred_{ij}$.

AN ITERATIVE ALGORITHM FOR CATEGORIZATION

In developing this iterative algorithm, mathematical results are taken from the Appendix on the ideal algorithm. This allows the iterative algorithm to be stated without long derivations or discussion of alternative assumptions.

The following is a formal specification of the iterative algorithm:

1. Before seeing any objects, the category partitioning of the objects is initialized to be the empty set of no categories.

2. Given a partitioning for the first m objects, calculate for each category k the probability P_k that the $m + 1$st object comes from category k. Let P_0 be the probability that the object comes from a completely new category.

3. Create a partitioning of the $m + 1$ objects with the $m + 1$st object assigned to the category with maximum probability.

4. To predict value j on dimension i for the $n + 1$st object, calculate

$$Pred_{ij} = \sum_k P_k \, P(ij|k) \tag{3-2}$$

where P_k is the probability that the $n + 1$st object comes from category k and $P(ij|k)$ is the probability of displaying value j on dimension i.

The basic algorithm is one in which the category structure is grown by assigning each incoming object to the category it is most likely to come from. Thus, a specific partitioning of the objects is produced. Note, however, that the prediction for the new $n + 1$st object is *not* calculated by determining its most likely category and the probability of j given that category. This calculation is performed over all categories. This gives a much more accurate approximation to the ideal $Pred_{ij}$, because it handles situations where the new object is ambiguous among multiple categories. It will weight these competing categories approximately equally.

It remains to come up with a formula for calculating P_k and $P(ij|k)$. Because $P(ij|k)$ is involved in the definition of P_k, we focus on P_k. In Bayesian terminology, P_k is a posterior probability $P(k|F)$ that the object belongs to category k given that it has feature structure F. Bayes formula can be used to express this in terms of a prior probability $P(k)$ of coming from category k before the feature structure is inspected and a conditional probability $P(F|k)$ of displaying the feature structure F given that it comes from category k:

$$P_k = P(k|F) = \frac{P(k)P(F|k)}{\sum_k P(k)P(F|k)} \tag{3-3}$$

where the summation in the denominator is over all categories k currently in the partitioning, including the potential new one. This then focuses our analysis on the derivation of a prior probability $P(k)$ and a conditional probability $P(F|k)$. The Appendix gives an extensive discussion relevant to both in the ideal case. Here, I just focus on stating the results that will be used in the iterative case. The iterative results can be derived rather directly from the ideal results.

Prior Probability

The critical assumption is that there is a fixed probability c that two objects come from the same category, and this probability does not depend on the number of objects seen so far. This is called the *coupling probability*. If one takes this assumption about the coupling probability between two objects being independent of the other objects and generalizes it, one can derive a simple form for *P(k)*:

$$P(k) = \frac{cn_k}{(1-c) + cn} \tag{3-4}$$

where c is the coupling probability, n_k is the number of objects assigned to category k so far, and n is the total number of objects seen so far. Note that for large n this closely approximates n_k/n, which means that there is a strong base rate effect in these calculations with a bias to put new objects into large categories. Presumably, the rational basis for this is apparent.

We also need a formula for *P(0)*, which is the probability that the new object comes from an entirely new category. This is

$$P(0) = \frac{(1-c)}{(1-c) + cn} \tag{3-5}$$

For large n, this closely approximates $(1-c)/cn$, which is again a reasonable form — that is, the probability of a brand new category depends on the coupling probability and the number of objects seen. The greater the coupling probability and the more objects, the less likely it is that the new object comes from an entirely new category.

Conditional Probability

As a major simplifying assumption, let us consider the probability of displaying features on various dimensions given category membership to be independent of the probabilities on other dimensions. Then we can write

$$P(F|k) = \prod P(ij|k) \tag{3-6}$$

The reader will recognize *P(ij|k)* from Equation 3-2, which is the probability of an object displaying value j on dimension i given that it comes from category k.

This independence assumption does not prevent us from recognizing categories with correlated features. Thus, we may know that retrieving sticks and being black are highly correlated for labradors. This would be represented by high probabilities of the stick-retrieving and the black features in the labrador category. What the independence assumption prevents us from doing is representing categories where values on two dimensions are either both one way or both the opposite. Thus, it would prevent us from recognizing a single category of animals that were either large and fierce or small and gentle, for instance. (This is the problem of representing a disjunction of two conjuncts.) Later, this chapter discusses how serious a limitation this really is. (Basically, we will see that we can deal with this by decomposing a large category into a number of smaller categories.)

The effect of Equation 3-2 is to focus us on an analysis of the individual *P(ij|k)*. Their analysis is discussed at considerable length in the Appendix for the ideal case and can again be easily generalized to the iterative case. There is one important complexity in that analysis. It requires a probability density that specifies our prior probabilities of various *P(ij|k)*. Conditional probabilities can be calculated for the observed feature distribution on dimension *i* given various sets of priors for *P(ij|k)*. Then the Bayesian formula can be used to calculate the posterior distribution of *P(ij|k)* from this prior distribution and these conditional probabilities. An important complexity in all this is that our priors and posteriors are probability densities of probabilities. This same complexity occurred in the previous chapter on memory, where there were probability densities of need probabilities.

Although other assumptions are considered, the assumption imported from the Appendix is that the prior distribution of probabilities is what is called, in Bayesian terminology (Berger, 1985), a *non-informative prior*. Effectively, this means that initially all possible probabilities are equally likely.

Given the assumption of non-informative priors, we can proceed to calculate a posterior density of probabilities and the mean of this density. That mean is the value of *P(ij|k)*:

$$P(ij|k) = \frac{n_{ij} + 1}{n_k + m_i} \tag{3-7}$$

where n_k is the number of objects in category *k* that have a value on dimension *i*; n_{ij} is the number of objects in category *k* with the same value as the object to be classified; and m_i is the number of dimensions to be classified. For large n_k, this approximates n_{ij}/n_k, which one frequently sees promoted as the rational probability. However, it has to have this more complicated form to deal with problems of small samples. For instance, if we have just seen one object in a category and it was red, we would not want to guess that all objects in the category are red. If there were seven colors that were equally probable on prior grounds, the above formula would give 1/4 as the posterior probability of red and 1/8 for the other six colors as yet unseen.

Basically, Equations 3-6 and 3-7 give us a basis for judging how similar an object is to the category's central tendency.

TABLE 3-2
Features I

Animals	HAIR	LIGHT COLOR	LAY EGGS	MAMMALS	FOUR LEGGED	FLIES	BIG	AGGRESSIVE	HAS A BEAK	GIVES MILK
WHALES	0	1	0	1	0	0	1	0	0	1
SEALS	0	1	0	1	0	0	1	0	0	1
DOGS	1	0	0	1	1	0	1	1	0	1
CATS	1	0	0	1	1	0	0	1	0	1
HORSES	1	0	0	1	1	0	1	0	0	1
BEARS	1	0	0	1	1	0	1	1	0	1
BATS	1	0	0	1	0	1	0	0	0	1
HUMANS	0	1	0	1	0	0	1	0	0	1
MICE	1	1	0	1	1	0	0	0	0	1
PLATYPUS	1	0	1	1	1	0	0	0	1	1
CHICKENS	0	1	1	0	0	0	0	0	1	0
PENGUINS	0	0	1	0	0	0	1	0	1	0
ROBINS	0	0	1	0	0	1	0	0	1	0
OSTRICHES	0	1	1	0	0	0	1	0	1	0
CROWS	0	0	1	0	0	1	0	0	1	0
PARROTS	0	0	1	0	0	1	0	0	1	0
SPARROWS	0	1	1	0	0	1	0	0	1	0
EAGLES	0	1	1	0	0	1	1	1	1	0
HAWKS	0	1	1	0	0	1	0	1	1	0
SEAGULLS	0	1	1	0	0	1	0	0	1	0

APPLICATION OF THE ALGORITHM

The major portion of this chapter surveys the application of this algorithm to results in the experimental literature. Before doing this, however, I would like to discuss issues involved in the application of this algorithm and illustrate its behavior applied to a couple of test cases.

The predictions of this algorithm are potentially order-sensitive, in that a different partitioning may be uncovered for a different ordering of instances. In actual practice, the behavior of the algorithm varies little with order of instances in cases where there is a strong category structure; but in cases of weak or ambiguous category structure, order can be important. The iterative algorithm is also extremely fast. A Franz LISP implementation categorized the 290 items from Michalski and Chilausky's (1980) data set on Soybean disease (each with 36 values) in 1 CPU minute on a Vax 780. This is without any special effort to optimize the code. It also diagnosed 93% of the test set of 340 soybean instances, which compares favorably with Michalski and Chilausky's handcrafted (but learned) solution, which got 98%. (This example is discussed in a little more detail later.)

Table 3-2 illustrates a toy problem used to test out the algorithm. Listed there are 20 animals with 10 binary features. I made up these feature assignments off the top of my head, and inspection shows some misjudgments on my part. The reader will note that the categorical label "bird" versus "mammal" is not given special status. Depending on the coupling parameter, c, the algorithm will merge all 20 animals into a single category, split them up into many categories, or divide them up into two or three categories. It extracts two or three categories for values of c in the range between .2 and .95. In this range, one category is always birds. Depending on the value of c and the ordering of the examples, it might extract a separate mammal category that includes human, seal, and whale (the reader will note that they have been given identical binary encodings) from the other seven mammals. If after observing 19 of the objects, the algorithm is asked to predict the category label of the last object (i.e., the value of the 4th dimension in Table 3-1) from the nine other features, it assigns a better-than-90% estimated probability to the correct category label. This example makes the point that the algorithm behaves sensibly, robustly, and does not require that the category label be treated differently than any other dimension.

Medin and Schaffer

The first experiment in Medin and Schaffer (1978) is a nice one for illustrating the detailed calculations of the algorithm. They had subjects study the following six instances each with binary features:

```
1 1 1 1 1
1 0 1 0 1
0 1 0 1 1
0 0 0 0 0
0 1 0 0 0
1 0 1 1 0
```

The first four binary values were choices in visual dimensions of size, shape, color, and number. The fifth dimension reflects the category label. After subjects learned to classify these six objects, Medin & Schaffer then presented the same 6 objects with their category labels missing plus six new objects without labels: 0111__ , 1101__ , 1110__ , 1000__ , 0010__ , and 0001__ . Subjects were to predict the missing category label.

We derived simulations of this experiment by running the program across various random orderings of the stimuli and averaging the results. Figure 3-1 shows the simulation with the presentation order 11111, 10101, 10110, 00000, 01011, 01000 using the coupling probability c = .5. What is illustrated in Figure 3-1 is the search behavior of the algorithm as it

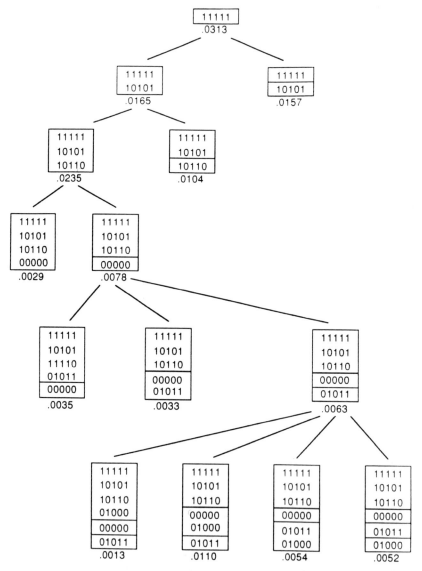

FIG. 3-1.   An illustration of the operation of the iterative algorithm in the material from the first experiment of Medin & Schaffer (1978). Boxes represent alternative partitionings, and bars within a box separate categories.

considers various possible partitionings. The numbers associated with each partition are measures of how probable the new item is given the category to which it is assigned in that partition. These are the values calculated by Equations 3-3 through 3-7. The quantities reported in Fig. 3-1 are the $P(k)P(F|k)$ — that is, the products of the prior probabilities and the conditional probabilities. Equation 3-3 specifies how to rescale them into posterior probabilities. The first item is 11111. There is only one possible partitioning for this item. Thus, $P(k) = 1$. $P(F|k) = (.5)^5 = .0313$, because this is the product of the five independent probabilities of getting 1 on each dimension, and Equation 3-7 gives these as .5 for a binary dimension with no instances seen in that category as yet (i.e., $n_{ij} = n_k = 0$).

There are two ways to expand this to include 10101 — either to merge it with the existing category or to create a new one. The 10101 is merged with the existing category, as this is more likely. Now let us consider in detail the calculation of the two possible ways of incorporating the next object, which is 10110. First, consider merging it with the existing category. Combining Equations 3-3, 3-4, 3-6, and 3-7 yields

$$P(k)P(F|k) = \frac{2c}{(1-c)+2c} \cdot \frac{n_{11}+1}{4} \cdot \frac{n_{20}+1}{4} \cdot \frac{n_{31}+1}{4} \cdot \frac{n_{41}+1}{4} \cdot \frac{n_{50}+1}{4}$$

where c is the coupling probability, n_{i0} is the number of zeros in dimension i, and n_{i1} is the number of 1s. Substituting $c = .5$, $n_{11} = 2$, $n_{20} = 1$, $n_{31} = 2$, $n_{41} = 1$, and $n_{50} = 0$, we get .0235. The probability of the object coming from its own unique category is

$$P(k)P(F|k) = \frac{1-c}{(1-c)+2c} \cdot (.5)^5 = .0104.$$

Thus, the third object is assigned to the existing category, even though its category label differs. This process continues with each new object incorporated into the partition by considering the possible extensions of the best partition so far. The algorithm ends up choosing the partition {11111, 10101, 10110}, {00000, 01000}, {01011}, which has three categories. Note that the system's categorization does not respect the categorization of Medin and Schaffer. The algorithm produces three categories, rather than two, and mixes category labels within one of its categories. In fact, the three-category structure obtained is, quite good. It is eight times more probable as an interpretation of the data than the experimenters' two-category structure, given the assumptions of the model and $c = .5$.

Having come up with a particular categorization, the algorithm was tested by presenting it with the 12 test stimuli and assessing the probabilities that it would assign to the two possible values for the fifth dimension, which is its label. Figure 3-2 relates the algorithm to their data. Plotted along the abscissa are the 12 test stimuli of Medin and Schaffer in their rank order

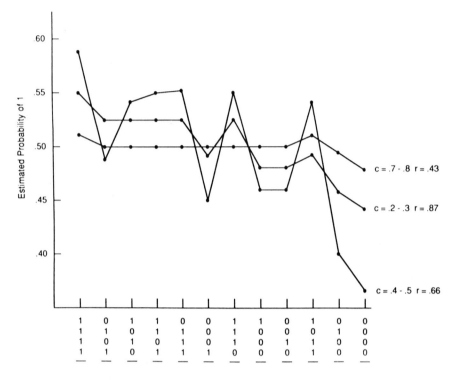

FIG. 3-2.   Estimated probability of category 1 for the 16 test stimuli in the first experiment of Medin & Schaffer (1978). Different functions are for different ranges of the coupling probability.

determined by subjects' confidence that the category label was 1. The ordinate is the algorithm's probability (calculated by Equation 3-2) that the missing value was 1. The figures illustrate three functions for different ranges of the coupling probability. The best rank order correlation was obtained for coupling probabilities in the range of .2 to .3. Throughout this chapter, .3 is used as the coupling probability in fitting data.

Using this coupling probability, the rank order correlation was .87. Using the same coupling probability, rank order correlations of .98 and .78 were obtained for two slightly larger experimental sets used by Medin and Schaffer. These rank order correlations are as good as those obtained by Medin and Schaffer with their many-parameter model. It also does better than the ACT* simulation I reported in Anderson, Kline, and Beasley (1979).

Note that the actual probabilities of category labels estimated by the model in Fig. 3-2 only deviate weakly above and below .5. This reflects the very poor category structure of these objects. With better structured material, such as the instances in Table 3-2, much higher prediction probabilities are obtained.

SURVEY OF THE EXPERIMENTAL LITERATURE

With the discussion of these general issues out of the way, the rational theory specified, and its application specified, this section surveys how well the rational theory can account for the empirical literature on categorization. A variety of experiments are considered that reflect the main themes in the literature — sensitivity to central tendency, effect of specific instances, sensitivity to correlated features, base rate effects, probability matching, emergence of basic-level categories, and effects of presentation order. All of these results can be predicted within the theory presented here. It would be tempting to claim that all of the results can be predicted from purely rational considerations without regard to mechanism, but the constraint of incremental learning means that the predictions are not totally mechanism-free. Nonetheless, many of the results are not sensitive to the constraint of incremental learning. Some I am unsure about. One of the results, concerning the effect of presentation order, does depend on incremental learning.

Central Tendencies, Specific Instances, and Multiple Modes

The strongest phenomenon in the literature on human categorization is that the reliability with which an instance is classified is a function of its distance from the central tendency of the category. This trend is so well established now that it is largely ignored in current research, which focuses on second-order effects. A rational analysis does predict this main effect: The probability that an item comes from a category is a function of its feature similarity (see Equations 3-6 & 3-7).

Posner and Keele. One of the classic studies on categorization that demonstrated this central tendency was research done by Posner and Keele (1968) in which subjects studied arrays of dot patterns. The dots were randomly distorted from four prototypes, and subjects were to learn to classify the study items into three categories. After reaching criterion performance on the study material, subjects were asked to classify test instances that included the actual prototypes (which had not been studied), old studied instances, new instances just as distorted as the old instances, and randomly generated instances. Subjects had the option of saying that an instance belonged to no studied category. A great deal of research on categorization has continued to use the Posner and Keele materials (e.g., Homa & Vosburgh, 1976; Homa & Cultice, 1984) and has consistently confirmed that subject's categorization behavior is a function of distance from prototype.

Recently, Hintzman (1986) has developed a scheme for encoding these

TABLE 3-3
Simulation of Posner & Keele Materials Using Hintzman's Representation:
Proportion of Instances Assigned by Model to the Category

Type of Test Instance	Category Size		
	3	6	9
New prototype	.46	.78	.98
Old	.37	.69	.95
New close distortion	.24	.61	.85
New far distortion	.11	.44	.67
New random	.06	.16	.25

materials into structures coded by 23 binary dimensions. I used his encoding scheme to try to simulate the Posner and Keele paradigm. Table 3-3 shows the probability of the simulation assigning various test instances to each of the three categories.[6] As has been done with the Posner & Keele materials, I manipulated the number of instances a subject saw in a category. As is typically found, categorization is more reliable with larger categories. This is a base rate effect. Note that there is an increased tendency to assign completely random instances to larger categories. Note, also, that the simulation categorizes the prototype of the category very well, often better than the instances that were studied. This illustrates the strong effect of the central tendency. However, the old instances are categorized better than new items equally distorted from the prototype. This shows an effect of memory for specific instances. Finally, the simulation classifies better new instances that are closer to the prototype than those that are distant from it.

In summary, this simulation reproduces all of the major phenomena associated with these materials: Classification is better for larger categories, old instances are classified better than new, new instances are better classified the closer they are to the prototype, and there is a tendency to falsely assign random instances to the larger categories.

Medin and Schaffer. The research of Medin and Schaffer just reviewed has received much attention, because it showed that there was an effect of similarity to specific examples as well as of central tendency. Experiments of this sort show that new instances are reliably classified if they are similar to a studied instance even if the studied instance is not close to the overall central tendency of the category. In the analysis of the Medin and Schaffer material in the previous section, we saw why. Subjects form multiple

---

[6]The simulation was run so that it assigned each instance to the most probable old category or to a new category. If an old category was chosen, the label associated with that category was given as the response.

categories — one that may incorporate the central tendency of the category and others for the odd-ball instances. This is how to maximize the overall predictive structure of the material. In short, subjects' categorization is not determined by the experimenter's category labels. They classify an instance reliably if it is similar to any category they have created with the correct category label.

Material like Medin and Schaffer's tends to have such poor category structure that the model comes close to creating a separate category for each instance. In the presence of a poor category structure, this rational algorithm will, in fact, create a separate category for each instance. With this category structure, it behaves isomorphically to the Medin & Schaffer model, measuring similarity between a test item and each study instance. Moreover, Equation 3-6 gives the same multiplicative rule for measuring similarity that Medin and Schaffer used. In summary, the Medin and Schaffer model is the rational model in the presence of poor category structure.

Elio and Anderson. As a further example of complications to the central tendency effect, consider a study by Elio and Anderson (1981) that has proven difficult for most theories of categorization, including past theories of my own. It shows the subtle combination of similarity to instances and categories. Subjects studied 16 instances defined by five dimensions with four possible values each plus a sixth binary-valued categorical dimension. In the *generalize condition,* pairs of items in a category overlapped on three of the noncategorical dimensions (plus the category), leading to substantial generalizations. Such overlaps did not exist in the *control condition.* Then, subjects were tested with stimuli that were equally similar to the individual test stimuli in the two conditions but that overlapped with the generalization in the generalize condition. So, for instance, subjects in the generalize condition might study a 11213 and a 11312 (yielding a 11-1-generalization) and be tested with a 11111 whereas subjects in the control condition would study a 11123 and a 13211 and be tested with the same 11111. In the control condition, the two studied instances overlapped on three features with the test, but, unlike the generalize condition, they were not the same three features. Subjects displayed substantially better performance in the generalize condition. This causes difficulties for models that claim that classification is a function of similarity between a test item and individual study items. On the other hand, Elio and Anderson also found that, holding overlap with the generalization constant, there was an effect of similarity to individual study stimuli. This causes difficulties for generalization-based models. Table 3-4 reports estimated probability in our current rational model that the test item belongs to the target category. Chance classification would be .50. The first

TABLE 3-4
Data Elio & Anderson (1981) and Probabilities from Model

	Generalize		Control	
	(Study 11213 and 11312)		*(Study 11123 and 13211)*	
	Subjects' *Ratings*	*Models'* *Probability*	*Subjects'* *Ratings*	*Models'* *Probability*
High overlap-generalization possible in generalize condition (test 11111)	2.48	.60	1.66	.55
High overlap-no-generalization possible (test 11233)	1.74	.56	.97	.51
Low overlap (test 12233)	.51	.49	−.36	.50

Note: Elio & Anderson had subjects assign the items as in one category or the other and give their confidence in the rating on a 5-point scale. The statistic reported here is mean confidence with incorrect assignments weighted negatively.

case on Table 3-4 involves testing with an item like 11111, which overlaps with the generalization in the generalize condition but which is equally similar to study stimuli (mean overlap is 3) in either the generalize or control condition. Here, both the subjects and the simulation rate higher the items in the generalize condition. This difference between conditions is preserved when we test with items like 11223, which only partially overlaps with the generalization. They also overlap less well (mean overlap is 2.5) with the study stimuli. The overall level of successful classification goes down for both simulation and human data. Finally, there are items like 12233, which have even lower overlap with study stimuli (mean overlap is 2.0) or with the generalization. Here, classification is not different from chance for either simulation or subjects. (Chance is .50 for simulation and 0 for subjects).

Like the Medin and Schaffer material, the Elio and Anderson material had a rather poor category structure. In the control condition, categories were built around specific instances, whereas in the generalize condition they were built around generalizable pairs. The advantage of the generalize condition turned on this difference. Note that subjects were, in effect, learning categories with multiple central tendencies.

Correlated Features: Medin, Altom, Edelson, and Freko

One of the questions we might ask about this model is how it deals with category structures defined by correlated features. In a representative experiment exploring this issue, Medin, Altom, Edelson, and Freko (1982) had subjects study the nine cases in Table 3-5, which were all supposed to represent instances from one disease category, burlosis. This was simulated by presenting these nine cases to the model with a sixth dimension, a disease label, which was always "burlosis." This was arbitrarily treated as a binary dimension. Note in Table 3-5 that for each symptom a 1 (denoting presence) is more often associated with the disease than not.

The critical feature of these materials from the perspective of correlated features concerns the fourth dimension, condition of eyes, and the fifth dimension, weight. Values are either both 1 or both 0. The first six items in Table 3-5 have two 1s; the last three have two 0s. The question is how one should go about representing such correlated features. When these stimuli were fed into the algorithm with $c = .3$, it typically extracted three categories—one to represent the first six items, one for the seventh, and one for the last two. Thus, the way it dealt with correlated features was to break out separate categories for the different possible values of the correlation. Thus, we see that this model can represent experimental categories with correlated features even though it treats features within a category as independent. The reason it can represent correlated features is that its internal categories do not have to correspond to the external categories, and it can create a separate internal category for every combination in the correlation.

Of course, there remains the issue of whether its behavior will correspond to that of subjects. To examine this, we have to consider the test that Medin and his colleagues used after subjects had been given 20 minutes to study the nine items. They presented their subjects with the test pairs in Table 3-6 and asked subjects which was more likely to have burlosis. It is not entirely clear how this task should be represented in the model or, indeed, what the subjects took to be their task. This was not a prediction task; rather, subjects were to consider what feature combinations were more diagnostic.

TABLE 3-5
Symptoms of Burlosis from Medin et al. (1982)

Case Study	Blood Pressure	Skin Condition	Muscle Condition	Condition of Eyes	Weight Condition
1. R.L.	0	1	0	1	1
2. L.F.	1	1	0	1	1
3. J.J.	0	0	1	1	1
4. R.M.	1	0	1	1	1
5. A.M.	1	1	1	1	1
6. J.S.	1	1	1	1	1
7. S.T.	1	0	0	0	0
8. S.E.	0	1	1	0	0
9. E.M.	1	1	1	0	0

Note: Zero denotes absence of the symptom and 1 denotes presence.

The way this was modeled was to present the model with the two descriptions in each pair plus the feature burlosis and ask it to judge the probability of each description — it calculated $P(k)P(F|k)$. Thus, the model delivered two probabilities, p_a and p_b, for the two disease descriptions a and b. Again, it is unclear how these should be related to choice behavior, but I calculated the ratio $p_a/(p_a + p_b)$ on the assumption that subjects' choice behavior should be at least monotonically related to this quantity. This is what is reported as the rational prediction in Table 3-6.

Table 3-6 also presents the predictions from the Medin and Schaffer model. Their model allows one to weight different dimensions differentially. This captures a lot of variance in the data, because subjects appear to be particularly sensitive to the dimensions of muscle condition and weight condition. This sensitivity to dimension can be handled by a generalization of the matching rule in Equation 3-7, which is an application of the more general model in the Appendix. This new equation is:

$$P(ij|k) = \frac{n_{ij} + \alpha_i}{n_k + \Sigma_i \alpha_i}$$

(3-7')

TABLE 3-6
Results from the Simulation of Medin et al. (1982)

Test Pair			Proportions of Choices of Alternative a		
a	vs.	b.	Observed	Medin et al. Prediction	Rational Prediction
1.	01110	11101	.37	.40	.45
2.	11001	11110	.43	.47	.43
3.	01010	11010	.50	.47	.49
4.	10001	10101	.23	.32	.39
5.	11100	11101	.57	.56	.55
6.	00111	11101	.57	.65	.61
7.	01011	11110	.70	.66	.61
8.	00100	00101	.53	.48	.53
9.	10000	10010	.63	.66	.55
10.	11000	01100	.33	.30	.31
11.	10100	01100	.33	.40	.37
12.	10011	11100	.50	.42	.46
13.	10011	01011	.40	.40	.45
14.	01111	11011	.60	.58	.60
15.	00011	01100	.37	.41	.42
16.	00100	10000	.57	.53	.53
17.	11100	01011	.50	.49	.49
18.	00111	01011	.60	.59	.55
19.	10111	11011	.53	.60	.55
20.	11001	01101	.40	.41	.42

where α_i is a parameter that reflects the sensitivity of dimension i. Smaller values of α_i are associated with greater sensitivity. The default value of 1 is used in Equation 3-7. We used the STEPIT program of Chandler (1965) to estimate these parameters.[7] The values of α_i for the five dimensions are 7.795, 1.801, .200, 2.850, and .001. The correlation between the rational model and the data is .91; between the Medin and Schaffer model and the data it is .92; and between the two models it is .93. Clearly, there is little to choose between in terms of the two models.

From the perspective of Medin and his colleagues, the critical feature of the data concerns the contrast between Tests 1 through 4 and Tests 5 through 9. In general, 1s are more diagnostic of burlosis than are 0s. In Cases 1 through 9, the b item contains more 1s. However, in Cases 5 through 9, the a item has the diagnostic feature combination—either two 1s or two 0s on the fourth and fifth dimensions. Correspondingly, subjects prefer the more diagnostic bs for Tests 1 through 4, but the as with correlated features for Tests 5 through 9. This change is also predicted by both the Medin et al. and the rational model. The rational analysis predicts the change because the a items better match the separate categories formed to represent each feature correlation. The Medin et al. model predicts the result because it assumes that subjects make their classifications by matching against specific instances. In summary, the rational model can capture feature correlation and can capture subjects' behavior in response to feature correlation.

Base Rate Effects: Medin and Edelson

As has already been observed with respect to the Posner and Keele simulation, the rational model produces a base rate effect. This base rate effect arises basically because of Equation 3-4, which weighs categories with more members more heavily. The general result in this literature is that there is a bias for larger categories—that is, members from larger categories are more reliably categorized, and items are more often misassigned to large categories. Recently, however, Medin and Edelson (1988) reported an experiment that showed a deviation from this general trend.

Table 3-7 illustrates the design of their materials. There were six possible diseases and nine possible symptoms. Subjects studied individuals who displayed a pair of symptoms and had a disease. One of these symptoms

---

[7]This program cannot usually be used, because in many applications there is not a fixed category structure. However, for these materials, the program always extracted the same three categories.

TABLE 3-7
Abstract Representation of Medin & Edelson (1988) Material

Learning: Relative Frequency	*Symptoms*	*Disease*
3	a,b	1
1	a,c	2
3	d,e	3
1	d,f	4
3	g,h	5
1	g,i	6

Transfer: Tests for base rate information

1. High frequency singles *b, e, h*
2. Low frequency singles *c, f, i*
3. Imperfect singles: *a, d, g*
4. Conflicting pairs: *bc, ef, hi*
5. Triples: *abc, def, ghi*

Note. The symptoms are represented in terms of single letters and the diseases in terms of numbers. The diseases differ in their relative frequency. See the text for concrete examples of symptoms and disease names.

was uniquely associated with the disease, whereas the other was associated with a pair of diseases. The two diseases in the pair occurred in a 3:1 ratio in terms of base rates: Subjects saw 192 cases about which they had to make predictions, 48 cases of each frequent disease and 16 cases of each infrequent disease.

We simulated this by creating feature descriptions of nine binary-valued dimensions for each symptom and a 6-valued dimension for the disease label. Exposed to the 192 cases with $c = .3$,[8] the model extracted six categories that corresponded to the six diseases. This is a case where the model agrees with the experimenter-defined categories, in contrast to the previous applications of the model.

At test, Medin and Edelson presented subjects with either single symptoms, pairs of symptoms, or triples of symptoms and asked them to predict the disease. Their data, along with the model's predictions, are shown in Table 3-8. In the case of ambiguous symptoms (imperfect single cues), there is a strong preference for the high-frequency disease in both the data and the model, replicating the standard base rate effect. The triples consisted of the two unique symptoms plus the ambiguous one. Again, both data and model agree on the base rate effect.

The interesting case concerns conflicting pairs, where one symptom is

---

[8]A similar partitioning is obtained over a considerable range of values for *c*.

TABLE 3-8
Results from the Medin & Edelson (1988) Experiment and Predictions of the
Rational Model (In Parentheses)

Test Item	Medin & Edelson (Model in Parentheses)	
	High-Freq. Category	Low-Freq. Category
High Frequency Single (e.g., b)	.812 (.897)	
Low Frequency Single (e.g., c)		.927 (.762)
Imperfect Single (e.g., a)	.781 (.553)	.146 (.325)
Conflicting Pair (e.g., bc)	.323 (.319)	.584 (.488)
Triple (e.g., abc)	.708 (.555)	.281 (.326)

Note: Rank order correlation = .94.

associated with a high-frequency disease and one is associated with a low-frequency disease. Here, data and model show a preference for the low-frequency disease, in contrast to the general base rate effect. The explanation within the rational model is interesting: When a conflicting pair is matched against the category for a disease, two mismatches are detected. First, the ambiguous feature is missing and, second, the conflicting feature is present. In contrast, when a single feature is matched against a category, there is only one mismatch—the second feature is absent. When a triple is matched, there is, again, only one mismatch—the conflicting feature is present. Equation 3-7 implies that such mismatches will be weighed more seriously for high-frequency diseases. Basically, every mismatch results in the probability being reduced by $1/(n + 2)$ where n is the category frequency. The advantage of category base rate more than makes up for one mismatch producing the advantage for ambiguous single cues and triple cues. However, the two mismatches in the case of ambiguous pairs overwhelms the base rate advantage. To an approximation, the difference between the low-frequency and high-frequency categories in conflict cases will be

$$\frac{4.8}{58.3} \times \left(\frac{1}{18}\right)^{m} \times \left(\frac{17}{18}\right)^{9-m} \times \frac{17}{22} \; versus \; \frac{14.4}{58.3} \times \left(\frac{1}{50}\right)^{m} \times \left(\frac{49}{50}\right)^{9-m} \times \frac{49}{54}$$

where the first term in each product represents the probability of the category (from Equation 3-4 with $c = .3$), the second and third terms reflect the feature mismatches and matches where m is the number of mismatches (from Equation 3-7), and the fourth term reflects the probability of the label in that category (also from Equation 3-7). The reader may confirm that, when there is one mismatch ($m = 1$), the advantage is given to the high-frequency category, but when $m = 2$, the advantage goes to the low-frequency category. In summary, although there is a bias in the priors for high-frequency categories, high-frequency categories are less tolerant of mismatches on dimensions where the values have been constant.

Probability Matching: Gluck and Bower

In certain situations, subjects' categorization behavior will display a probability matching character. An experiment by Gluck and Bower (1988) is a nice case in point. Their task was one where subjects saw from one to four symptoms (bloody nose, stomach cramps, puffy eyes, and discolored gums) and had to predict whether the patient had one of two diseases. The two diseases differed by a 3:1 ratio in base rates. Patients with a particular disease would display symptoms probabilistically. Patients with the rare disease displayed the first symptom with probability .69, the second symptom with probability .44, the third symptom with probability .35, and the fourth symptom with probability .23. In the case of the common disease, the probabilities were .23, .35, .46, and .69, respectively. Within the constraint that they had no symptomless patients, the symptoms occurred independently within a disease category.

Two key features of this experiment are that subjects were exposed to a lot of instances (250) and that a particular feature configuration was associated with a disease only probabilistically. Under these kinds of conditions one sees probability matching in the behavior of subjects. Figure 3-3 presents a plot of the objective probability of the rare disease given one of the 15 ($2^4 - 1$) possible symptom configurations against the proportion of assignments by subjects to the rare category. As can be seen, the proportion of assignments by subjects closely mirrors the objective probabilities.

This was simulated by presenting the model with 250 instances generated according to the specifications of Gluck and Bower. They were represented as five binary-valued dimensions where the first four dimensions were the symptoms and the fifth dimension was the disease label. The coupling probability was set to .3.

The behavior of the model in this situation is somewhat unstable across simulation runs. It winds up creating somewhat different categories that represent the accidents of random item construction and presentation order. So, in the first two runs, it created four main categories described in the following presentation by size (n) and estimated probability of a symptom or the common disease label:

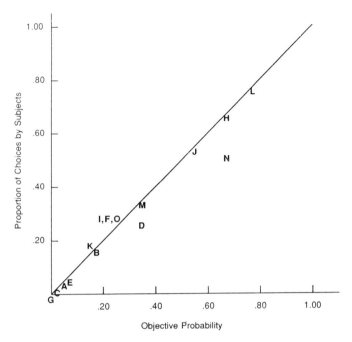

FIG. 3-3. Match of the Gluck and Bower data against the predictions of probability matching. Letters correspond to various of the 15 patterns — see Gluck and Bower (1988) for explanation.

run 1

Category A $n = 28$, $p_1 = .27$, $p_2 = .83$, $p_3 = .83$, $p_4 = .03$, $p_5 = .37$
Category B $n = 59$, $p_1 = .38$, $p_2 = \underline{.98}$, $p_3 = .16$, $p_4 = \overline{.72}$, $p_5 = .98$
Category C $n = 127$, $p_1 = .24$, $p_2 = \underline{.01}$, $p_3 = .53$, $p_4 = .72$, $p_5 = \overline{.97}$
Category D $n = 29$, $p_1 = \underline{.97}$, $p_2 = \overline{.35}$, $p_3 = .13$, $p_4 = .29$, $p_5 = \underline{.03}$

run 2

Category A $n = 27$, $p_1 = .24$, $p_2 = .03$, $p_3 = \underline{.97}$, $p_4 = .03$, $p_5 = .90$
Category B $n = 127$, $p_1 = .19$, $p_2 = \overline{.29}$, $p_3 = \overline{.33}$, $p_4 = \overline{.99}$, $p_5 = .97$
Category C $n = 29$, $p_1 = .03$, $p_2 = \underline{.97}$, $p_3 = .33$, $p_4 = \underline{.01}$, $p_5 = \overline{.97}$
Category D $n = 59$, $p_1 = \underline{.98}$, $p_2 = \overline{.49}$, $p_3 = .31$, $p_4 = \overline{.18}$, $p_5 = \overline{.07}$

Thus, for instance, 28 patients were placed in the first category, A, of run 1. Seven of these displayed symptom 1, leading to an estimated probability (according to Equation 3-7) of $(7 + 1)/(28 + 2) = .27$; 24 displayed symptom 2, leading to $p_2 = .83$; 24 displayed symptom 3, leading to $p_3 = .83$; 0 displayed symptom 4, leading to $p_4 = .03$; and 10 were classified as the common disease, leading to $p_5 = .37$.

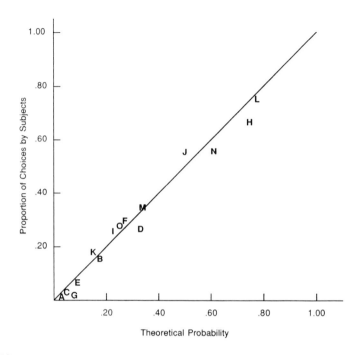

FIG. 3-4. Match of the probabilities from the rational model against the data of Gluck and Bower (1988). Letters correspond to various of the 15 patterns — see Gluck and Bower (1988) for explanation.

It turns out that each run produces one category that looks like the rare disease pattern, has symptom 1 present, symptom 4 absent, and is labeled as the rare disease. These are categories D in both runs just illustrated. The simulation produces one or more categories that look like the common disease, have symptom 1 absent, symptom 4 present, and are labeled as common disease. These are categories B and C for run 1 and category B for run 2. Finally, there are categories that are, in one way or another, amalgams.

So, by way of summary, the simulation extracts a crude approximation to the categorical structure that the experimenter had in mind. It turns out that, from such a category structure, the model produces behavior that looks like probability matching in the aggregate. Figure 3-4 compares the predictions of the model against those of the data, and the strong correspondence is apparent.

It is interesting to explore why the model predicts probability matching. The key to understanding this comes from the earlier observation that the model approximately extracts the experimenter's category structure. Suppose the model perfectly extracted the category structure and had formed just the two experimenter categories. Combining Equations 3-2 and 3-3, we get:

$$P(\text{rare label}) = \sum_k \frac{P(k)P(F|k)}{\sum_l P(l)P(F|l)} \, P(\text{rare label}|k)$$

Under the idealization of a perfect sort, there are just two categories being summed, and *P(rare label|k)* is effectively 1 for the rare category and 0 for the common category. Thus,

$$P(\text{rare label}) = \frac{P(\text{rare category})P(F|\text{rare category})}{P(\text{rare category})P(F|\text{rare category}) + P(\text{common category})P(F|\text{common category})}$$

The model estimates *P(F|rare category)* and *P(F|common category)* by Equations 3-6 and 3-7. Given that the experiment makes the features independent and the sample is large, this means that the model's estimate will be the objective conditional probability. Similarly, given the large sample, the model will objectively estimate the base rates for *P(rare category)* and *P(common category)* by Equation 3-4. Thus, given that its estimates of base rates and conditional probabilities are accurate, it will predict the objective probability of a disease label. In summary, if (a) the model identifies the experimenter categories, (b) the features are independent, and (c) the samples are large, then the model estimates will match the objective probabilities. The first condition is approximately met, and the second and third conditions are satisfied by experimental design. The model thus does predict, in a parameter-free way, that subject behavior will be controlled by objective probability in this situation. So, if we assume that subjects choose a label with a probability that matches their internal probability, we can predict the probability-matching behavior.

The Symptom Rating Task.   Guided by their own theory, Gluck and Bower made light of this probability matching, which, in my view, is the most interesting part of their data. Rather, they focused on another aspect of the data, which involves a posttest. Here, they presented subjects with an individual symptom and asked them, "Of all the patients in the hospital exhibiting [symptom], what percent of these patients would you expect to suffer from [disease]?" Here, subjects are being asked to assign a number rather than predict whether the disease will be rare or common. Gluck and Bower's analysis treats this task as basically equivalent to the earlier prediction task, although, as we will see, subjects assign estimated values different from the proportions of choice on the training task.

What did subjects take as their task in this part of the experiment? Figure 3-5 provides the relevant analysis. It contains the data and three quantities that might predict the data. Gluck and Bower claimed that, normatively, the subjects should be reporting $P(R|S)$, the probability of the rare disease

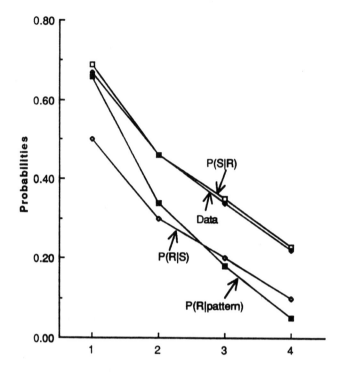

FIG. 3-5.   Subject ratios of symptom diagnosticity and various potential predictors for the Gluck and Bower (1988) experiment.

given the symptom. These probabilities are to be aggregated over all of the patterns. Clearly, subjects are not doing this. Gluck and Bower's theory predicts that subjects should be responding in the same way as they did in the prediction task. Because subjects probability match in the prediction task, this is reflected by the curve $P(R|pattern)$, where pattern refers to a pattern with a single feature present. Gluck and Bower, however, did not assume that subjects are probability matching in this task and so were content with ordinal predictions. In particular, they took great comfort in the fact that symptom 1 had an estimated probability greater than .5 in contrast to the normative predictions.

The interesting theoretical quantity is the other one plotted in Fig. 3-5, which is the probability of the symptom given the disease$-P(S|R)$. The correspondence is so remarkable with the data that there can be little doubt that this is what the subjects are reporting. Thus, it seems that subjects are interpreting instructions to rate the probability of a category given the symptom as instructions to rate the probability of the symptom given the category.

Does the rational analysis predict this? If we provide the model with the category label and ask it for the probabilities of the various symptoms, it will again probability match. However, the model has no stance on how subjects interpreted their instructions, so there is no way within the model to predict in advance that this is what the subjects would do. Still, it has been shown in other research (e.g., Eddy, 1982) that subjects sometimes interpret instructions to rate the diagnosticity of a cue for a category as $P(cue|category)$. Therefore, there is prior reason to model the task this way in a rational analysis. It is just that the reason for doing so comes from outside rational analysis.

Subjects' estimates do not always reflect $P(S|R)$, however. It does not appear that subjects were reporting this in the third experiment of Gluck and Bower. Estes, Cambell, Hatsopoulos, and Hurwitz (1989) attempted to replicate this aspect of the data of Gluck and Bower in Fig. 3-5 and failed. The behavior they found did not correspond to any of the theoretical curves in Fig. 3-5 and disconfirmed the Gluck and Bower claims. The actual behavior of subjects in this rating task proves to be quite variable. In contrast, the result of probability matching in the experiment proper, which the rational model does predict, appears to be robust across experiments.

Basic Level Categories

As noted earlier, the rational model strives to find a level of categorization that maximizes the predictive structure of the objects. This is the motivation behind Rosch's basic-level categories. Rosch's idea of a basic level is that it is the level in the generalization hierarchy to which we first assign objects. For instance, she argued that we would first see an object as a bird, not as a sparrow or a bird. Gluck and Corter (1985) reported an attempt to model studies (Murphy & Smith, 1982; Hoffman & Ziessler, 1983) that have been done of experimentally trained category structures, where the phenomenon of basic-level categories emerged. In the following subsections the rational model will be applied to these studies.

Murphy and Smith. One experiment that Gluck and Corter considered is a study by Murphy and Smith that used materials such as those illustrated in Fig. 3-6. The stimuli consisted of 16 objects identified for subjects as examples of fictitious tools. The structure of the material, as encoded by Gluck and Corter, is illustrated in Table 3-9. There were two superordinate categories, which were divided into four intermediate categories and into eight subordinate categories. Table 3-9 gives the attribute description of each category. Subjects were fastest to classify the material at the intermediate level, which Murphy and Smith intended to be the basic level. Objects

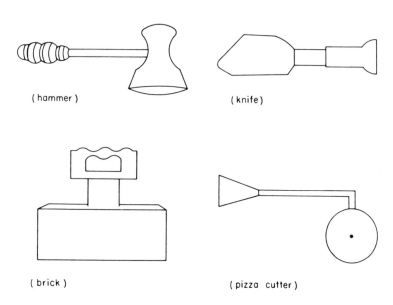

(hammer)   (knife)

(brick)   (pizza cutter)

FIG. 3-6.   Examples of the experimental material used by Murphy and Smith (1982).

at this level had two attributes plus two labels in common. Only one additional feature and label was gained at the subordinate level, and all features were lost at the superordinate level except for their feature of being a pounder or a cutter.

We modeled this material by encoding the stimuli as seven-dimensional objects with dimensions for the superordinate label (two values), the intermediate label (four values), the subordinate label (eight values), handle (five values), shaft (five values), head (six values), and size (two values). The category structure that was obtained depended on the value of the coupling probability. For $c > .96$, all were merged into one category; for $.95 > c > .8$, the two superordinate categories emerged; for $.8 > c > .4$, the model fluctuated between the superordinate and intermediate categories, depending on presentation order; for $.4 > c > .2$, it extracted just the intermediate categories; for $.2 > c > .05$, it basically extracted the intermediate categories with an occasional singleton category or subordinate category; for $c < .05$, it extracted only singleton categories. In summary, the subordinate categories never emerged, and only at very high levels of c did superordinate categories dominate. At the value of c used in the simulations of this chapter ($c = .3$), only the basic-level categories emerged. Thus, it seems fair to conclude that the analysis agrees with the subjects as to what the basic level is.

TABLE 3-9
Gluck and Corter's Analysis of the Feature Structure of the Material from
Murphy & Smith (1982)

Item #	Categories			Attributes			
	Super-ordinate	Inter-mediate	Sub-ordinate	Handle	Shaft	Head	Size
1.	Pounder	Hammer	Hammer1	2	2	0	0
2.				2	2	0	1
3.			Hammer 2	2	2	1	0
4.				2	2	1	0
5.		Brick	Brick1	0	3	4	0
6.				0	3	4	1
7.			Brick 2	1	3	4	0
8.				1	3	4	1
9.	Cutter	Knife	Knife1	3	4	2	0
10.				3	4	2	1
11.			Knife2	3	4	3	0
12.				3	4	3	1
13.		Pizza C.	P.C.1	4	0	5	0
14.				4	0	5	1
15.			P.C.2	4	1	5	0
16.				4	1	5	1

Hoffman and Ziessler. The second experiment that Gluck and Corter addressed is one by Hoffman and Ziessler (1983) that used the stimulus sets in Fig. 3-7. The Gluck and Corter representation of this material is shown in Table 3-10. The first hierarchy has the property that, in addition to the category label, there is a visual feature that can be predicted from superordinate membership—the contour of the stimuli. For the second hierarchy, contour and the inside shape can be predicted from intermediate category, but nothing except category label can be predicted from superordinate category. For the third hierarchy, nothing except category labels can be predicted from superordinate or intermediate category. Hoffman and Ziessler found evidence that the basic level was the superordinate level for hierarchy 1, the intermediate level for hierarchy 2, and subordinate for hierarchy 3.

I modeled this experiment, using the Gluck and Corter encodings—two values for the superordinate label, four for the intermediate, eight for the subordinate, two for contour, four for inside shape, and four for bottom. However, it seemed a bit extreme to claim, as do the Gluck and Corter encodings, that the stimuli in Hierarchy 3 have nothing in common. All the Hoffman and Ziessler stimuli in Fig. 3-7 resemble each other more than they do the stimuli in Fig. 3-6, for instance. They all have a global shape in common. This was represented by adding one more dimension on which all

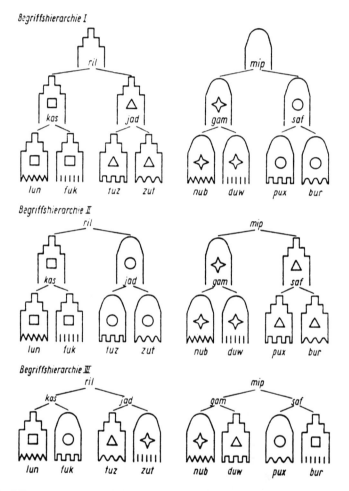

FIG. 3-7. Structure of the experimental material used by Hoffman and Ziessler (1983) in various experimental conditions. The three conditions are illustrated in the three rows. Each row consists of eight stimuli in a hierarchical structure. Illustrated at higher levels of the hierarchy are what those stimuli have in common—a name and perhaps some shape features.

TABLE 3-10
Gluck & Corter's Analysis of the Feature Structure of the Material from
Hoffman & Ziessler (1983)

HIERARCHY 1

	Categories			Attributes		
Item #	Superordinate	Intermediate	Subordinate	Contour	Inside	Bottom
1.	High 1	Mid 1	1	0	0	0
2.			2	0	0	1
3.		Mid 2	3	0	1	2
4.			4	0	1	3
5.	High 2	Mid 3	5	1	2	0
6.			6	1	2	1
7.		Mid 4	7	1	3	2
8.			8	1	3	3

HIERARCHY 2

	Categories			Attributes		
Item #	Superordinate	Intermediate	Subordinate	Contour	Inside	Bottom
1.	High 1	Mid 1	1	0	0	0
2.			2	0	0	1
3.		Mid 2	3	1	3	2
4.			4	1	3	3
5.	High 2	Mid 3	5	1	2	0
6.			6	1	2	1
7.		Mid 4	7	0	1	2
8.			8	0	1	3

HIERARCHY 3

	Categories			Attributes		
Item #	Superordinate	Intermediate	Subordinate	Contour	Inside	Bottom
1.	High 1	Mid 1	1	0	0	0
2.			2	1	3	2
3.		Mid 2	3	0	1	3
4.			4	1	2	1
5.	High 2	Mid 3	5	1	2	0
6.			6	0	1	2
7.		Mid 4	7	1	3	3
8.			8	0	0	1

stimuli had the same value. Somewhat arbitrarily, I proposed that there are
10 discriminable values on this dimension of overall shape. Again, the value
of c used was .3. With this value of c, the model categorized according to
superordinate level for hierarchy 1, intermediate for hierarchy 2, and
subordinate for hierarchy 3.

Comparison to Gluck and Corter. As the Gluck and Corter model reproduces these effects also, it is worth commenting on the similarities and differences between their model and the rational model. They took an information-theoretic approach that views category structure as optimizing the amount of information that can be communicated. Thus, their analysis is very much tied up with the notion of category labels as special. They tried to choose a category that would maximize the following metric:

$$[P(c) \sum_{i=1}^{n} P(f_i|c)^2 + (1-P(c)) \sum_{i=1}^{n} P(f_i|notc)^2] - \sum_{i=1}^{n} P(f_i)^2$$

where the summations are over the nonlabel features, $P(c)$ is the probability of the category, and $P(f_i|c)$ is the probability of a feature given the category. These two probabilities are like the quantities defined in Equations 3-5 and 3-7. They are, however, based on observed frequencies, rather than on Bayesian estimates of the probabilities. Still, it is not surprising that there should be a strong correlation between their metric and the one developed here. Indeed, Fisher (1987) has developed a categorization algorithm that uses the Gluck and Corter metric. It is quite similar to the iterative rational algorithm described here.

The fact that two independent "rational" analyses should come to similar predictions should be comforting. In contrast to the situation with mechanistic models, where similar predictions from different theories are a cause for concern, we can feel all the more certain of the correctness of the analysis.

Order Sensitivity

As noted periodically, the iterative algorithm is order-sensitive, in that initial similarity among the first objects may cause certain categories to be formed that would not be formed if other objects were first seen. Once seeded with these categories, the algorithm tends to stick with them. Work has been done in artificial intelligence on how to revise such initial commitments (Fisher, 1987; Lebowitz, 1987); however, there is experimental evidence that people are indeed sensitive to order of presentation (Elio & Anderson, 1984; Kline, 1983).

Table 3-11 illustrates the material that Mike Matessa and I used in an unpublished study to explore this issue of order-sensitivity. Subjects studied a set of 16 strings presented in one of two orders. Subjects initially studied the material without any idea that they were in a categorization task. Rather, they thought that they were in a memorization task. They saw a string on the screen, it disappeared, and they had to reproduce it. They went through the 16 strings in four sets of 4. When they were able to

TABLE 3-11
Presentation Order in the Anderson & Matessa
Experiment

Front-Anchored Order	End-Anchored Order
scadsporm	snadstirb
scadstirm	snekstirb
sneksporb	scadsporm
snekstirb	sceksporm
sneksporm	sneksporm
snekstirm	snadsporm
scadsporb	scekstirb
scadstirb	scadstirb
snadsporm	sceksporb
sceksporb	snekstirm
scekstirb	snadstirm
snadstirm	scadsporb
snadsporb	scekstirm
sceksporm	sneksporb
scekstirm	snadsporb
snadstirb	scadstirm

reproduce a set of four twice without errors, they went into the next phase. After completing the 16, they were shown the full set of 16 on a sheet of paper in the order studied and were asked to divide them into two categories of 8, according to whatever basis seemed appropriate. We used this procedure of hiding the true purpose of the experiment during initial stimulus exposure because we did not want to evoke conscious hypothesis-testing procedures. Rather, we wanted to determine how subjects would spontaneously organize a set of materials.

The same 16 strings were presented in either the front-anchored order or the end-anchored order, both of which are illustrated in Table 3-11. The first eight strings in the front-anchored order could be divided into four that began sneks_ _ _ _ and four that began scads_ _ _ _. This was the categorical structure that our model would extract. After the remaining eight, the generalization would be pared down to either become sn_ _ _ _ _ _ _ versus sc_ _ _ _ _ _ _ or _ _ ads_ _ _ _ versus _ eks_ _ _ _ _. Thus, we predicted that subjects in the front-anchored condition would sort the 16 stimuli according to one of these regularities. Eleven out of 20 subjects did.

In contrast, after the first eight stimuli in the end-anchored ordering, the model would emerge with the generalization_ _ _ _stirb versus _ _ _ _ sporm. After the next eight, this would either become _ _ _ _stir_ versus _ _ _spor_ or _ _ _ _ _ _ _rb versus _ _ _ _ _ _ _rm. Thus, we predicted that subjects in the end-anchored condition would sort according to one of these regularities. Fourteen out of 20 subjects did.

In total, 25 out of 40 subjects behaved according to our hypothesis. This is marginally greater than a .5 chance ($z = 1.67$; $p < .05$, one-tailed), providing some support for order sensitivity. What was apparent to us was that subjects had strong priors as to where regularities should be found, which often overrode our experimental manipulation. In particular, many subjects looked for regularities at the ends of strings, even in the front-anchored condition. It was also noted in the earlier discussion of the Medin et al. (1982) experiment that subjects had a strong tendency to focus on certain features. There, I developed a generalization of the rational model (Equation 3-7′), which incorporated this attentional sensitivity. Indeed, it is entirely in the spirit of a Bayesian analysis to have priors obscure the effect of the regularities in the data.

CONCLUSION

This concludes the effort to show the correspondence between the model and the empirical literature on categorization. The only bounds on the size of this section are my good sense and time. It seems that one could go on endlessly simulating results within the rational model. Hopefully, the choice of experiments has been informative in terms of highlighting features of the literature and features of the rational model.

Comparisons to Shepard's Theory of Generalization

It is of interest to compare this rational theory with the analysis of Shepard (1987). He was concerned with deriving what he calls the Universal Law of Generalization. When a response is learned to a stimulus with a particular value on one or more dimensions, the response will generalize to stimuli with similar dimensional values. The probability and strength of generalization varies with the distance between the original and test stimulus. Shepard originally explored this phenomenon with respect to continuous dimensions such as size or hue but has since (Shepard, 1989) extended this analysis to discrete dimensions such as are the focus of this chapter. Because generalization of a response to a new stimulus can be conceived of as placing the new stimulus in the same category as the old, there is a clear relationship between this generalization analysis and categorization.

Shepard conceives of the organism's tendency to generalize as a function of the probability that the two stimuli are in the same "consequential space" where this can be read as a category. In Shepard's view a consequential space is some region in a multidimensional space. The probability that the test stimulus and the original stimulus are in the same consequential space is, according to Shepard, a function of the distance between the two and the systems' priors (expressed as a probability density) about the size of the consequential space. He produces basically a Bayesian analysis of this generalization process and comes up with the prediction of an exponentially decaying generalization function.

This can be extended to discrete stimuli by simply regarding difference between stimuli as a sum of the number of dimensions on which they differ. This leads to a prediction that the strength of generalization increases exponentially with the number of dimensions two stimuli share. The current rational model makes essentially the same prediction on the basis of the product rule in Equation 3-6. The two efforts are coming to the same conclusion from routes that are quite different in detail but in abstract both derivations are of the same kind. That is, both start with minimal, reasonable assumptions about the structure of the environment, then derive the probability that a generalization is valid given that structure, and then make the assumption that behavior will reflect this objectively derived probability. The fact that the details of the derivational route do not matter to the conclusion should give us greater cause for accepting the conclusion.

Performance on Complex Tasks

Although not much time has been invested in this regard, it does appear that this algorithm has some substantial value as an artificial intelligence (AI) algorithm. This goal is distinguished from the goal that occupied the previous section, in that the goal of an AI algorithm is to get good performance in domains that are so complex that they overwhelm the human system. A good example is the data base of soybean diseases used by Michalski & Chilausky (1980), consisting of 290 study instances of 15 soybean diseases and 340 test cases. Each case is potentially described by values on 35 dimensions (in addition to the disease label), although some cases have missing values on some dimensions. Some of the dimensions have ordered values (like month of the year), but this ordering information was not used, and these values were treated as cardinal.

Given that the goal here is not to simulate human learning but just to predict category membership, I prevented the algorithm from putting members of two diseases into the same category.[9] However, it was possible for categories with dissimilar members to split up into subcategories. With a

---

[9]Putting members with two disease labels into a single category might increase the predictiveness of the overall feature structure, but it would not improve ability to predict category labels. Because predicting category labels was the goal of this AI application, I imposed this restriction so as to have results more comparable to other efforts.

coupling probability of .01, the rational algorithm extracted 18 categories from the original 290 instances. These categories were then used to predict the disease label of the 340 test instances. The model correctly classified 93%, which compares favorably with the 98% reported by Michalski and Chilausky for their algorithm and the 72% reported for rules derived from experts.

This example nicely illustrates the limits of the rational analysis as a predictor of human behavior. Although it is not the best machine algorithm for this data base, it was outperforming human classifiers. This algorithm has no representation of working memory limitations. There is no way that humans are going to be able to simultaneously hold 35 features in working memory. Most of the empirical research on human categorization has not pushed human capacity beyond the working-memory limit. However, real-world situations do. Here, much of the story on human categorization may turn of the way humans break down a complex stimulus array into manageable pieces.

Emile Servan-Schreiber (e.g., Servan-Schreiber & Anderson, in press) has been working on this complexity problem. His analysis is that we take complex stimuli and decompose them into chunks of manageable size. We strive to find regularities in these chunks. Finding such regularities, we may then look for regularities in chunks of chunks, and so on. In other words, his basic analysis is that, faced with the limits of working memory, we decompose a stimulus into a hierarchy of manageable chunks and work on this. This can be easily incorporated within the rational framework. We would have a second computational constraint, working-memory limitation, in addition to the constraint of incremental learning.

Implementation Considerations

This discussion has proceeded with little regard for how this categorization process might actually be implemented in a mechanistic theory like ACT*. This testifies to the autonomy and sufficiency of the rational level of analysis. Still, I cannot help speculating.

The categorical structure can be easily implemented in an ACT* declarative network, basically of the same character as the one proposed in the previous chapter on memory. Figure 3-8 shows such a network to implement the category structure associated with the first run of the program over the Gluck and Bower materials (p. 121). In the center of the figure are the four categories. I have illustrated associations from each of the 10 features (eight symptoms and two diseases) to each category and from the category to each feature. Activation will spread from the input feature nodes to the category nodes and then to the output feature nodes.

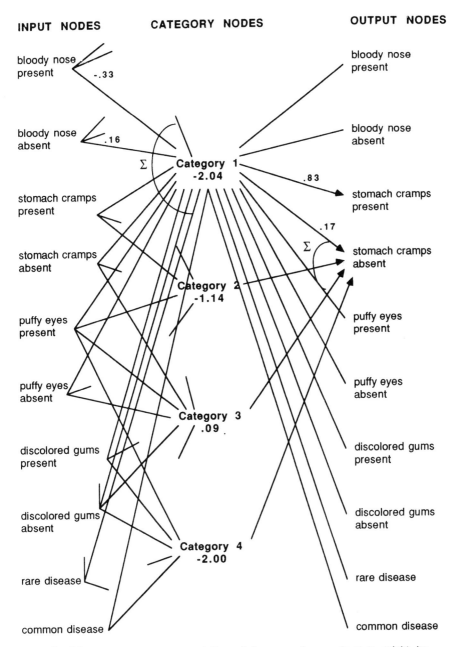

INPUT NODES

bloody nose present

bloody nose absent

stomach cramps present

stomach cramps absent

puffy eyes present

puffy eyes absent

discolored gums present

discolored gums absent

rare disease

common disease

CATEGORY NODES

Σ

Category 1
-2.04

Category 2
-1.14

Category 3
.09

Category 4
-2.00

-.33

.16

Σ

OUTPUT NODES

bloody nose present

bloody nose absent

stomach cramps present

stomach cramps absent

puffy eyes present

puffy eyes absent

discolored gums present

discolored gums absent

rare disease

common disease

.83

.17

FIG. 3-8. A schematic representation of how a category structure might be represented in an ACT declarative network.

Let us first consider calculation of the activation levels of the category nodes. The two relevant probabilities are $P(k)$ for each category and $P(ij|k)$ for each link from feature j to category k. As in the memory chapter, we will take logarithms of odds ratios and make $ln(P(k)/P(\bar{k}))$ as the strength or base activation level of the category nodes and $ln(P(ij|k)/P(ij|\bar{k}))$ as the strength of the j-to-k links. For instance, for category 1, $P(k) = .115$, and $ln(P(k)/P(\bar{k})) = -2.04$, which is what is shown in Fig. 3-8. Similarly, for category 1 and bloody nose, $P(ij|k) = .27$, and $P(ij|\bar{k}) = .39$, and $ln(P(ij|k)/P(ij|\bar{k})) = -.33$, which is what is given in Fig. 3-8. Activation spreading from presented features would calculate

$$ln(P(k)/P(\bar{k})) + \sum_j ln(P(ij|k)/P(ij|\bar{k}))$$

which is the log odds of the object coming from the target category. Thus, spreading activation would calculate the log-odds version of Equation 3-3. The real purpose of categorization is not to assign objects to categories but rather to make predictions. This requires spreading activation out of the category nodes to the feature nodes and accumulating activation there. According to the rational analyses, we want to calculate Equation 3-2. This requires converting the log-odds, which is what the node activation represents to probability, which is what the output activation should represent. Thus, we need the following formula, which relates a nodes' activation, A, to the amount of activation output, O.

$$O = 1/(1 + e^{-A})$$

This output activation is multiplied by $P(ij|k)$, which represents outgoing link strength, to determine the amount of activation arriving at features j from category k. This contrasts to the strengths assigned to the incoming links, which were $ln(P(ij|k)/P(ij|\bar{k}))$.

The activation-based scheme just described will deliver a level of activation to node j, which represents $Pred_{ij}$. If we assume an implementation scheme that makes probability of making a prediction a function of this level of activation, then we will have an ACT architecture that produces the categorization results we reviewed. Indeed, the ACT* theory is such an instance of an ACT* architecture. In ACT* probability of matching a pattern in a production's condition is a function of level of activation. The sort of production rules that would be used in categorization would be of the form:

IF the goal is to predict the value on dimension i for object X
    and X is in category k
    and category k has feature j on dimension i
THEN predict j.

Matching the clause "*X* is in category *k*" will determine the category assignment of the object. The category chosen will be the most active category node. Similarly, matching the clause "feature *j* on dimension *i*" will determine the prediction. The feature selected will be the most active feature node.

Category Learning Algorithm. Given this mapping of the categorization process into an ACT architecture, one can specify the category learning algorithm. New category nodes have to be created in declarative memory every time an object cannot be assigned to an existing category (or equivalently, fails to get activation of a category node above threshold). Every time an object is assigned to an existing category, the link strengths between the category and features have to be updated so that they reflect either $ln(P(ij|k)/P(ij|\bar{k}))$ for incoming links or $P(ij|k)$ for outgoing links. Also, the base level activation of the category node has to be updated.

Thus, category learning in this ACT implementation is totally declarative. This contrasts sharply with the ACT* analysis, which assigned category learning to production learning. As noted elsewhere (Anderson, 1986, 1987c), there are independent reasons for being dissatisfied with the ACT* analyses. In particular, the ACT* production implementation does not allow for conscious awareness of category structure. In contrast, this would be possible in a declarative implementation.

There is one distinction between the network for memory suggested in the previous chapter and this network for categorization. The categorical network has to be variabilized so that it can apply simultaneously to multiple objects. Thus, we want to be able to simultaneously classify one object as a cat and predict that it will scratch and another object as a dog and predict that it will bark. Thus, we are not just activating a feature node for scratch or bark but a node instantiated for a particular object. Such a capacity to spread object-instantiated activation represents a difference from ACT*.

As a final comment, we see once again, as in the memory chapter, that a rational analysis can guide an implementation within the ACT framework. Again, it appears that an implementation with this guidance promises to be more accurate than the ACT* implementation.

There are striking similarities between this network and PDP networks with hidden units, which are learned by the backprop algorithm (Rumelhart, Hinton, & Williams, 1986). The category nodes are like hidden units, and the calculations in which they participate are similar, if not identical. The real difference occurs in the learning algorithm. Whereas it takes huge numbers of iterations to get the backprop algorithm to learn a category structure, this algorithm basically gives asymptotic structure after each trial. The speed of learning of this procedure is gained by its strong priors about the structure of the environment, whereas the backprop algorithm assumes—unrealistically, I think—a much less structured environment.

Learning algorithms are not optimal in and of themselves. They are optimal with respect to environments. There are imaginable environments in which the backprop algorithm would do better. A rational approach encourages us to inquire as to the structure of our actual environment and design an algorithm that is optimal for it, rather than design algorithms that would only be optimal in some bizarre world.

APPENDIX: THE IDEAL ALGORITHM

This appendix considers the ideal but computationally intractable categorization model described in the body of the chapter. There are two functions to this Appendix besides intellectual curiosity. First, this algorithm serves as a standard against which the iterative approximation should be measured. Second, its analysis provides the basis for the mathematical results asserted in the statement of the iterative algorithm.

Equation 3-1 stated the basic computation that the ideal algorithm should use for predicting the probability of value j on dimension i:

$$Pred_{ij} = \sum_x P(x|F)P(ij|x) \tag{3-1}$$

where the summation is over all possible partitionings x of the objects into categories. The combinatorial problem is that the number of such partitionings explodes exponentially with the number of objects. As in the iterative algorithm, the key is analyzing $P(x|F)$, and we can give it a Bayesian expression similar to Equation 3-3:

$$P(x|F) = \frac{P(x)P(F|x)}{\sum_x P(x)P(F|x)} \tag{3-8}$$

The difference is that the summation is over partitionings of the objects into categories, not over categories, as in Equation 3-3. (Each partition is a decomposition of the objects into a different set of categories.) Again, we can break our investigation into a study of a prior probability, $P(x)$, and a conditional probability of a feature structure, $P(F|x)$. However, now we are investigating the prior probability of an entire partitioning and the conditional probability of the feature structure of all the objects given the partitioning.

Prior Probabilities

We are interested in the prior probability of a partitioning of a set of objects before we consider the feature structure. Because we are ignoring the feature structure, the only thing that can influence this prior probability is the number of categories and the number of objects in each category. The model assumes that there is a probability, c, that any two objects will be in the same category, which we call the *cohesion* or *coupling* probability. Suppose we have partitioned the n objects into s categories, where each category k has n_k objects. It can be shown that the probability of the partitioning is:

$$P(x) = \frac{\displaystyle\prod_{k=1}^{s} (1-c) \prod_{i=1}^{n_k-1} ci}{\displaystyle\prod_{i=0}^{n-1} [(1-c)+ci]} \tag{3-9}$$

For example, given three objects, x, y, and z, the probability that all three will be in one category is $2c^2/(1 + c)$; the probability that they are split into two categories (which can happen in three ways) is $c(1 - c)/(1 + c)$; and the probability that they are in separate categories is $(1 - c)^2/(1 + c)$. The probability that x and y are in the same category is the probability of either of the partitions (xyz) and (xy, z) which the reader may confirm is c.

Equation 3-9 is one of the few cases in this book where I have not be able to find an established mathematical treatment. It probably exists somewhere but, just in case, I included the one I developed. Equation 3-9 can be derived if we make three reasonable assumptions:

1. Summed over all partitions, the probability that any pair of objects are in the category is c.
2. Let x be a partition of n objects and x_i denote various extensions of it to $n + 1$ objects.

$$P(x) = \sum_i P(x_i).$$

3. Let x_1 and x_2 be two partitions of n objects such that both have i objects in one category. Let x_1' and x_2' be two partitions obtained by deleting that category of i objects. $P(x_1)/P(x_2) = P(x_1')/P(x_2')$.

We first show that Equation 3-9 satisfies the preceding three criteria and then show that the three criteria imply Equation 3-9.

Part A: Equation 3-9 Implies Criteria

Criterion 1. The reader can confirm that this is true in the case of $n = 2$. This fact and Criterion 2 imply that this is true for all n.

Criteria 2.   If there are s categories in x, then there are s extensions of x formed by adding an object to one of the categories plus one partition created by adding the object to a new category. Let x_i be the partition formed by adding an object to the ith category. According to Equation 3-9:

$$P(x_i) = P(x) \frac{cn_i}{(1-c)+nc}$$

Let x_0 be the partition formed by creating a new category for the new object:

$$P(x_0) = P(x) \frac{1-c}{(1-c)+nc}$$

Then it can be easily confirmed that

$$\sum_{i=0}^{s} P(x_i) = P(x)$$

Criteria 3.   Without loss of generality, let 1 index the category deleted. Then it can be confirmed that:

$$P(x_i) = \frac{(1-c) \displaystyle\prod_{i=1}^{n_1-1} ci}{\displaystyle\prod_{i=n-n_1}^{n-1} [(1-c)+ci]} P(x_i')$$

The ratio relating x_i to x_i' depends only on the number of objects in category 1 and not the other categories. Thus, for any two partitions x_1 and x_2 that share a category of i objects $P(x_1)/P(x_2) = P(x_1')/P(x_2')$.

Part B: Criteria Imply Equation 3-9

Proof by induction on the number of objects.

This equation is implied by Criterion (1) for $m = 2$.

Assume that this is true for all numbers of objects from 2 to $n - 1$, and prove that this equation is true when the number of objects is n.

We will prove that Equation 3-9 holds for all partitions of the n objects except the partition that assigns all n objects to one category. Then, because the sum of the probabilities of the partitions must sum to 1, Equation 3-9 will hold for that partition also. This argument is a bit complex. Figure 3-9

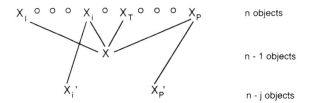

FIG. 3-9.   An illustration of the logic of the proof by induction. x_T is a partition of n objects derived from a partition of $n - 1$ objects. $x_1 \ldots x_p$ are all possible partitions of n objects derived from x, x_i' and x_p' are partitions of $n - j$ objects from x_i and x_p by deleting a common category of j objects.

provides a representation of the partitions involved to help the reader. Take any partition x_T of the n objects except the one that assigns all objects to a single category. It can be derived as an extension of a partition x of $n - 1$ objects where x has at least two categories. Such an extension involves adding an object to one of the categories in the partition of $n - 1$ objects or by creating a new category for the one object. Let $x_1, \ldots, x_p$ be the partitions that are extensions of x by adding the nth object to one of the categories of x or by creating a new category. x_T will be one of them. By Criterion 2,

$$\sum_{i=1}^{P} P(x_i) = P(x)$$

Without loss of generality, let x_p be the partition of x that involves creating an extra category. x_p will share a category with any other x_i that is an extension of x (because at least one category in x stays unchanged in going from x to x_i, and all categories stay the same in going from x to x_p). By Criterion 3,

$$\frac{P(x_i)}{P(x_p)} = \frac{P(x_i')}{P(x_p')}$$

where x_i' is gotten by deleting the common category of j objects from x_i and x_p' is gotten by deleting that same common category from x_p. By the inductive hypotheses, Equation 3-9 holds for x_i' and x_p'. Let n_i be number of objects in the category augmented in forming x_i from x (i.e., the category has n_i objects in x and $n_i + 1$ in x_i). Then, because Equation 3-9 holds for x_i' and x_p',

$$\frac{P(x_i')}{P(x_p')} = \frac{n_i c}{1 - c}$$

Hence,

$$P(x_i) = \frac{n_i c}{1 - c} P(x_p)$$

Hence, by Criterion 2, we can write:

$$P(x) = \sum_{i=1}^{p-1} P(x_i) + P(x_p)$$

$$= \sum_{i=1}^{p-1} \frac{n_i c}{1-c} P(x_p) + \frac{(1-c)}{1-c} P(x_p)$$

$$= \frac{P(x_p)[(n-1)c + (1-c)]}{1-c}$$

Hence,

$$P(x_p) = \frac{(1-c}{(n-1)c + (1-c} \cdot P(x)$$

$$= \frac{\displaystyle\prod_{k=1}^{s} (1-c) \prod_{i=1}^{n_k - 1} ci}{\displaystyle\prod_{i=0}^{n-1} [(1-c) + ci]}$$

and

$$P(x_i) = \frac{\displaystyle\prod_{k=1}^{s-1} (1-c) \prod_{j=1}^{n'_k - 1} cj}{\displaystyle\prod_{i=0}^{n-1} (1-c) + ci} \quad \text{for } i < p$$

where $n'_k = n_k$ if $k \neq i$ $n'_k = n_k + 1$ if $k = i$

Thus, $P(x_i)$ has the right form for all x_i that are extensions of x including x_T.

Conditional Probabilities

Now let us turn to $P(F|x)$, the probability that the objects would display the feature structure that they do under partitioning x. Assuming that the categories and dimensions are independent, we can write this as:

$$P(F|x) = \prod_{k=1}^{s} \prod_{i=1}^{r} Prob_{ki} \tag{3-10}$$

where $Prob_{ki}$ is probability of the distribution of features for the ith dimension of the kth partition. Let $n_1, n_2, \ldots, n_m$ be frequency counts for the number of objects showing each of the m values on dimension i. Let P_1, $P_2, \ldots, P_m$ be the prior probabilities of displaying values $1, \ldots, m$ of dimension i. Note that

$$\sum_j P_j = 1.$$

What we have observed is n multinomial trials corresponding to the objects, and the probability of this sequence is described by

$$m(n_1, n_2, \ldots, n_m | P_1, P_2, \ldots, P_m) = \prod_{j=1}^{m} P_j^{n_j} \tag{3-11}$$

The complication occurs because we cannot start out with known prior probabilities P_i for an unknown category. What we can start out with is a probability density of possible probabilities. The conjugate prior density for a multinomial distribution is the Dirichlet density (Berger, 1985):

$$D(P_1 \ldots, P_m | \alpha_1, \ldots, \alpha_m) = \frac{\Gamma(\alpha_0)}{\prod_{j=1}^{m} \Gamma(\alpha_j)} \prod_{j=1}^{m} P_j^{\alpha_j - 1} \tag{3-12}$$

where $\Gamma(X) = (X - 1)!$ and $\alpha_0 = \Sigma \alpha_j$.

In this distribution, the mean expected value for P_j is $\alpha_j | \alpha_0$. If one does not have any expectations that some values are more likely than others and one does not have any other expectations about possible values, it is best to use the noninformative prior, which is obtained by setting all $\alpha_j = 1$. This was what is used throughout the main body of the chapter on the iterative algorithm.

The posterior distribution of probabilities is also a Dirichlet distribution, but with parameters $\alpha_j + n_j$. This implies that the mean expected value of displaying value j in dimension i is

$$(\alpha_j + n_j) / \sum_j (\alpha_j + n_j)$$

This is $P(ij|k)$ for Equation 3-7 where all α_i have been set to 1 which is the simplest assumption. $Prob_{kj}$ from Equation 3-10 is to be calculated as the probability of that series of multinomial trials over all possible values of the P_j, and is calculated as

$Prob_{ki} =$
$$\int_0^1 \int_0^{1-P_1} \ldots \int_0^{1-P_1-\ldots-P_{m-2}} m(n_1, \ldots, n_m | P_1 \ldots P_m) D(P_1, \ldots, P_m | \alpha_1, \ldots, \alpha_m) dP_1 \ldots dP_{m-1}$$

which has the solution:

$$Prob_{ki} = \frac{\Gamma(\alpha_0)}{\Gamma(\sum_j \alpha_j + n_j)} \prod_{j=1}^{m} \frac{\Gamma(\alpha_j + n_j)}{\Gamma(\alpha_j)} \tag{3-13}$$

Representing Extremity

A complication is that categories may tend to have all or none of their instances display a particular feature, rather than have intermediate probabilities of features. Thus, even if 50% of the world's animals are brown, it may be the case that most species have almost all of their members brown or almost none of their members brown.

This situation can be captured by complicating the prior distribution of P_i to have the form

$$p(P_1, P_2, \ldots P_m) = \sum_a p_a d(P_1, \ldots, P_m | \alpha_{1a}, \alpha_{2a}, \ldots, \alpha_{ma}) \tag{3-14}$$

where

$$\sum_a p_a = 1.$$

Thus, we have a set of separate Dirichlet distributions where we can make the priors in each one as extreme as we choose. Then,

$$Prob_{ki} = \sum_a p_a \frac{\Gamma(\alpha_{0a})}{\Gamma(\sum_j \alpha_{ja} + n_j)} \prod_{j=1}^{m} \frac{\Gamma(\alpha_{ja} + n_j)}{\Gamma(\alpha_{ja})} \tag{3-15}$$

As a special case of this, we might have m distribution parameters such that there is a one-to-one mapping between parameters α_{ja} and α_{jb} for any a and b such that one of α_{ja} equals one of α_{jb}. For instance, we might have three distributions with $\alpha_{11} = 1$, $\alpha_{21} = 2$, $\alpha_{31} = 10$ for one distribution, $\alpha_{12} = 10$, $\alpha_{22} = 1$, $\alpha_{32} = 2$ for another, and $\alpha_{13} = 2$, $\alpha_{23} = 10$, $\alpha_{33} = 1$ for another. If, further, the $p_a = 1/m$, the posterior of value j would be:

$$\sum_a^m \frac{\alpha_{ja} + n_j}{\sum_j (\alpha_{ja} + n_j)} * \prod_j \frac{\Gamma(\alpha_{ja} + n_j)}{\sum_a \prod_j \Gamma(\alpha_{ja} + n_j)}$$

If, in the preceding example, $n_1 = 1$, $n_2 = 0_1$, $n_3 = 0$ (i.e., we observe just one instance of value 1), the estimate of the probability of a 1 rises from .33 to .65. This is a more radical shift than the rise from .33 to .5, which would occur with the no-extremity model used in the main part of the chapter.

Hominids of East Turkana: An Example

Although it is not possible to apply this algorithm to complex cases, it is worthwhile to consider how it might be applied to a simple case. As an example case, consider Shafer & Tversky's (1985) rendition of the Hominids of East Turkana (Walker & Leakey, 1978):

> In the August, 1978 issue of *Scientific American,* Alan Walker and Richard E. T. Leakey discussed the hominid fossils that had recently been discovered in the region east of Lake Turkana in Kenya. These fossils, between a million and 2 million years of age, show considerable variety, and Walker and Leakey were interested in deciding how many distinct species they represent.
>
> In Walker and Leakey's judgment, the relatively complete cranium specimens discovered in the upper member of the Koobi Fora Formation in East Turkana are of three forms:
>
> (I) A "robust" form with large cheek teeth and massive jaws. These fossils show wide-fanning cheekbones, very large molar and premolar teeth, and smaller incisors and canines. The brain case has an average capacity of about 500 cubic centimeters, and there is often a bony crest running fore and aft across its top, which presumably provided greater area for the attachment of the cheek muscles. Fossils of this form have also been found in South Africa and East Asia, and it is generally agreed that they should all be classified as members of the species *Australopithecus robustus.*
>
> (II) A smaller and slenderer (more "gracile") form that lacks the wide-flaring cheekbones of I, but has similar cranial capacity and only slightly less massive molar and premolar teeth.
>
> (III) A large-brained (c. 850 cubic cm) and small-jawed form that can be confidently identified with *Homo erectus* specimens found in Java and northern China.
>
> The placement of the three forms in the geological strata in East Turkana shows that they were contemporaneous with each other. How many distinct species do they represent? Walker and Leakey admit five hypotheses:
>
> 1. I, II, and III are all forms of a single, extremely variable species.
> 2. There are two distinct species: One, *Australopithecus robustus,* has I as its male form and II as its female form; the other, *Homo erectus,* is represented by III.

3. There are two distinct species: One, *Australopithecus robustus,* is represented by I; the other has III, the so-called *Homo erectus* form, as its male form, and II as its female form.
4. There are two distinct species: One is represented by the gracile-form II; the other, which is highly variable, consists of I and III.
5. The three forms represent three distinct species.

Here are the items of evidence, or arguments, that Walker and Leakey use in their qualitative assessment of the probabilities of these five hypotheses:

(i) Hypothesis 1 is supported by general theoretical arguments to the effect that distinct hominid species cannot coexist after one of them has acquired culture.

(ii) Hypotheses 1 and 4 are doubtful because they postulate extremely different adaptations within the same species: The brain seems to overwhelm the chewing apparatus in III, while the opposite is true in I.

(iii) There are difficulties in accepting the degree of sexual dimorphism postulated by Hypotheses 2 and 3. Sexual dimorphism exists among living anthropoids, and there is evidence from elsewhere that hints that dental dimorphism of the magnitude postulated by Hypothesis 2 might have existed in extinct hominids. The dimorphism postulated by Hypothesis 3, which involves females having roughly half the cranial capacity of males, is less plausible.

(iv) Hypotheses 1 and 4 are also impugned by the fact that specimens of type I have not been found in Java and China, where specimens of type III are abundant.

(v) Hypotheses 1 and 3 are similarly impugned by the absence of specimens of type II in Java and China. (pp. 313–314)

This is a nice example for illustrating the categorization analysis, although, as becomes apparent, we are assigning probabilities arbitrarily, not having adequate knowledge ourselves. Shafer & Tversky (1985) can be read for another interesting but equally arbitrary analysis.

Rational Analysis

We can view this as a problem of forming a partitioning of three objects I, II, and III. The five hypotheses correspond to the five possible partitionings of these three objects. The two relevant binary dimensions are brain size and robustness:

$$I = 500, \text{ robust}$$
$$II = 500, \text{ gracile}$$
$$III = 850, \text{ gracile}$$

Now let us consider how we will incorporate the considerations (i)–(v) listed by Tversky & Shafer:

(i) There is a high coupling factor to the effect that all coexisting specimens be of one species. For argument's sake, let $c = .75$.

(ii) This just makes the point that members of the same category should share the same features. It comes out in the mathematics of our calculations.

(iii) This makes the point that brain size has a high extremity factor, whereas robustness does not. Hence, for brain size, let us set

$$f_1(P_1,P_2) = \frac{1}{2} d(P_1,P_2|11,1) + \frac{1}{2} d(P_1,P_2|1,11),$$

and for robustness, let us set

$$f_2(P_1,P_2) = d(P_1,P_2|1,1).$$

In both f_1 and f_2, P_1 and P_2 are variables ranging over possible probabilities of the binary values.

(iv) & (v) These make the point that there are already specimens like III. Let us represent this by proposing another specimen from Java and China:

IV = 850, gracile

However, let us set the probability of coupling of this with the other 3 at $c = .50$, because it comes from a different location. There are some 15 partitionings of the objects I through IV. We can proceed to calculate the probability of each according to the Bayesian formula and project these probabilities down to the five partitionings of the objects I through III. Table 3-12 reproduces that analysis. Critically, what we need to do is calculate $P(x)$, the probability of each partitioning; $P(F_1|x)$, the probability of the distribution of brain sizes given the partitioning; and $P(F_2|x)$ the probability of the distribution of robustness given the partitionings. Then we need to calculate the product of these three probabilities to get the numerator of the Bayesian formula for the posterior probability $P(x|F_1,F_2)$. The denominator will be the sum of all of these products.

Table 3-12 gives all of these quantities. I cannot go through each case, but let us consider 12,34 which is the most likely partition. Using Equation 3-9, the prior probability can be calculated:

$$P(x) = \frac{(1-.75)^2(.75)(.50)}{(1-.75)(1-.75+.75)(1-.75+1.5)(1-.5+1.5)} = .027$$

TABLE 3-12
Analysis of the Probability of Various Partitions of the Specimens 1–4 in the
Example of the "Hominids of East Turkana"

	Priors $P(x)$	Dimension1 $P(F_1|x)$	Dimension2 $P(F_2|x)$	$P(x)P(F_1|x)\,P(F_2|x)$
1,2,3,4	.009	.063	.063	.000035
1,4,2,3	.009	.018	.041	.000006
1,24,3	.009	.018	.084	.000013
1,2,34	.009	.107	.084	.000080
1,2,3 Summary				.000135
12,3,4	.027	.107	.041	.000118
124,3	.054	.018	.041	.000020
12,34	.027	.185	.055	.000273
12,3 Summary				.000412
13,2,4	.027	.018	.041	.000019
134,2	.054	.018	.041	.000039
13,24	.027	.001	.055	.000002
13,2 Summary				.000060
1,2,3,4	.027	.009	.084	.000020
14,23	.027	.001	.055	.000002
1,234	.054	.035	.126	.000236
1,23 Summary				.000258
123,4	.161	.035	.041	.000234
1234	.482	.004	.050	.000096
123 Summary				.000330

Using Equations 3-13 and 3-15,

$$p(F_1|x) = Prob_{11} \cdot Prob_{21} = \left(\frac{1}{2}\frac{11!}{13!}\frac{12!}{10!}\frac{0!}{0!} + \frac{1}{2}\frac{11!}{13!}\frac{10!}{10!}\frac{2!}{0!}\right)^2 = .185$$

$$p(F_2|x) = Prob_{12} \cdot Prob_{22} = \left(\frac{1!}{3!}\frac{1!}{0!}\frac{1!}{0!}\right)\left(\frac{1!}{3!}\frac{2!}{0!}\frac{0!}{0!}\right) = .055$$

The product of these three probabilities is .000273. The conditional probability of the 12,34 partition is .000273/.0001195 = .228. The total probability of the various ways 1 and 2 could cluster into one group separate from 3 is .345. This contrasts with the least likely hypothesis, which is that 1 and 3 cluster separately from 2, which has a probability of only .050.

In no way should this be taken seriously as a resolution of the issue of how to cluster the specimens. However, it should be taken seriously as a procedure for how to perform the clustering. What is missing from this application of the procedure is sufficient evidence about the underlying probabilities and the actual counts of fossils in various locations.

4 Causal Inference

Contents
Preliminaries   149
Basic Formulation of the Causal Inference Problem   151
Causal Estimation   155
    Analysis of 2 × 2 Contingency Tables   157
    Schustack & Sternberg Experiment   159
Cues for Causal Inference   161
    Formalization of Spatial and Temporal Contiguity   163
    Bullock, Gelman, & Baillargeon Experiment   164
    Similarity   165
    Cues to Causality: A Summary   167
Integration of Statistical and Temporal Cues   168
    Modelling the Siegler Experiment   169
Discrimination   172
    Modeling the Rescorla Experiment   173
Abstraction of Causal Laws   177
    Individual-Based Generalization   179
    Category-Based Generalization   179
    Relational Generalization   181
    An Experiment   183
Implementation in a Production System   186
Conclusion   187
Appendix   187

PRELIMINARIES

In writing about causality, I feel like a lamb going out among wolves. The philosophers have argued for centuries about what causation means and when we are justified in making causal attributions. Modern physics has, in effect, eliminated causation and replaced it by sets of constraint equations, although there are forever efforts to introduce causation back into physical analyses (e.g., DeKleer & Brown, 1984). While cognitive psychologists

busied themselves elsewhere, social psychologists have developed a sophisticated body of data and theory about causal attribution in person
perception (e.g., Hilton & Slugoski, 1986; Jaspars, Hewstone, & Fincham,
1983; Kelley, 1973, 1983; Orvis, Cunningham, & Kelley, 1975). Developmental psychologists seem to have been the only ones to have given much
thought to the issue of causal attribution in cognition, led, as always, by
Piaget (1974). For a long time, the one major piece of research relating to
adult perception of causation in a nonsocial setting has been the classic
work of Michotte (1946). Causal relationships do play an important part in
modern theories of text processing (e.g., Trabasso, Secco, & van den Broek,
1984). Here, the emphasis is how a causal rule such as "lightning causes fire"
is used to understand a text. However, there has been little concern in
cognitive psychology with how such rules are inferred in the first place. This
is the principal concern of the present chapter.

It is peculiar that causal inference does not get more play in mainstream
cognitive psychology because it has to be one of the key organizing
constructs of human cognition. It is central to problem solving, and some
of us (Anderson, 1983; Newell, 1980b; Tolman, 1932) see problem solving
as particularly central to human cognition. In solving a problem, we are
basically trying to do something that will cause a particular state of affairs.
Surely, how we reason about causality must be central to how we organize
our problem solving. Still, the standard practice, of which I have been
guilty, is to talk about problem solving and ignore causality. Indeed, this
chapter was not originally intended in the design of this book. It came to be
when I realized that it was necessary if I was going to do a rational analysis
of problem solving.

My thinking about this topic has strongly been influenced by Holland,
Holyoak, Nisbett, and Thagard's (1986) distinction between diachronic and
synchronic relations. Synchronic relations refer to predictive relationships
that exist among features and were the focus of the previous chapter on
categorization. Diachronic relations refer to predictive relationships between things present and things in the future. They are the focus of causal
analysis. To be neutral to philosophic controversies about the nature of
causation, I might say that this chapter is concerned with diachronic
relations and avoid making any reference to the concept of cause.

In terms of a rational analysis, the goal that the system is trying to
optimize is accuracy of its predictions about the future.[1] In general, it is
valuable to be able to achieve this goal. A particularly important case is
problem solving, where we are trying to determine what action will cause a
desired state of affairs.

The basic logic of the rational analysis of causal inference is very similar

---

[1]For a philosophical development that emphasizes statistical prediction see Suppes (1970).

to the logic of the rational analysis for categorization in the previous chapter. The goal of the system has already been stated: that is prediction. A certain structure is assumed of the environment that the system tries to exploit in its Bayesian inference scheme for forming causal rules. This is like the categorical structure assumed in the previous chapter. As in the previous chapter, the goal of this chapter is to show that this approach covers a wide range of empirical phenomena.

However, I feel that the developments in this chapter are not as definitive as in the previous chapter, for two reasons. First, there is not as rich an empirical literature on causal inference as there is on categorization. Second, the structure of the world relevant to causal inference is much more complex than in the categorization case. Nonetheless, this chapter displays a promising set of results, and there is the potential for real enlightenment by a rational approach. Table 4-1 contains a summary of the mathematical notations that are used in this chapter.

BASIC FORMULATION OF THE CAUSAL INFERENCE PROBLEM

The fundamental two equations for a rational analysis of causal inference are perfect analogs of the central two equations from chapter 3. To repeat, the central goal of causal inference is to predict events that will happen in a particular situation. A situation can be conceived of as presenting a set of cues, C, that might be relevant to predicting an event, E, occurring. The prediction task is to come up with a probability $P(E|C)$ of an event E conditional on the cues C. The relevant intervening constructs are causal rules i that we have inferred. $P(E|C)$ can be calculated by the following rule:

$$P(E|C) = \sum_{i=0} P(i|C) \, P(E|i) \tag{4-1}$$

where $P(i|C)$ is the probability of causal rule i applying in the presence of cues C, and $P(E|i)$ is the probability of event E should rule i apply. This rule is the analog of Equation 3.2 from the previous chapter.

It is necessary to include the possibility that there is no known causal rule at work. The situation of no cause is denoted as the 0th causal rule. Thus, $P(0|C)$ is the probability of no known rule in presence of cues C, and $P(E|0)$ is the probability of the event E spontaneously occurring without any known cause.

To illustrate, suppose there were just two rules, (a) flipping a switch would cause a light to go on and (b) stomping our feet would cause a house

TABLE 4-1
Mathematical Notations Used in Chapter 4

Conditional Probabilities

$P(E\|C)$	Probability of event E conditional on cues C. See Equation 4-1.
$P(i\|C)$	Probability of causal rule i applying in the presence of cues C. See Equations 4-2 and 4-3.
$P(C\|i)$	Probability that cues C would occur if rule i applied.
$P(E\|i)$	Probability of event E, should rule i apply.
$P(m,n\|p)$	Probability of m successes and n failures, given that the probability of success is p. See Equation 4-5 in Table 4-2.
$Prob(m,n\|\alpha,\beta)$	Probability of m successes and n failures, given a prior Beta distribution of probabilities with parameters α and β. See Equation 4-8 in Table 4-2.
$\mu(p\|m,n)$	Expected probability given m successes and n failures.
$P(i\|n_1,n_2,n_3,n_4)$	Probability of a causal rule i, given values n_1, n_2, n_3, and n_4 from Table 4-3.
$P(\bar{i}\|n_1,n_2,n_3,n_4)$	Probability of no causal rule i, given values n_1, n_2, n_3, and n_4 from Table 4-3.
$P(n_1,n_2,n_3,n_4\|i)$	Probability of values n_1, n_2, n_3, and n_4 from Table 4-3, given that there is a causal rule i.
$P(n_1,n_2,n_3,n_4\|\bar{i})$	Probability of values n_1, n_2, n_3, and n_4 from Table 4-3, given that there is no causal rule i.
$P(t,d\|i)$	Probability of a transfer-of-force cause having its effect t time units and d distance units away.
$P(D\|n_i)$	Probability that feature D is a discriminating feature for a causal law, given a set of numbers n_i from Table 4-7. See Equation 4-16.
$P(\bar{D}\|n_i)$	Probability that D is not a discriminating feature, given a set of numbers n_i from Table 4-7.
$P(n_i\|D)$	Probability of a set of numbers n_i from Table 4-7, given that D is a discriminating feature.
$P(n_i\|\bar{D})$	Probability of a set of numbers n_i from Table 4-7 given that D is not a discriminating feature.

Probabilities

$P(i)$	Probability that a causal rule i is applicable in the current situation.
$Con(i)$	Probability that a causal rule i exists.
$Prior(i)$	Prior probability of a causal rule relating a potential cause i and an effect.
$Prior(\bar{i})$	Prior probability of no causal rule relating a potential cause i and an effect.
$Prior(D)$	Prior probability of a feature D being relevant to a discrimination of a causal law.
$Prior(\bar{D})$	Prior probability of a feature D not being relevant to a discrimination of a causal law.

Conventions

i	Indexes causal rules.
0	Denotes the unknown cause.
p	Probability of an event.

(Continued)

TABLE 4-1 *(Continued)*

Conventions (continued)

m	Number of successes.
n	Number of failures.
n_1	Number of co-occurrences of a potential cause and an effect.
n_2	Number of occurrences of a potential cause without an effect.
n_3	Number of occurrences of an effect without a potential cause.
n_4	Number of times neither effect nor potential cause occur.
t	Time between cause and effect.
d	Distance between cause and effect.
R	Ratio of probability between two competing causes.
D	Discriminating feature for a causal law.
P_a	Probability of a causal law reapplying to an individual.
P_b	Base probability of an event.
P_i	Probability of a causal law generalizing to all members of category i.
P_r	Probability of a causal law generalizing to individuals linked by a particular relationship.

Probability Densities

$\Pi(p)$	Prior distribution of probability that a causal law will produce its effect. See Equation 4-4.
$\Pi(p\|m,n)$	Posterior distribution of probability, given that m successes and n failures are observed. See Equation 4-6.

Parameters

α, β	Parameters of the beta distribution — see Equation 4-4.
α_N, β_N	Parameters of the beta distribution for the model of no cause.
α_C, β_C	Parameters of the beta distribution for the presence of a cause.
α_A, β_A	Parameters of the beta distribution for the absence of a cause.
a	Parameter of the exponential distribution of times between causes and effects — see Equation 4-13.
b	Parameter of the exponential distribution of distances between causes and effects — see Equation 4-13.

of cards to collapse. Suppose C is the act of flipping a switch. Let us assume the following totally hypothetical probabilities:

$$P(0|C) \quad = .04$$
$$P(1|C) \quad = .95$$
$$P(2|C) \quad = .01$$
$$P(light|0) \quad = .01$$
$$P(light|1) \quad = .95$$
$$P(light|2) \quad = .01$$
$$P(house\ of\ cards\ collapsing|0) \quad = .05$$
$$P(house\ of\ cards\ collapsing|1) \quad = .05$$
$$P(house\ of\ cards\ collapsing|2) \quad = .90$$

Then we can use Equation 4-1 to calculate $P(light|C) = .90$ and $P(house\ of\ cards\ collapsing|C) = .06$

Equation 4-1 focuses on $P(i|C)$, the probability of a causal law applying in a situation, and $P(E|i)$, the probability of an event should a causal law apply. $P(E|i)$ will be basically derived from how often the event occurs when the rule is applicable. Thus, the fact that $P(light|1)$ is less than 1 reflects the fact that the light is a bit flaky. Much of the interest focuses on $P(i|C)$, which includes in its analysis the considerations relevant to determining $P(E|i)$. Basically, $P(i|C)$ involves an induction from prior experience and prior beliefs.

Analogous to Equation 3-2, the relevant equation for $P(i|C)$ is:

$$P(i|C) = \frac{P(i)\ P(C|i)}{\sum_i P(i)\ P(C|i)} \tag{4-2}$$

where $P(i)$ is the probability of rule i holding before we consider the cues (i.e., its base rate), and $P(C|i)$ is the probability that cues C would occur in an application of i. Thus, to continue with the two-cause analysis, suppose:

$$
\begin{aligned}
P(0) &= .5 \\
P(1) &= .25 \\
P(2) &= .25 \\
P(C|0) &= .02 \\
P(C|1) &= 1.0 \\
P(C|2) &= .01
\end{aligned}
$$

Then,

$$
\begin{aligned}
P(0|C) &= .04 \\
P(1|C) &= .95 \\
P(2|C) &= .01
\end{aligned}
$$

Equation 4-2 assumes that there is an established set of mutually exclusive rules in which we have complete confidence but that vary in their frequency of applicability according to $P(i)$. However, it is often the case that there are causal rules about which we are uncertain — for instance, does jogging lead to back pain. In many experimental situations, we have rules that are equally frequent but that vary in their certainty. In this case, the following formula is applicable:

$$P(i|C) = \frac{Con(i) \ P(C|i)}{\sum\limits_{i} Con(i) \ P(C|i)}$$ (4-3)

where $Con(i)$ denotes the confidence that i exists. Note that the sum of $P(i)$ must equal 1, but the sum of the confidences need not. This equation can be equivalent to Equation 4-2 if we set $P(i) = Con(i)/\Sigma Con(i)$, which is reasonable in cases of equally applicable rules.

Equation 4-3 focuses on two issues — one of which is $Con(i)$, the confidence that causal rule i exists, and the other of which is $P(C|i)$, which is the match of the current situation to the situation assumed by the causal rule. The second is the more problematical, because it requires spelling out a model of the universe. I tackle these in order of their difficulty. The next section considers causal estimation, which is concerned with how we determine our degree of confidence that a causal rule exists. As part of this, I introduce a Bayesian framework relevant to estimating both $P(E|i)$, the probability that a rule will produce its effect, and $Con(i)$, the probability that the rule exists.

After discussing $P(E|i)$, the chapter tackles the issue of $P(C|i)$, the match of the rule to the context. There are three sections devoted to different aspects of this topic. One is the role of classic Humean cues to causality — temporal contiguity, spatial contiguity, and similarity. The second is how discriminating features get attached to a causal rule. The third is how we determine the range of generalization of a causal rule. The overall analysis is by no means totally integrated. The major goal of each discussion is to identify what factors are relevant to a rational analysis and show that these factors do, indeed, predict behavior.

The goal of this chapter is to convince the reader that we can understand human causal inference by assuming that it is rational. As was the case for previous chapters, this chapter concludes with some speculations about how this rational analysis can be achieved in an ACT framework.

CAUSAL ESTIMATION

Whether we are trying to estimate the probability that a causal law produces an effect or the probability that the causal law exists at all, the first step is to specify some prior probability of the law (if it exists) producing the effect. Again, we assume that there is a prior distribution of probabilities of causal laws producing their effects. We use the Beta distribution, which is a special case of the Dirichlet distribution used in the prior chapter. It is the standard prior distribution assumed in Bayesian analyses of binary events, and there are just two events of relevance in a causal law — either we get the effect or we don't. Taking a probabilistic view, there is a probability p of an effect and a probability 1-p of no effect.

Table 4-2 reviews the basic mathematical results that are used in this chapter. They are based on the assumption of a prior Beta distribution. A Beta distribution is defined by two parameters, α and β, and has mean $\alpha/(\alpha + \beta)$. This reflects the mean prior probability of the effect in question. The Bayesian inference procedure takes the observation of m "successes" when the cause is followed by the effect and n "failures" when it is not and

TABLE 4-2
Summary of Mathematics of Bayesian Inference of the Probability
of A Binary Event

Let $\Pi(p)$ be the prior distribution of the probability p of a success. The beta distribution of p is given by:

$$\Pi(p) = \frac{\Gamma(\alpha+\beta)p^{\alpha-1}(1-p)^{\beta-1}}{\Gamma(\alpha)\Gamma(\beta)} \tag{4-4}$$

where $\Gamma(X) = (X-1)!$. The mean of this distribution is $\alpha/(\alpha + \beta)$, and the variance is $\alpha\beta / (\alpha + \beta)^2 (\alpha + \beta + 1)$.

Conditional on a particular probability p from the prior distribution, the probability of a sequence of events involving m successes and n failures is described by the formula for a Bernoulli sequence:

$$P(m,n|p) = p^m(1-p)^n \tag{4-5}$$

The posterior distribution can then be calculated:

$$\Pi(p|m,n) = \frac{\Pi(p)P(m,n|p)}{\int_0^1\Pi(x)P(m,n|x)dx} \tag{4-6}$$

This turns out also to be a Beta distribution with parameters $\alpha + m$ and $\beta + n$.

It is also possible to calculate the probability of m successes and n failures given a prior Beta distribution with parameters α and β. This quantity is $Prob(m,n|\alpha,\beta)$ and can be calculated as:

$$Prob(m,n|\alpha,\beta) = \int_0^1 x^m(1-x)^n\beta(x|\alpha,\beta)dx \tag{4-7}$$

$$= \frac{\Gamma(m+\alpha)\Gamma(n+\beta)\Gamma(\alpha+\beta)}{\Gamma(m+n+\alpha+\beta)\Gamma(\alpha)\Gamma(\beta)} \tag{4-8}$$

where $\beta (x|\alpha,\beta)$ is a Beta distribution of x with parameters α and β (see Equation 4-4).

a posterior distribution of probabilities. This turns out to also be a Beta distribution but with parameters $\alpha + m$ and $\beta + n$. The mean of the posterior distribution, therefore, is:

$$\mu(p|m,n) = (\alpha + m) / (\alpha + \beta + m + n) \qquad (4\text{-}9)$$

The value of $\mu(p|m,n)$ is $P(E|i)$ for Equation 4.1. This is the probability of effect E.

Note that Equation 4-9 converges to observed proportion of successes $m/(m + n)$ as m and n become large. Thus, Equation 4-9 specifies a rational scheme for moving from the prior estimate of the probability, $\alpha/(\alpha + \beta)$, to the empirical proportion, $m/(m + n)$. The size of the parameters α and β reflect an "inertia" factor. The larger they are, the less influenced is the estimation procedure by the data and the more observations it will take to converge on the empirical proportion.

Analysis of 2 × 2 Contingency Tables

This Bayesian model can be used to estimate $Con(i)$, the probability that rule i actually exists. One standard formulation of this issue concerns the analysis of 2 × 2 contingency tables (e.g., Arkes & Harkness, 1983; Crocker, 1981; Jenkins & Ward, 1965; Lipe, 1982; Shaklee & Tucker, 1980; Smeldslund, 1963). Such a contingency table is illustrated in Table 4-3, where n_1, n_2, n_3, and n_4 are the frequencies in the various cells. Sometimes, just the tables are presented, but it seems more often that actual events are presented according to the frequencies in one of these 2 × 2 tables. These tend to be situations where considerations of the cues relevant to causal inference, such as temporal contiguity or similarity, are not applicable. Thus, the purported cause might be jogging, and the effect might be a backache. The subject is told of cases where the patient jogs and has a backache (n_1), jogs and has no backache (n_2), does not jog and has a backache (n_3), and neither jogs nor has a backache (n_4). The number of experimental variations of this experimental paradigm are many, and it is

TABLE 4-3
The Classic 2 × 2 Contingency Table for
Causal Estimation

Cause	Effect	
	present	absent
present	n_1	n_2
absent	n_3	n_4

unlikely that the analysis of causation developed here would be appropriate for them all. In cases where the subject is trying to induce a causal relationship from experience, predictions can be derived from the rational model developed in this section.

Basically, one has to compare two hypotheses. The first is that the frequency of the effect is the same in the presence or absence of the suspected cause i. The second is that there is a causal relationship, and the frequency of the effect is higher in the presence of the cause i. The odds ratio for the probability of the NULL hypothesis versus the CAUSAL hypothesis, given the data (n_1, n_2, n_3, n_4), can be calculated as:

$$\frac{P(i|n_1,n_2,n_3,n_4)}{P(\bar{i}|n_1,n_2,n_3,n_4)} = \frac{Prior(i)}{Prior(\bar{i})} \cdot \frac{P(n_1n_2,n_3,n_4|i)}{P(n_1,n_2,n_3,n_4|\bar{i})} \tag{4-10}$$

where $P(i|n_1,n_2,n_3,n_4)$ is *Con(i)* for Equation 4-3, *Prior(i)* is the belief in the causal relationship before any data, $P(n_1,n_2,n_3,n_4|i)$ is the conditional probability of the data given the rule, and the quantities in the denominator have corresponding definitions. The conditional probabilities depend on the prior probabilities of the effect under the causal and null models. If we assume that the prior probability of a success is described by a Beta distribution with parameters α and β, then the critical quantity becomes the probability of m successes and n failures, given that prior distribution. This is the quantity *Prob(m,n|α,β)* derived in Table 4.2.

The formula for *Prob(m,n|α,β)* can be used to calculate the conditional probabilities in Equation 4-10. Note that if there is no causal law at work there, the two rows of Table 4-3 can be collapsed, and we are simply interested in the probability of $n_1 + n_3$ successes and $n_2 + n_4$ failures under the null hypothesis. Let α_N and β_N describe the prior distribution of probability of an event when there is no identified causal law at work, and we get:

$$P(n_1,n_2,n_3,n_4|\bar{i}) = Prob(n_1+n_3,n_2+n_4|\alpha_N,\beta_N) \tag{4-11}$$

Let α_C, β_C be the parameters that describe the distribution when the cause is present and α_A, β_A describe the distribution when the cause is absent. Then,

$$P(n_1,n_2,n_3,n_4|i) = Prob(n_1,n_2|\alpha_C,\beta_C)Prob(n_3,n_4|\alpha_A,\beta_A) \tag{4-12}$$

A reasonable, minimal constraint on these parameters is that the probability of the event be greater with an identified cause than the probability without an identified cause and that this be greater than the probability in the absence of an identified cause. With respect to the parameters of Beta distribution, this means:

$$\alpha_C / (\alpha_C + \beta_C) > \alpha_N / (\alpha_N + \beta_N) > \alpha_A / (\alpha_A + \beta_A)$$

There has been a great deal of empirical research on the effect of the various values n_1, n_2, n_3, and n_4 (Crocker, 1981; Seggie & Endersby, 1972; Arkes & Harkness, 1983; Schustack & Sternberg, 1981). A general summary of this research is that subjects tend to be particularly sensitive to manipulations in n_1 and particularly insensitive to manipulations in n_4. This is often characterized as non-normative, because it is assumed that n_1 and n_4 should be treated symmetrically. However, according to the rational model sketched out above, these quantities should be treated symmetrically only if $\alpha_C = \beta_A$ and $\beta_C = \alpha_A$—which implies that the prior probability of an effect in the presence of the cause equals the prior probability of the effect not occurring in the absence of the cause. There is no reason to make such a symmetric assumption.

The sensitivity of Bayesian model is a function of the sum of α and β. The larger this is, the less the model weights the empirical proportion and the more it weights its prior estimate. It seems reasonable to assume that the prior estimate of the probability of an event on absence of an identified cause (determined by α_A and β_A) should be low and more stable than the prior estimate of the probability of an event in the presence of prior cause. Some causes are nearly certain in their effect and others terribly unreliable. Thus, it seems reasonable to assume $\alpha_A + \beta_A > \alpha_C + \beta_C$. In this case we would predict greater sensitivity to n_1 than n_4. In summary, the assumption that subjects should be equally sensitive to n_1 and n_4 depends on an unreasonable assumption about priors.

Schustack and Sternberg Experiment

Experiment 3 from Schustack and Sternberg[2] provides a good example to pursue this issue. They presented their subjects with 60 test items of the form

$$
\begin{array}{ccccc}
S & W & N & T \rightarrow & R \\
-Q & N & Z & S \rightarrow & -R \\
T & W & S & Z \rightarrow & R \\
T & -S & -Q & -N \rightarrow & -R \\
& & S & \rightarrow & R
\end{array}
$$

where the first four are abstract characterizations of possibly casual events. The first says that when S, W, N, and T were present, R occurred; the

---

[2]Miriam Schustack has generously provided me with the raw data from this experiment.

second says that when Q was absent, N, Z, and S were present, R did not happen; and so forth. The last item is the one subjects are asked to judge — in this case, they are asked to judge the likelihood that S leads to the outcome of R. (Subjects assigned a value of 34.7% to that example.) Such problems can be described in terms of the values of n_1, n_2, n_3, and n_4. In the case just given, $n_1 = 2$, $n_2 = 1$, $n_3 = 0$, and $n_4 = 1$ where these reflect the co-occurrence pattern of S and R. Schustack and Sternberg did a regression analysis of how well n_1 through n_4 predicted subjects' rated likelihood. Consistent with other results, they found strongest correlations with n_1 and weakest with n_4.

This model was fit to the Schustack and Sternberg data, using the Stepit program of Chandler (1965). This program finds the values of the parameters α_C, β_C, α_N, β_N, α_A, β_A, and $Prior(i)$, which gives $P(i|n_1,n_2,n_3,n_4)$, which best correlates with the rated likelihoods provided by subjects. The correlation between the data and the model is .96, which is slightly higher than that obtained by Schustack and Sternberg. It is of interest to consider the parameter estimates:

$$
\begin{aligned}
\alpha_C &= 1.79 \\
\beta_C &= .74 \\
\alpha_N &= 1.76 \\
\beta_N &= 4.67 \\
\alpha_A &= .98 \\
\beta_A &= 6.87 \\
Prior(i) &= .40
\end{aligned}
$$

Thus, these estimates satisfy the earlier constraint that the largest prior probability is of an effect in the presence of a cause ($\alpha_C/(\alpha_C + \beta_C) = .71$), the next largest with no cause ($\alpha_N/(\alpha_N + \beta_N) = .27$), and the least in absence of a cause ($\alpha_A/(\alpha_A + \beta_A) = .12$). The absolute values of these probabilities seem reasonable also.

Schustack and Sternberg get correlations of .81, $-.58$, $-.59$, and .12 between their data on n_1, n_2, n_3, and n_4, respectively; the predictions of the rational model produce correlations of .82, $-.61$, $-.54$, and .11. The relatively large value of β_A in contrast to α_C means that there is less sensitivity to occurrences n_4 than n_1 — recall that the size of the α and β parameters determine the sensitivity to frequencies in experience. This result makes the point that there need be no discrepancy between a rational analysis and differential weighting of the cells in a 2 × 2 contingency table. The critical issue is what prior model is adopted in a rational analysis.

CUES FOR CAUSAL INFERENCE

We now turn to an examination of the problematical $P(C|i)$, the probability of a set of cues given that i is the cause. Hume (1740) argued that we tend to see a causal relationship to the degree that cause and effect are temporally contiguous (provided cause does not follow effect), spatially contiguous, and similar. These ideas are found in a number of modern models of causal inference (e.g., Einhorn & Hogarth, 1986). However, other theorists (e.g., Shultz, 1982) have argued that these cues receive too much play and that what really matters are models of causal mechanisms. The current approach sees the mechanism-versus-cues issue as a false dichotomy. Under the current framework, there are different possible models of mechanisms that make different cues more or less probable. Thus, $P(C|i)$ should be analyzed differently depending on the mechanism assumed in the cause. In an unpublished study, Mike Matessa, Ross Thompson, and I set out to explore this with respect to the role for cues of spatial and temporal contiguity in causal inference. The two experimental situations are illustrated in Figs. 4-1A and 4-1B.

In all cases, the event to be explained is a trap door opening and a ball rising out of the hole at the right of the box. Prior to this, an event occurs to the left of the hole. The subjects' task is to judge whether or not the first event appears to be the cause of the door opening and the ball coming out. In Fig. 4-1A, a weight is dropped onto the box, and the subjects are told that it may have jarred loose a latch that opens the door and releases the ball. Subjects are asked to judge how likely it is that the weight is responsible. The time between the dropping of the weight and the opening of the box is varied, as is the distance between where the weight drops and the door. In this case, subjects judge the weight more probably the cause the closer in time and space it is to the effect, just in accord with Hume's prescription. In Fig. 4-1B, subjects see a ball go in another hole and are told that there might be a passage in the box through which it goes and comes out at the trap door. In this case, subjects use the velocity of the ball to find the right combination of distance and time so that the ball would have traveled that far in time.

Thus, temporal and spatial contiguity cues are filtered through a model of the situation. It is assumed that vibratory waves diminish over time and space in Fig. 4-1A. A ball continues its initial velocity and takes a certain time to move a certain distance in Fig. 4-1B.

Why, then, is it commonly thought that we are more likely to perceive causality the closer objects are in time and space? Presumably, the default model for causal interaction between objects is through some sort of force transmission like the situation in Fig. 4-1A. In many situations, the exact

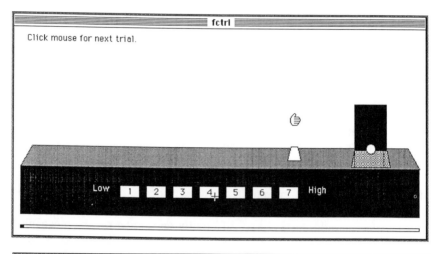

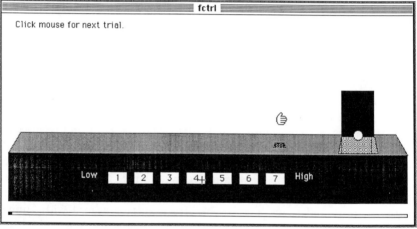

FIG. 4-1. Two conditions used by Anderson, Matessa, & Thompson.
(A) promotes a vibratory wave model
(B) promotes a projectile model

mechanisms of causality are obscure, and we fall back on the default one. This is particularly likely if the purported cause involves some force. Thus, if I drop a book on the floor and a nearby ball begins to spin, exactly how this came about is surely obscure, but a transfer of force model seems plausible. Thus, the right analysis of spatial and temporal contiguity is not that they are absolute cues to causality, as some have argued; rather, it is that they are rational cues to causal attribution when a transfer of force model is appropriate, and such models are most typically appropriate.

Formalization of Spatial and Temporal Contiguity

Given that spatial and temporal contiguity are relevant in a transfer of force model, and that such models are most often applicable, it is useful to offer a formalization of these cues in order to have a formula for calculating $P(t,d|i)$, where i is a cause involving transfer of force from a cause removed t units in time and d units in distance from its purported effect.

In some cases, very precise models can be brought to bear in determining $p(t,d|i)$. Consider the situation where one object collides with a second and causes the second to move off. Here, t is the time between the first object touching the second and the second moving, and d is the gap between the two objects. In this case, $P(0,0|i) = 1$ and $P(t,d|i) = 0$ for all t and d greater than zero. Michotte (1946), in his famous experiments, found that the objects had to touch and the movement had to be instantaneous for causality to be perceived.

A case that can be modeled with much less precision is the traveling of waves, as in the weight example (Fig. 4-1A) where a wave loosens some mechanism to produce an effect. This is much like the situation where an earthquake causes a building to collapse. How does the probability of a building collapsing vary with distances and time from the source of the earthquake? Depending on the medium, the force at a particular location will decrease with something between $1/d$ and $1/d^2$, where d is the distance. The shock waves travel very rapidly, producing near instantaneous effects at short distances, but, depending on the construction of the object, it might take some time for it to collapse.

In many situations, only very vague scientific models can be brought to bear. For instance, consider trying to blow a house of cards over. Who can say how the collapse of the house will vary with time and distance from the puff of air. Nonetheless, time and distance do have an effect on that probability.

It is of interest to inquire what model can be adopted for time and distance in cases where there is little information. Because effects cannot precede their causes, both time and space are variables in causation that vary from zero to infinity. The standard noninformative Bayesian (Berger, 1985) prior for such spaces is the exponential probability density, which has the property of favoring closer things. Thus, if t and d are variables ranging over times and distances between causes and effects,

$$p(t,d|i) = abe^{-at}e^{-bd} \tag{4-13}$$

which gives mean time $1/a$ and mean distance $1/b$ between cause i and the effect.

Bullock, Gelman, & Baillargeon Experiment

There have been a number of studies (e.g. Bullock, Gelman, & Baillargeon, 1982; Shultz, Fischer, Pratt, & Rulf, 1986) in the literature that have pitted spatial and temporal contiguity against each other. The results are not consistent in identifying which factor is more important. Equation 4.13 implies that either factor can dominate, depending on the size of the differences on the two dimensions and in the parameters a and b. Shultz and colleagues (1986) found that, when spatial and temporal contiguity are in conflict, subjects attribute the cause to the temporally closer cause, whereas Bullock, Gelman, & Baillargeon found that subjects preferred the spatially closer factor. The data in the latter study are presented in a somewhat better way for modeling. Therefore, I have attempted to model it with Equation 4-13. The connections were obscure in their experiment, but I assume that the vague transfer of force model is appropriate in this circumstance.

There were four conditions in their experiment. In each case, subjects had to choose between two possible causes for an effect (see Fig. 4-2). Two balls rolled down the tubes, and a Jack-in-the-Box appeared out of the center box. One condition, as illustrated in Fig. 4-2, involved the two potential causes equally far away but one closer in time than the other. In the second condition, the two potential causes occurred at the same time, but one cause was further away. In the third condition, one cause was closer in both space and time, and in the fourth condition the two cues conflicted. The statistic of interest concerned the relative choice of the two potential causes as the true cause. Because the prior probabilities for the two causes will be the same, this is essentially a function of the relative conditional probabilities of the two causes:

$$R = \frac{P(C_1|1)}{P(C_2|2)} = \frac{ae^{-at_1} be^{-bd_1}}{ae^{-at_2} be^{-bd_2}} \tag{4-14}$$

where t_1 and t_2 are the two times and d_1 and d_2 are the two distances. Taking logarithms yields:

FIG. 4-2. The apparatus used by Bullock, Gelman, & Baillargeon (1982)

$$ln(R) = a(t_2 - t_1) + b(d_2 - d_1) \qquad (4\text{-}15)$$

There were basically three values for $t_2 - t_1$: Δt when t_2 was further away, 0 when simultaneous, and $-\Delta t$ when t_2 was closer. Similarly, $d_2 - d_1$ will take on values Δd, 0, and $-\Delta d$. Table 4-4 reports the net difference between the two conditions and the choice behavior of the subjects. The data are consistent with a larger value of $b\Delta d$ than $a\Delta t$. Note that this does not mean that distance is more important than time, in general; it is just that the difference in distance used in this experiment was more important than the difference in time used. Indeed, as noted earlier, Shultz and his colleagues found evidence for greater preference for time in their experiments. The study that needs to be done is one that performs a more parametric manipulation of space and time.

Similarity

So far, we have looked at the causal cues of spatial and temporal contiguity and shown that they are rationally justified in many situations, and in situations where they are not justified people do not pay attention to them (see discussion with respect to Fig. 4-1). The situation with respect to Hume's third cue of similarity is much more problematical. Why should causes and effects resemble each other? I think, as a statistical fact, that cause and effect tend to resemble one another more than chance, but similarity is by no means a perfect cue, and in some situations we do ignore it. To begin to see why causes resemble their effects, we need to begin to explore the issue of what is meant by similarity. We next consider two types of similarity between cause and effect. One is when they share values on some dimensions, and the other is when they share components.

1. Dimensional. The cause may share a value on a dimension like color or size with an effect. If we are in a strange world and see a red flash and a green flash of lightening, and a stone turns the same hue of green as the green flash, we are more likely to attribute it to the green flash. If we

TABLE 4-4
The Experimental Apparatus Used by Bullock, Gelman & Baillargeon (1982)

	Ln(R)	*Adults' Choice Behavior*
Condition 1	$a\Delta t$	65% to temporally closer.
Condition 2	$b\Delta d$	100% to spatially closer.
Condition 3	$a\Delta t + b\Delta d$	100% to spatially & temporally closer.
Condition 4	$b\Delta d - a\Delta t$	70% to spatially closer.

encounter a big and a small animal in this world, and a small glow the same size as the small animal appears in the air, we are more likely to attribute it to the small animal. What is the basis for these attributions?

These attributions turn on the fact that causes sometimes do confer their properties on their effects. Some objects color other things with their color. For example, blue jeans color other objects in the wash with their color. When we lie on the snow, we leave an image in our size and shape. To analyze what is happening here, let p be the probability of conveying a value on a dimension, and let n be the number of discriminable values on that dimension that we assume are equally probable. Suppose we are trying to choose between two possible causes, A and B, where A shares a value with the effect. The posterior ratio of these two causes is:

$$\frac{P(A|\textit{effect shares a value with A})}{P(B|\textit{effect shares a value with A})} = \frac{P(A)}{P(B)} \cdot \frac{P(\textit{effect shares a value with A}|A)}{P(\textit{effect shares a value with A}|B)}$$

In the case that B is the cause, the probability of the effect sharing a dimension with A is, presumably, chance. Thus, if there are n discriminable values, P *(effect shares a value with $A|B$)* $= 1/n$. Let p be the probability that A confers a dimension on the effect when A is the cause. Then, *P(effect shares a value with $A|A$)* $= p + (1-p)/n$. Thus,

$$\frac{P(A|\textit{effect shares a value with A})}{P(B|\textit{effect shares a value with A})} = [(1-p)+np] \frac{P(A)}{P(B)}$$

Clearly, if the number of possible discriminable values (n) is large there can be a major increment to A as the cause, even in the face of relatively small probability, p, of conferring a dimension on the effect.

2. Shared Components. A second basis for similarity is that the cause shares components with the effect. Thus, to return to the example of chapter 1, in medieval times, lungs of foxes were thought to cure asthma, in part because they both involved breathing. This example certainly seems bizarre today, but other examples of such causal attribution can still be fairly compelling. For instance, Lewis (1988) described a number of situations where subjects overwhelmingly infer causality on this basis (which he called the identity heuristic).

The situations where cause and effect actually do share components are numerous, but we can easily overlook them. When one person does something to another person (e.g., injury), and the other person does something in return (e.g., lawsuit), the first event that is the cause shares components (i.e., the people) with the second event. When we key 100 into the money machine, and $100 comes out, there is a clear causal connection between the category of 100 units in the cause and 100 units in the effect.

Indeed, it is statistically rare for cause and effect not to share components. In past ages, when such instances occurred, it was considered magical; in the current age, we assume hidden wires and such. The reason for such causal attributions is that things tend to interact through their components. Therefore, effects will tend to possess some of the pieces of their causes. This is really just a componential derivative of the fact that causes tend to be spatial and temporally close to their effects.

Note that, as in the case of temporal and spatial contiguity, similarity is not an absolute and is filtered through a theory. Consider the image in the snow that resembles a person. Suppose there was a second image in the snow that also resembled the person. We are unlikely to attribute one image as the cause of the other, even though the two images are physically more similar than either is to the person. This is because we know that people produce images in the snow, and images in the snow do not produce other images.

Cues to Causality: A Summary

To summarize the discussion about cues to causality: Under certain models of causality, spatial contiguity, temporal contiguity, and similarity are valid cues to causality. Note that there is no reason why we should restrict ourselves just to these cues. Under some models, there are other valid cues. For instance, in variations on Michotte's experiment where one object collides with a second and the second is seen to move, Kaiser and Proffitt (1984) showed that subjects use cues of velocity and angle to judge causality. When the transfer of momentum was physically anomalous (such as an impossible direction or rate of acceleration), subjects failed to perceive causality. Subjects could also judge relative mass of the two objects from the velocity and angle at which the objects separated.

An interesting issue concerns how these prior models develop and whether the development of such prior models can be incorporated into a rational framework. For instance, it does appear that there is some developmental trend in the ability of subjects to apply the correct kinematic model to the object collisions (Kaiser & Proffitt, 1984).

There are situations where subjects' judgments are not so in tune with the correct scientific model. Consider the situation where an object moves off a surface, such as when a ball rolls off a table. The correct scientific model is one in which the trajectory of the object after it leaves the table is a curve reflecting a combination of the original horizontal velocity and the downward negative force due to gravity. Some people believe the object will go directly down, and others predict an L-shaped trajectory in which the object initially goes forward and then goes down. Judgments in this domain show a definite developmental trend, with older subjects showing fewer miscon-

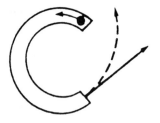

FIG. 4-3. C-Shaped Tube problem used by Kaiser, McCloskey, &
Proffitt (1986). Copyright (1986) by
the American Psychological Asso-
C-SHAPED TUBE PROBLEM   ciation. Reprinted by permission.

ceptions. Apparently, people come to tune their models with experience (Kaiser, Proffitt, & McCloskey, 1985).

Even more interesting are judgments about the trajectory of an object after it leaves a curve-shaped tube, such as the one in Fig. 4-3 (Kaiser, McCloskey, & Proffitt, 1986; McCloskey, 1983). A common misconception is that it will show a curved trajectory, rather than a straight one. This belief shows a curious U-shaped developmental trend, with children around the sixth grade showing the most misconception and preschoolers and college students about equivalent and somewhat better.

These results and developmental trends indicate that we are not born with all the laws describing our environment; rather, we induce at least some of them from experience. The actual process by which we learn to incorporate such theories is an interesting issue, but one that I do not pursue in this chapter.

INTEGRATION OF STATISTICAL AND TEMPORAL CUES

Thus far, two types of experimental situations have been considered: First, there were experiments like Schustack and Sternberg (1981), which manipulated over multiple observations how often causes and possible effects co-occurred. Second, there were experiments like that of Bullock, Gelman, and Baillargeon (1982), which gave subjects a single observation of a cause–effect pairing and manipulated various cues to causality. This, naturally, raises the question of what happens when both things are manipulated simultaneously. The experiment by Siegler (1976) is an appropriate one for discussing this potential interaction between physical and statistical cues. He varied what he termed the necessity and sufficiency conditions. Necessity referred to the fact that the effect only occurred in the presence of the purported cause. Sufficiency referred to the fact that when the purported cause occurred, the effect always occurred. In his experiment, the effect to be explained was the flashing of a light. The two possible causes were a card reader being fed and a computer operating. The reader was turned on every 20 seconds, and he varied the sufficiency and necessity relationships between the card reader and the light. The visible operations of the computer were random with respect to the light.

The matrices in Table 4-5 show the actual frequencies utilized by Siegler. The no-no cell (signified by ?) illustrates the practical difficulty of counting events that lacked both the purported cause and effect. How often was it the case that the card reader was neither turned on nor the light flashed? Depending on how one counts events, this could be anything from zero to infinity. We specify a method for counting events in this cell after we have further specified how to model his experiment.

Modeling the Siegler Experiment

1. Given that the subjects had to choose between the computer and the reader, we have to specify when computer events occurred, as well as card reader events. With the computer operating (blinking lights) more or less continuously, this question becomes one of when a subject chooses to encode a computer event. I choose to model this as a random encoding event that was a Poisson process with a mean of 1 encoding every 10 seconds. Thus, on average, computer events occurred twice as frequently as card reader events, which occurred once every 20 seconds on a regular basis.

2. On Siegler's advice, we decided to include an attentiveness process to reflect that children would not always encode the events. We set the probability of encoding any event (light, computer, or reader) at .7.

3. Causal attribution requires that we have a prior probability *Prior(i)* in Equation 4-10 of a cause-and-effect link in advance of a causal law. Siegler

TABLE 4-5
Frequency Matrices Used by Siegler (1976)

	matrix 1 (necessity & sufficiency)		matrix 2 (necessity only)	
	light	no light	light	no light
card reader on	6	0	6	6
card reader not on	0	?	0	?
	matrix 3 (sufficiency only)		matrix 4 (neither sufficiency nor necessity)	
	light	no light	light	no light
card reader on	3	0	0	8
card reader not on	3	?	6	?

claims that the computer–light relationship seemed more plausible a priori than the reader–light link. Therefore, I set *Prior(i)* to be .25 for the computer and .10 for the card reader.

4. When a light occurred, a decision had to be made about whether to attribute it to the card reader or computer. The past was searched for the most recent computer and reader events if there were any. Equation 4-3 was used to calculate posterior probabilities $P(i|C)$ where i indexes causes (either computer or card reader) and C is the cue of time between the cause and the light. This involved calculating a conditional probability, $P(C|i)$, and a confidence, *Con(i)*, in the cause i. The cue used to calculate $P(C|i)$ was distance in time between the light and i (either the reader or the computer) and was calculated by means of Equation 4-13, ignoring the spatial distance factor. The parameter a from Equation 4-13 was set at .4. *Con(i)* was calculated using Equation 4-10. This involved assigning values to n_1, n_2, n_3, and n_4. As we have discussed, it is problematical to determine n_4, the frequency of events, without effect on the purported cause. We set this as the number of times the other possible cause occurred without the effect, assuming that these were the only other events being encoded. Calculating *Con(i)* by this means requires that we specify the α and β parameters that were set at $\alpha_C = 4.0$, $\beta_C = 1.0$, $\alpha_N = 1.0$, $\beta_N = 1.0$, $\alpha_A = 1.0$, and $\beta_A = 4.0$.[3] This scheme for estimating *Con(i)* builds into the system a kind of snowball effect. The greater *Con(i)*, the more likely the subject is to attribute i as the cause. The more such attributions, the greater *Con(i)*.

5. At the end of the experiment, *Con(i)* was calculated for both computer and card reader, and the ratio $R = Con(reader)/Con(computer)$ was calculated. If R was greater than a threshold, T, the card reader was chosen; if R was less than $1/T$, the computer was chosen; otherwise, the program refused to choose.

The random encoding of computer events created a random character to the actual causal attribution. Therefore, we ran 1000 simulations of each of Siegler's conditions. Table 4-6 presents the results from our simulations and from Siegler's experiment. Siegler ran two groups of subjects, 5-year-olds and 8-year-olds. Data is given in terms of number of children who ascribe causality to the card reader, number who ascribe causality to the computer, and number of equivocal subjects who say it was sometimes one and sometimes the other. Eight-year-olds are much more cautious in ascribing causality to either device. We modeled this developmental difference by varying the extremity of the threshold T before giving a response. For the

---

[3]These parameters are arbitrary guesses. A mildly amusing observation was that I set $\alpha_C = \beta_A$ and $\beta_C = \alpha_A$, which is the implicit symmetry error assumed in theoretical analyses of human inference from 2×2 contingency data. I doubt that this experiment is sensitive to that symmetry assumption.

TABLE 4-6
Siegler Experiment and Simulation

	Subjects					
	5 Years			8 Years		
	Card Reader	One or Other	Computer	Card Reader	One or Other	Computer
Necessity & Sufficiency	10	0	2	10	1	1
Necessity Only	11	0	1	5	3	4
Sufficiency Only	9	2	1	1	10	1
Neither	4	1	7	4	3	5

	Simulations					
	T < 2			T < 10		
	Card Reader	One or Other	Computer	Card Reader	One or Other	Computer
Necessity & Sufficiency	11.20	.41	.40	9.20	2.59	.20
Necessity Only	10.16	.53	.31	8.28	2.00	1.72
Sufficiency Only	7.45	1.54	3.01	5.23	4.99	1.78
Neither	3.28	2.43	6.30	1.75	6.46	3.78

5-year-olds, T was set at 2.0, whereas for 8-year-olds, it was set at 10.0. These numbers were chosen to roughly match the overall numbers of subjects giving equivocal responses across conditions in an age group.[4]

The numbers at the bottom of Table 4-6 reflect the predicted frequencies of our simulation. The correlation between data and prediction was .82. To get a different measure of fit, we did a chi-square test of deviation from prediction. In applying this test, we aggregated cells in a column that had expected frequencies less than 1. The cells combined are boxed on Table 4-6. Given that we estimated two ratios to fit the equivocal column and given that the numbers must sum to 48 for each age group, there are 15 degrees of freedom (19 boxes − 4 constraints). The χ-square statistic was $\chi^2_{15} = 23.47$, which indicates a very good fit with no significant deviation between data and theory. Note that this fit was obtained without estimating best-fitting parameter values (and I have not subtracted these from my degrees of freedom).

---

[4]Siegler, in personal communication, agrees with this interpretation of 8-year-olds as more cautious.

Besides indicating that we can account for causal attribution in the Siegler experiment from this rational framework, these results give us an interesting perspective on developmental trends. They indicate that these young children were behaving as optimally as we can expect, given their prior assumption about which was the more plausible cause and given how often they chose to attend to the computer as a possible cause. The only developmental trend was the increased caution displayed by the 8-year-olds in making any causal attribution. As we shortly see, not only do young children appear rational in their causal attributions; so do rats.

DISCRIMINATION

The causal rules that we have considered have proposed links between single causes and their effects. Often, however, multiple factors have to be in place for a factor to have its effect. Thus, a bolt of lightning may be the cause of a forest fire, but this will only happen if the forest is in a particularly dry state. A fair amount of philosophical discussion is given to the issue of whether the cause is just the bolt of lightning or whether it is the conjunction of features, such as lightning plus dryness of forest. For purposes of our organism trying to maximize the success of its prediction, this philosophical discussion is irrelevant. The critical point is that there are circumstances where prediction will be enhanced by adding additional features to causal laws.

Although there may be circumstances where one could start out with causal laws with multiple factors, I consider the situation where laws start out with a single factor and other discriminating features are added. This seems a likely situation: One starts out in a particular situation where the relevant conditions are satisfied, discovers a cause-and-effect relationship, and, as new situations are explored, discovers what features about the original situation were critical.

By now, the logic I propose for when to discriminate should have a familiar pattern. Let us suppose that we have a causal law and want to consider restricting it to situations where feature d is present. Our choice about whether to do this should be a function of the relative probability of our experience, given the discriminated law (D) versus the nondiscriminated law $(\overline{D})$: In making this decision, we will have to make reference to eight frequencies defined by a crossing of the binary factors of discriminating feature present or absent, cause present or absent, and effect present or absent. Table 4-7 organizes these frequencies in matrix form. Our odds ratio is:

$$\frac{P(D|n_i)}{P(\overline{D}|n_i)} = \frac{Prior(D)}{Prior(\overline{D})} \frac{P(n_i|D)}{P(n_i|\overline{D})} \tag{4-16}$$

TABLE 4-7
Relevant Numbers for Assessing a Discriminating Feature in Equation 4-16

	Discriminating Feature Present		Discriminating Feature Absent	
	Effect	*No Effect*	*Effect*	*No Effect*
Cause	n_1	n_2	n_5	n_6
No Cause	n_3	n_4	n_7	n_8

where

$$P(n_i|D) = Prob(n_1,n_2|\alpha_C,\beta_C)\ Prob(n_3+n_5+n_7,n_4+n_6+n_8|\alpha_N,\beta_N)$$

$$P(n_i|\overline{D}) = Prob(n_1+n_5,n_2+n_6|\alpha_C,\beta_C)\ Prob(n_3+n_7,n_4+n_8|\alpha_N,\beta_N)$$

where n_i refers to the set of eight numbers from the matrices. In general, it is reasonable to assume that the prior odds ratio $Prior(D)/Prior(\overline{D})$ is low because there are numerous potential discriminating features, and the probability of any particular feature being relevant must be low. Nonetheless, if the frequencies change sharply conditional on some such feature, the conditional probabilities would overwhelm any difference in prior probabilities.

Modeling the Rescorla Experiment

An interesting illustration of the discrimination process is an experiment by Rescorla (1968) on classical conditioning. Animal conditioning is an interesting domain, because it can be shown that animals are sensitive to the probability of a conditioned stimulus. Holland, Holyoak, Nisbett, & Thagard (1986) have argued that animals are forming a causal theory that an unconditioned stimulus causes the conditioned stimulus. They have presented an analysis of Rescorla's experiment in the context of their theory.

In Rescorla's experiment, hungry rats were placed in a box with a bar that could be pressed to obtain food. The total period of an experimental session was 2 hours, which could be conceptualized as consisting of sixty 2-minute periods. In a random 12 of these periods, a tone was presented for the duration, whereas the other 48 periods were silent. Rescorla varied the probability of a shock during the tone periods and the silent periods. This continued for 5 training days. Then, he administered 6 days of 2 hours of extinction in which the shock was never present. The tone was present on a random four of the sixty 2-minute periods in an extinction session.

The critical data concern what is termed the *suppression ratio* over the extinction sessions. The suppression ratio is a measure of how much bar pressing is suppressed in the presence of the tone, presumably because the animal is expecting a shock. Figure 4-4 shows Rescorla's data plotted as a function of extinction session. Each panel corresponds to a different probability of shock in the presence of a tone, and each curve within a panel corresponds to a different probability of a shock in the absence of the tone. A suppression ratio of .5 indicates no suppression of bar pressing in the presence of a tone relative to the rate in silence. As can be seen, the suppression ratio is a function of the difference between probability of a shock in the presence of a tone versus the probability in the absence. The suppression decreases as extinction progresses.

The first part of the analysis of this experiment should be to determine in which conditions the animals are likely to form causal laws during training, linking the tone to the shock. This is a good case for the analysis of 2×2 contingency tables and Equation 4-10. There were 60 tone periods and 240 silent periods. Let p be the probability of a shock during tone and q during silence. Combining Equations 4-8 through 4-12, the ratio of the null hypothesis to the causal hypothesis should be:

$$\frac{P(CAUSAL|n_i)}{P(NULL|n_i)}$$

$$=\frac{Prior(CAUSAL)}{Prior(NULL)} \cdot \frac{Prob(60p,60(1-p)|\alpha_C,\beta_C) \; Prob(240q, \; 240(1-q)|\alpha_A,\beta_A)}{Prob(60p+240q, \; 60(1-p) + 240(1-q)|\alpha_N,\beta_N)}$$

$$(4\text{-}17)$$

We set $\alpha_C = 1$, $\beta_C = 1$, $\alpha_A = 1$, $\beta_A = 4$, $\alpha_N = 1$, $\beta_N = 3$ and $Prior(CASUAL)/Prior(NULL) = .5$. Again, these represent first guesses as to parameters and are not results of extensive parameter searches. The α and β values were set to approximate, on average, the frequency of shock on average in the Rescorla condition. The values calculated by Equation 4-17 for the various conditions are given in Table 4-8. As can be seen, it is reasonable to assume a causal relationship in all cases except the cases where $p = q$ when a causal relation is improbable and the one case where $p = .2$ and $q = .1$, where the evidence is equivocal.

The next issue to address is the extinction data in those conditions where a causal law will be formed. This is where the discrimination analysis we developed is relevant. The rat must discriminate the fact that its tone-implies-shock law was relevant to the training context and not to the extinction context. To address Rescorla's data on extinction also requires specifying what quantity would be related to the suppression ratio. It seemed to me that this quantity should be the amount of increase in expected probability of shock in the presence of a tone.

The discrimination that the animal has an opportunity to make is one in

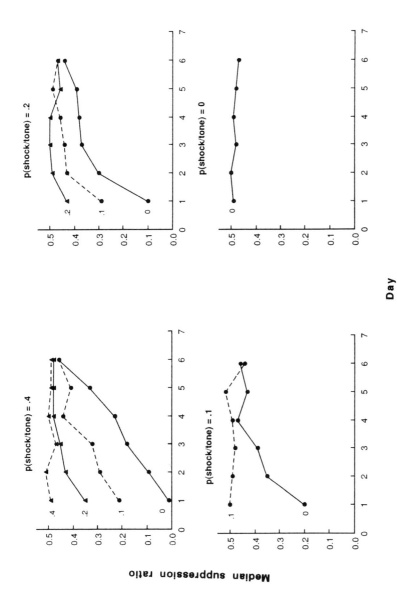

FIG. 4-4. Median suppression ratios for each group over six extinction test sessions. Within each panel, all groups had the same probability of the shock (US) during the tone (CS); the parameter in each panel is the probability of the US in the absence of the CS. From Rescorla (1986).

TABLE 4-8
Probabilities of a Causal Rule in the Various Conditions of Rescorla's
Experiment

Probability of Shock in Absence of Tone	Probabilities of Shock in Presence of Tone			
	.4	.2	.1	0
.4	.08			
.2	.94	.11		
.1	1.00	.50	.01	
.0	1.00	1.00	1.00	.00

which some aspect of the extinction trial blocks the causal law or, equivalently, the negation of that aspect enables the causal law. Thus, for purposes of Equation 4-16, the relevant matrices are those given in Table 4-9, where s is the number of extinction sessions. I set $Prior(D)/Prior(\overline{D}) = .1$ to represent the low a priori odds of a discrimination.

Then, I calculated the mean expected increase in the probability of a shock during extinction trials, which is:

$$P(Causal|Tn_i) \, P(\overline{D}|En_i) \, [(P(Shock|Cause+\overline{D}) - P(Shock|\overline{Cause}+\overline{D})]$$

where $P(Causal|Tn_i)$ is the probability of a causal law given the n_i during training (Tn_i denotes these are counts during training); $P(\overline{D}|En_i)$ is the probability calculated from Equation 4-16 of not making a discrimination, given the n_i during extinction (En_i denotes these are counts in Table 4-9 for extinction); $P(Shock|Cause + \overline{D})$ is the probability of a shock in the presence of the cause, given no discrimination; and $P(Shock|\overline{Cause} + \overline{D})$ is the probability of a shock in the absence of a cause, given no discrimination. This gives the product of the probability of a cause from training, the probability of no discrimination, and the difference between probability of a shock in the presence of a cause versus the absence. We can define

Table 4-9
Number of Events of Each Type Calculation of Discrimination Numbers for
the Rescorla Experiment

	Training Context		Extinction Context	
	Shock	No Shock	Shock	No Shock
Tone	$n_1 = 60p$	$n_2 = 60(1\text{-}p)$	$n_5 = 0$	$n_6 = 4s$
No Tone	$n_3 = 240q$	$n_4 = 240(1\text{-}q)$	$n_7 = 0$	$n_8 = 56s$

Note: s is the number of extinction sessions.

$P(Shock|\text{Cause} + \overline{D})$ and $P(Shock|\overline{Cause} + \overline{D})$ in terms of eight cells of Table 4-9:

$$P(Shock|Cause + \overline{D}) = \frac{n_1 + n_5 + \alpha_C}{n_1 + n_2 + n_5 + n_6 + \alpha_C + \beta_C}$$

$$P(Shock|\overline{Cause} + \overline{D}) = \frac{n_3 + n_7 + \alpha_A}{n_3 + n_4 + n_7 + n_8 + \alpha_A + \beta_A}$$

The predictions of the theory based on these equations are plotted in Fig. 4-5. There is a substantial correspondence to Rescorla's data, and the overall correlation is .82. There is one systematic discrepancy between the data and the theory that is seen best in the curve for the $P(shock) = .4$ with tone and $P(shock) = 0$ without tone. This curve most rapidly converges on zero because the evidence for a discrimination is very strong—a 40% shock has been replaced by 0%—a clear difference. In contrast, the rat's suppression ratio stays low long after there is overwhelming evidence that the shock is no longer in effect. This may reflect that my conception of the discrimination is too simple. I assume that the rat is discriminating on a simple binary feature of before or after day of onset of extinction. It might be more realistic to assume that each day becomes less similar than the rest on a more continuous scale, and the discrimination is taking place on this continuous scale.

Although the match-up is not perfect, this exercise does show that, at least to an approximation, rats are responding rationally to the statistics about shock presentation. It remains an open question whether the fact that it is only an approximation reflects faults in the rats or faults in the assumptions of the analysis.

ABSTRACTION OF CAUSAL LAWS

So far, the discussion has proceeded as if it were obvious where a causal law was to be applied. For instance, in the Rescorla experiment, it was essentially the same tone predicting the same shock. However, the class of situations to which a causal rule should generalize is often far from obvious. Suppose a tone of a somewhat different frequency is presented—should the rule generalize or not? As research on stimulus generalization in conditioning has shown (e.g., Guttman & Kalish, 1956; Jenkins & Harrison, 1958), there are generalization gradients on dimensions such as the frequency of a tone such that the degree of conditioning decreases as a function of the difference between the original stimulus and the test stimulus.

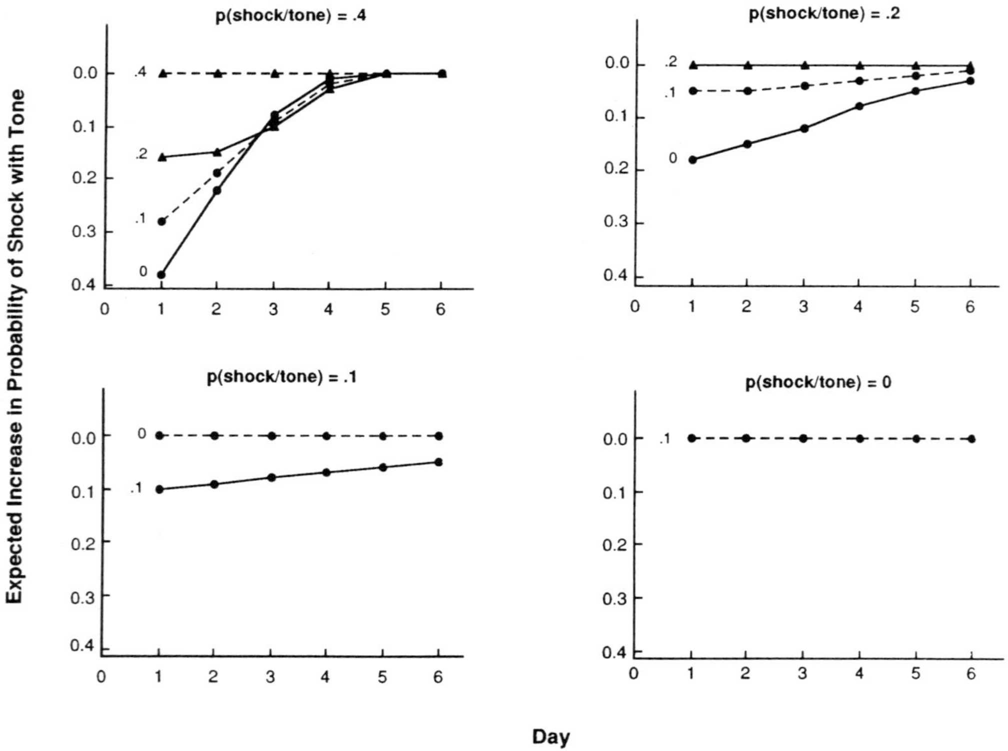

FIG. 4-5. Data from the simulation of Rescorla's Experiment. Compare with Fig. 4-4.

178

This section of the chapter considers the issue of how causal rules generalize. However, the focus is not on continuous dimensions but rather on categorical and relational dimensions, because of their relevance to the next chapter on problem solving. It turns out that rational principles for generalizing are very much like those developed in the PUPS model of analogical generalization (Anderson & Thompson, 1989). PUPS was developed to account for what seemed to us to be the salient empirical features of analogical generalization without any guidance from a rational framework. This is another instance of a strong correlation between a mechanistic model generated from data and rational derivations. The PUPS model and this rational analysis also correlate fairly well with other theories of analogy (e.g., Carbonell, 1985; Gentner, 1983; Holyoak & Thagard, 1989; Winston, Binford, Katz, & Lowry, 1983) in terms of what analogies are expected.

Individual-Based Generalization

Perhaps the clearest case of justified generalization is when we are predicting a causal connection involving the same individuals. For instance, suppose we saw an event of Russ (a dog) observing Sylvester (a cat) and then chasing Sylvester. Suppose further, on whatever grounds, we had made the inference that the first event caused the second. If we again see Russ observe Sylvester, we are certainly justified in predicting that Russ will chase Sylvester. Also, if, for whatever reason, we want Russ to chase Sylvester, we would be justified in trying to get Russ to observe Sylvester. Of course, in both cases, we may be wrong in our prediction or problem-solving effort, but, if so, this is best interpreted as reflecting the fact that the Russ–Sylvester causal law, like most, only holds probabilistically.

It is reasonable to assume that the individuals, Russ and Sylvester, will obey the same causal relations over time. This assumption is part of the concept of an enduring individual, (although I am ignoring the issue of how we determine that it is the same individual in one situation as the other). We can assume that individuals will participate in the same causal laws across situations. Individual people, animals, and objects do tend to show constancy in their behavior. The interactions between my dog and his favorite ball do display a remarkable predictability.

Category-Based Generalization

The question is whether we are justified in extrapolating beyond Russ and Sylvester. For instance, if my best friend observes my wife, I am not justified in predicting that he will chase her. On the other hand, if Fido, another dog, observes Mittens, another cat, the extrapolation seems reasonable. Basically, we have put Fido and Russ into the same category, *dog,* because they are similar. We have done the same with Sylvester and Mittens. It is a reasonable, if less certain, extrapolation from the Russ–Sylvester instance to the generalization that dogs will chase cats.

In this case, the generalization just flows from last chapter's analysis of categorical structure. That analysis can be applied to get from Russ–Sylvester to Fido–Mittens in two steps. First, the causal law of chasing Sylvester can be regarded as a property of Russ. In the terminology of the previous chapter, it is a binary dimension with two possible values, true and false. The category of dogs has some probability that its members will obey this law. There is a prior distribution of probabilities that members of a category will have the property of obeying this law. Conditional on observing one or more members of the category display this property, a posterior probability can be calculated that the members will display this property.

Because there has been no careful experimental research on such categorical generalizations, a precise mathematical model would be an excessive formalism. However, a couple of points can be made with reference to the model of chapter 3. First, unlike the default assumption of no extremity and noninformative priors in the previous chapter, it seems quite the other way for causal laws. That is, rather than a category displaying a property like chasing Sylvester with a mean prior probability of .5, the prior probability of such a causal law is presumably much lower. Second, in the terminology of the previous chapter, the prior distributions should be ones of considerable extremity. That is, the assumption is that particular categories will tend to a 0 or 1 probability of obeying a causal law rather than intermediate values.

The posterior distribution of the probability of a causal law will have some mean, P_1, for the category—that is, the probability that all dogs will tend to chase Sylvester is P_1. The actual causal law will have an associated probability, P_a, that the predicted effect will occur where the causal law applies in contrast to the base probability of P_b. That is, the probability that Russ will chase Sylvester is P_a, and the probability that a random creature will chase Sylvester is P_b. We can use P_1, P_a, and P_b to express the expected probability that a dog like Fido will chase Sylvester. This is $P_1 P_a +$ $(1 - P_1)P_b$, in contrast to P_a for Russ and P_b for a non-dog. So, the probability P_1 captures the strength of the categorical generalization. Of course, once we observe Fido chasing or not chasing Sylvester upon sight, we no longer have to make a prediction about whether the causal law extends to Fido. This observation can also be used to adjust the posterior probability that it applies to other members of the dog category.

So far, the analysis has only gotten to Fido chasing Sylvester. What about Fido chasing Mittens, another instance of the cat category: What emerges from the first round of analysis is a probability that dogs engage in Sylvester chasing. This can be treated as a binary-value feature of Sylvester, and a probability can be calculated as to whether it extends to cats. The same kind of analysis will deliver a second probability, P_2, that this applies to another cat.[5] Thus, the probability that Fido will chase Mittens is $P_1 P_2 P_a$ + $(1 - P_1 P_2)P_b$. If we must generalize over n categories to make our generalization, the probability is

$$\prod_{i=1}^{n} P_i P_a + (1 - \prod_{i=1}^{n} P_i)P_b$$

where the P_i are the probabilities of generalization over each category. If there are n individuals involved in a casual law, there are $2^n - 1$ potential generalizations, depending on which individuals are replaced by their categories. Assuming that generalization to any category is independent of generalization to any other category, this analysis can be extended to all of these potential generalizations.

There is a complex joint estimation problem involved here, but the result that should emerge is straightforward—a set of probabilities that the causal law will apply to members of each category and a probability that the prediction of the causal law will be true in a particular situation where it applies.

Relational Generalization

It is worth examining more carefully the causal law involving Russ and Sylvester or dogs and cats. It relates a cause, *a observes b,* to an effect, *a chases b.* Note that it is the same *a* and *b* in cause and effect. This identity of the individuals made the generalization straightforward. However, suppose I inferred, for whatever reason, a causal linkage between events that did not share the same elements. Then, the generalization is more difficult. For instance, suppose we observe Fred spurned by Mary and then see him propose to Jill, and we infer that the spurning caused the proposal. Suppose we observe Ted spurned by Diane. We might want to generalize the rule and predict that Ted will propose to someone, but who? Without further knowledge, all we can do is predict that some woman will be proposed to. In the preceding case, the reader presumably may have some theory about how to instantiate this category. However, in absence of such a theory, one is stuck with a weak prediction that specifies only the category of the proposee.

In some cases, it can be sufficient to predict the category of the object identified, but in other cases—particularly problem-solving situations—this

---

[5]Note that we are using *cat* and *dog* to refer to the internal categories of the previous chapter and not the category labels, which are just a feature of the internal category.

may not be adequate. Suppose we observe a computer screen with three objects arranged—an orange, an apple, and a banana. We observe a computer user type the letter "p", and the apple disappears, and we infer that the first event caused the second—that is, typing "p" caused the apple to disappear. Suppose we want to remove the orange. Making a generalization that typing a letter causes a fruit to disappear does not do us much good. We need to know which letter will remove the orange.

It turns out that people will tend to type the "p" again in a situation like this (Lewis, 1988). Lewis has called this "superstitious copying." The next chapter on problem solving explores the rational basis for superstitious copying. Here, I want to explore what would happen when we have additional knowledge. Suppose, for instance, that we know that this is a French computer and the French word for apple begins with a "p." Then, we might try an "o", because the French word for orange begins with an "o." This attempt involves inferring a linkage between the events *"p" is typed* and *apple disappears*. That linkage is caught by the fact that *apple begins with "p"* in French.

The rational justification for this inference has to be some generalization of the basic rule of no effect at a distance. If there is a causal link between the letter and fruit, there has to be some prior connection between the two through which the causation "travels." The inference is probabilistic that the French spelling of the fruit provides the prior link. Thus, the probability that typing "o" will cause the orange to disappear will depend on:

1. The probability P_1 that the rule will generalize to other letters.
2. The probability P_2 that the rule will generalize to other fruits on the screen.
3. The probability P_r that one has identified the correct relation that connects cause and effect—that is, the French spelling.
4. The probability P_a that the rule will work when applicable. Presumably, in the case of deterministic computers, this probability is near 1.
5. The probability P_b that the orange would disappear even if there were no causal connections. Presumably in this case, the probability must be near 0.

The probability of the prediction now becomes

$$(P_1P_2P_r)P_a + (1 - P_1P_2P_r)P_b$$

and, to the extent that $P_a = 1$ and $P_b = 0$, this becomes simply $P_1P_2P_r$, which is to say the product of the probabilities of generalizing the rule across the categories of letters and fruits and the probability that the appropriate relation has been identified.

It turns out that, in cases where there is no relationship between a causal element and an effect element, subjects will invent one. In an experiment, Lewis (1988) showed subjects a situation where "67m" was typed into a computer and then "truck." A truck turned red on the computer screen. When asked what "67m" did, most subjects said it specified "red." He contrasted this with a situation where "67m" was typed and then "red." Again, a truck turned red. In this situation, subjects inferred that "67m" designated "truck." Lewis called the heuristic that does this identification a "loose ends" heuristic: If something in the cause is unconnected to anything in the effect, and if something in the effect is unconnected to anything in the cause, then assume that they are connected to each other.

This heuristic can enable interesting generalizations, as Lewis demonstrated in another example. Subjects first saw "NNA" typed on the keyboard followed by "ladder", and they saw a ladder rotate 45 degrees, from which they should infer that "NNA" designates "rotate 45 degrees." Then they saw "NNA" typed on the keyboard, followed by "da9," and saw a tree rotate 45 degrees. This not only confirmed the initial hypothesis but led them to the hypothesis that "da9" denoted "tree." Then, they saw "nb6" typed on the keyboard, followed by "da9," and saw a tree shrink to half its size. Again, this confirmed an earlier hypothesis and generated a new hypothesis that "*nb6*" denoted "shrink to half size." The subjects were asked, "What would you do to make the ladder shrink?" More than three-fourths of the subjects spontaneously put all the inferences together and said "*nb6* ladder."

An Experiment

I could not find in the experimental literature any test of subject's tendencies to generalize causal rules across categories or to extract relational linkages. Therefore, I decided to perform an experimental test. I had 14 subjects read the experimental materials that are reproduced verbatim in the Appendix.

The material describes some islanders who have pet boars. Among the islander-boar pairs are the following:

Timothy and his pet Tusk
Benjamin and his pet Bristles
Samuel and his pet Snort

The following critical event is described:

Timothy, quite by accident, bumps into Bristles
and Bristles flees to Benjamin.

Subjects were asked to extrapolate from a single event to predict the
probability of 20 other events, such as "If Timothy accidently bumps into
Snort, will Snort flee to Samuel?". These other events could be classified
according to three dimensions. The agent could be identical to Timothy in
the seed event, in the same human category as Timothy, or in the boar
category. The object could be identical to the seed object Bristles, in the
same boar category, or in a human category. Finally, the person fled to
could be in the same relationship of owner to the boar; could be Benjamin,
as in the seed event, but not in the owner relationship to the boar; or could
be neither Benjamin nor the owner of the boar. Some cells are impossible in
this 3 × 3 × 3 design. In addition, we missed one cell by accident and
consequently reduplicated another. Table 4-10 shows the mean probabilities
assigned by subjects to the existing cells where they were asked to give these
as percentages in a 0–100 scale where 0 meant impossible and 100 meant
certain.

TABLE 4-10
Mean Percentage Rating of a Causal Generalization

Matrix 1: Flee to Owner

Agent	Object		
	Bristles	Boar	Human
Timothy	87.5	75.6	X
Human	81.4	75	X
Boar	56.1	51.4	X

Matrix 2: Flee to Benjamin when He Is not Owner

Agent	Object		
	Bristles	Boar	Human
Timothy	X	8.4	4.5
Human	X	8.4	4.0
Boar	X	14.5	1.5

Matrix 3: Flee to Human other than Benjamin and Owner

Agent	Object		
	Bristles	Boar	Human
Timothy	16.2	X	3.6
Human	17.9	12.2	3.4
Boar	4.9	X	4.5

Statistical test shows that there are three overall significant factors: (a) Subjects show much higher ratings that the boar will flee to its owner than to a non-owner, (b) the ratings for fleeing to the non-owner do not depend on whether it is the identical Benjamin (2nd matrix in Table 4-10) or another person (3rd matrix in Table 4-10), and (c), the other two effects are that subjects show higher ratings when the agent is in the same human category as Timothy and when the object is in the same Boar category as Bristles.

The analysis developed in this section only applies to the four cells in Table 4-10 where the boar flees to its owner, the agent is a human, and the object is a boar. These cells are a 2 × 2 submatrix defined by whether the agent is Timothy or some other human and by whether the object is Bristles or some other boar (top left 4 cells of Matrix 1). The values in this submatrix are much higher than anywhere else, confirming the proposal that this would be the domain of generalization. There is a significant variation within this matrix, indicating that strength of inference decreases when categorical or relational generalizations are required. According to the analysis developed earlier (if we assume $P_b = 0$), the probability of generalization — if the individuals are the same — is P_a; if the agent is only in the human category, $P_a P_1$; if the object is only in the boar category, $P_a P_2 P_r$; and if agent and object are only in the same categories, $P_a P_1 P_2 P_r$. One can get a good fit to the data setting $P_a = .86$, $P_1 = P_2 = P_r = .95$. The high value of P_1, P_2, and P_r indicates the high level of generalization.[6]

There is one discrepancy between the theoretical analysis and these data, which is that subjects did not totally abandon the rule when one feature was violated. They rated cases involving boars bumping boars that preserved the owner relationship as much more probable than cases that also violated the owner relationship. Similarly, they rated cases that kept the categories and violated the owner relation as more probable than cases that both violated the categories and the owner relationship. Thus, subjects preferred cases that violated just one dimension of generalization to those cases that violated multiple dimensions of generalization. This preference seems rational, but the formal model developed in this section assumed that the probability would go down to a low base level as soon as one dimension was violated.

In summary, the experiment establishes that subjects do use categories and relationships to define causal generalizations. There are mechanistic models (for instance, the PUPS model — Anderson & Thompson, 1989) that predict these generalizations. What this analysis does is expose the rational bases for these generalizations. That is, these generalizations are justified

---

[6]Of course, with this many parameters and this few data points, the ability to fit the data per se is uninteresting. The interesting result is the value of the parameters.

on the reasonable assumptions that causal rules generalize across members of a category and that the causation involves objects that bear some prior relation.

IMPLEMENTATION IN A PRODUCTION SYSTEM

Whereas categories map onto nodes in the ACT architecture, causal rules map onto production rules, because they require complex pattern matching that cannot be achieved even by spreading of instantiated activation. There are two types of production rules possible—those that predict an effect given a cause and those that prescribe a cause given a desired effect. Informal instances of the first kind of production rules are:

P1: IF one stomps his feet
    and there is a house of cards near by
    THEN the house of cards will collapse.

P2:   IF one turns on a switch
    and the switch is attached to a lamp
    THEN the lamp will go on.

Productions of the other variety are problem-solving rules, such as:

P3:   IF one wants a house of cards to collapse
    THEN get near the house of cards
        and stamp one's feet.

P4:   IF one wants a lamp to go on
      and there is a switch attached to the lamp
    THEN turn on the switch.

The analysis in this chapter was really concerned with production rules like P1 and P2. According to Equations 4-1 and 4-2 (pp. 151,154) at the beginning of this chapter, the critical quantities are $P(E|i)$, which is the probability of an event if the causal rule applies, $P(i)$ or $Con(i)$, which is one's confidence in the rule, and $P(C|i)$, which is the probability of the cues if the rule applies. The quantity $P(i)$ can be mapped into the strength of such a rule. The quantity $P(C|i)$ can be mapped into the degree of match between the rule and the situation. Finally, $P(E|i)$ can be mapped into the level of activation of the resulting prediction created in memory.

Equation 4-1 (See p. 151) potentially creates a dilemma for a production rule architecture. It prescribes summing over all causal rules and, hence, under the proposed mapping into the ACT* architecture, all production rules. This violates the general assumptions of production rule architecture that just a single rule in a conflict sets fires. However, it is unlikely in any situation that there will be substantial match of more than one causal rule that predicts the same event. Therefore, it is a reasonable approximation to simply fire the single production that matches best.

The rational theory prescribes how to build such causal rules, assign strengths to them, calculate degrees of match, and assign levels of activations to the structures they create. New production rules should be created when events occur for which no probable prior interpretation (calculated by Equation 4-3 p. 155) exists. This is like creating new categories for unusual objects, but calculating such quantities is a bit more problematical than the analogous activity of creating categorical elements. This is because it is necessary to invoke a scientific model to formulate the structure of production rules. Thus, in the case of an electrical model, one would pay attention to connectivity, whereas in the case of a mechanical wave model, one would pay attention to spatial and temporal contiguity.

CONCLUSION

In the spirit of previous chapter, this chapter is an attempt to show that we can predict causal inference from the assumption that it is an optimal attempt to predict future events. This chapter shows the promise of such an approach, but it has not been as thorough as the chapters on memory and categorization. Part of the reason for lack of thoroughness comes from the relative paucity of relevant empirical data. The other reason for lack of thoroughness is the complexities associated with the role of prior models and how these models are acquired.

Given the widespread bias against the rationality of human causal inference, this chapter constitutes considerable progress. It has shown the fallacies in criticisms of human use of 2×2 contingency information and human use of classic cues of temporal contiguity, spatial contiguity, and similarity. It has shown the near optimality in the behavior of children and rats. Using the models developed in this chapter, precise predictions were obtained about behavior that were as good as those from existing mechanistic models. Much work remains to be done, but there is promise.

APPENDIX: EXPERIMENTAL MATERIALS FOR EXPERIMENT WHOSE RESULTS ARE GIVEN IN TABLE 4-10

Suppose you find yourself suddenly given an all-expenses-paid trip to Bora Bora. On the plane out there, you read a short travel brochure that is not very informative but does tell you this little about the inhabitants of the island:

On the Island of Bora Bora, natives are very attached to an indigenous island boar, which is different than species of boars elsewhere and, if we are to believe the natives, is as intelligent as a human. The natives would not think of killing or eating such a boar. Rather, every native has at least one (and usually just one) boar that follows him or her around like a devoted pet. Each boar has its own name and comes quite obediently when called by its owner. It turns out that natives give their boars names that begin with the same letter as their first name. The natives, all members of the Seventh Day Adventist Church, have biblical names.

When you arrive on the island, you immediately meet the following natives and their boars:

Timothy and his boar Tusk
Benjamin and his boar Bristles
Samuel and his boar Snort

You find the island and its inhabitants sufficiently unusual that you are unsure whether these natives are like any group of people you have met before or whether the boars are like any creature you know about. All you know about them is what you read in the travel brochure. Then the following critical event occurs:

***You observe Timothy, quite by accident, bump into Bristles
and Bristles flees to Benjamin.***

I want you to assign probabilities to the following events happening. Use a percentage scale from 0 to 100 where 0 means impossible and 100 means certain.

1. If Timothy again accidently bumps into Bristles, will Bristles flee to Benjamin?
Prob =

2. If Samuel accidently bumps into Bristles, will Bristles flee to Timothy?
Prob =

3. If Snort accidently bumps into Tusk, will Tusk flee to Timothy?
Prob =

4. If Tusk accidently bumps into Benjamin, will Benjamin flee to Samuel?
Prob =

5. If Timothy accidently bumps into Samuel, will Samuel flee to Benjamin?
Prob =

6. If Benjamin accidently bumps into Tusk, will Tusk flee to Samuel?
Prob =

7. If Tusk accidently bumps into Samuel, will Samuel flee to Benjamin?
Prob =

8. If Tusk accidently bumps into Bristles, will Bristles flee to Samuel?
Prob =

9. If Samuel accidently bumps into Tusk, will Tusk flee to Timothy?
Prob =

10. If Samuel accidently bumps into Benjamin, will Benjamin flee to Timothy?
Prob =

11. If Timothy accidently bumps into Snort, will Snort flee to Benjamin?
Prob =

12. If Benjamin accidently bumps into Samuel, will Samuel flee to Timothy?
Prob =

13. If Samuel accidently bumps into Bristles, will Bristles flee to Benjamin?
Prob =

14. If Snort accidently bumps into Bristles, will Bristles flee to Benjamin?
Prob =

15. If Snort accidently bumps into Tusk, will Tusk flee to Benjamin?
Prob =

16. If Timothy again accidently bumps into Bristles, will Bristles flee to Samuel?
Prob =

17. If Timothy accidently bumps into Benjamin, will Benjamin flee to Samuel?
Prob =

18. If Samuel accidently bumps into Tusk, will Tusk flee to Benjamin?
Prob =

19. If Samuel accidently bumps into Timothy, will Timothy flee to Benjamin?
Prob =

20. If Timothy accidently bumps into Snort, will Snort flee to Samuel?
Prob =

5 Problem Solving

Contents
Preliminaries   191
Making a Choice Among Simple Actions   194
  Subjective Utility and Subjective Probability   196
  Problem Framing   199
Combining Steps   201
  Iterative Plan-and-Act Structure   202
  Choice of Partial Plans   203
  Mathematical Simplifications   205
  Use of Similarity   207
  Effort Spent So Far   209
  Estimation of Probability and Cost   209
  Generation of Moves: Satisficing   214
Studies of Hill Climbing   215
  Jeffries, Polson, Razran, & Atwood   215
  Atwood & Polson   218
Mean–Ends Analysis   221
  Tower of Hanoi   222
  Modeling Kotovsky, Hayes, & Simon   224
  Comparisons with the Kotovsky, Hayes, & Simon Model   227
Instantiation of Indefinite Objects   228
Conclusions on Rational Analysis of Problem Solving   229
Implementation in Act   230
  Conflict Resolution   231
Appendix: Problem Solving and Clotheslines   232
  The Clothesline Scenario   232
  Contrasts with the Received Model of Problem Solving   233
  Simulation of the Clothesline Scenario   234

PRELIMINARIES

The previous chapters offered rational analyses of various information-processing goals that the system had. In particular, they were concerned with how to order retrieval from memory and how to make predictions about unseen features of objects and forthcoming events. The underlying assumption was that accurate and appropriate information was useful. We turn now to the question of "useful for what?" The answer is that it is useful for deciding what action to take. This is the heart of the matter. Everything else is just serving a supporting role. Unless we take action, all of the fine information-processing in the world would be worthless. We would be in the situation of Tolman's apocryphal rat (Guthrie, 1952; p. 143), lost in thought in the maze of life.

Problem solving is the generic term that is used herein to cover deciding what action to take. Decision making might also be appropriate. That term emphasizes the evaluation of alternatives, whereas research on problem solving has traditionally focused on the combinatorial explosion of sequences of actions that occur in problem-solving search.

Problem solving is a major field of research in artificial intelligence and a substantial field in cognitive psychology. From an adaptionist perspective, both areas have chosen a strange set of tasks to focus on: There are the puzzles and games — such as chess, Tower of Hanoi, Rubics cube, and the eight puzzle — and there are the academic activities, like mathematical and scientific problem solving (to which I have devoted much of my research). Such problem solving has little adaptive value, and one can question whether our problem-solving machinery has evolved to be adapted to such tasks. Indeed, one might argue, in the case of puzzles and games, that they are played because they are challenging, and they are challenging precisely because we are not adapted to succeed in such domains.

This is not to argue that research on such domains is not without value. There is applied value in understanding academic problem solving (even if academic problem solving has no relationship to adaptation). Also, these problems often are nice laboratories for studying problem solving, just as a vacuum is useful for studying physics. However, there is a danger of letting these tasks place the stamp of their character on one's theory of problem solving. This has happened in the field of problem solving, and I am certainly one of the guilty parties.

One day I asked the members of a research seminar to "Name a problem you tried to solve in the last 24 hours." Their answers are listed in Table 5-1.[1] These problems provide a startling contrast with what is usually studied in research on problem solving. They involve problems in domains where we typically induce causal rules rather than are explicitly told them. This is part of the motivation for the study of causal inference in the previous chapter. They also differ from research problems in that the rules

---

[1] I should also say that the problems they mentioned involved real difficulties in keeping with the character of the problems involved in research. Thus, for instance, finding a rest room might not seem like much of a problem but in this case it was (details purposely omitted).

Table 5.1

Answers to "Name a problem you tried to solve in the last 24 hours"
finding the rest room
finding a route from a hotel to a restaurant
planning a project with my advisor
debugging someone else's code
addressing a reviewer's comments
getting my car registered
picking up a car from a service station
deciding on a birthday card for brother
getting subjects to sign up for my experiment
finding a new house
writing a presentation for Midwestern Psychological Association
deciding timing of in-laws' visit
deciding whether to buy an expensive zoom lens
figuring out how to get from where I am staying to friend's house
getting two diet Cokes from Coke machine
writing a letter to a potential au pair
figuring a price to ask for my car

tend to be probabilistic and the problem solving involves fairly explicit considerations of varying costs and benefits.

A rational analysis of problem solving requires specifying three components—the goal of the system, the structure of the environment, and a set of computational constraints. With respect to the first, the assumption is simply that the goal of the system is to have various states of affairs true in the environment. This may be to get out of the rain, marry one's love, solve an algebraic expression, or escape a tiger.

As for the structure of the environment, the analysis of problem solving includes the assumptions of chapters 2 through 4, which describe the reoccurrence of knowledge and the predictive structure of the environment. Central is the causal analysis of the previous chapter. In essence, if we want a particular state of affairs to exist, we are looking for some action that will cause that state of affairs. In addition to these, I introduce some assumptions about how the current state of problem solving predicts the future prospects. Under the current state of problem solving, I consider similarity of the current state to the goal and amount of effort spent so far. Under future prospects, I consider probability of success and amount of further effort needed to attain success.

Finally, one major computational limitation is imported from the discussion in chapter 2 of memory span. This assumption is that there is no memory buffer to reliably hold partial products, and, consequently, reliable storage of such partial products depends on the recency portion of the memory function. This lack of a memory buffer produces the extreme short-term memory limitations in problem solving. I also assume a cost associated with considering a possible problem-solving move.

The major organizing principle in this chapter is one of complexity. I start with the simplest problem-solving situation and then incrementally complicate it. Again, this chapter is somewhat mathematical, and Table 5-2 summarizes the notations that it uses.

MAKING A CHOICE AMONG SIMPLE ACTIONS

The typical problem-solving situation is where one must put together a sequence of problem-solving steps to achieve a goal. Each such step corresponds to a causal link, as discussed in the previous chapter, but *step* is the term of choice in this chapter. A sequence of such steps that one plans will be called a *move*. However, before considering multistep problem solving, let us consider the simplest situation in which the goal can be achieved in a single step.

Consider the situation where one has the goal to achieve a certain state of affairs and has one or more steps, i, which claim to be able to deliver that state of affairs. For instance, one might be hungry and have the goal of satiation. Among the steps at hand might be going to a restaurant, going home, or asking a friend if he or she has some food. These are all actions that can cause us to be satiated. From the previous chapter, each of these steps has some probability, P_i, of achieving the goal. It was not developed in the previous chapter, but each of these steps has a cost, C_i. What is involved in these costs is complex, and I consistently ignore exploring this in detail, but it would include things such as time, energy, and money. Finally, let G be the value of achieving the goal.

There are a number of possible relationships among the alternative steps. One is that these steps are independent — for example, asking a friend and failing does not preclude going home. The prescriptions of rational theory for this situation are straightforward. The system should order its choices of steps by the ratio P_i/C_i and stop when it finds a successful method or reaches a method i such that $C_i > P_iG$. Another possibility is that the alternatives are mutually exclusive and that doing one excludes the remainder. In this case, the system should choose the alternative with maximum value of $P_iG - C_i$, provided that this expected value is positive. There can be more complex dependencies among the alternatives, which, in the limit, might require separately evaluating every possible sequence of choices.

Ignoring the cases of complex dependencies, we can ask whether people behave rationally in the simple situations. This question has been most systematically explored in people's preferences for gambles where probabil-

TABLE 5-2
Mathematical Notations

Conventions

i	Indexes causal rules, problem-solving moves, steps, plans, or operators.
P_i	Probability that move i or plan i will achieve the goal.
p_i	Probability that move i will have its intended effect.
p_i''	Probability of satisfying the precondition of move i.
p_i'	The probability that move i will have its intended effect if its precondition is satisfied for move i.
q_i	Probability that we can achieve the goal if move i has its intended effect.
C_i	Expected cost associated with achieving the goal by move i or plan i.
a_i	Cost of move i.
a_i''	The cost of satisfying the precondition for move i.
a_i'	Cost of executing move i if its precondition is satisfied.
c_i	Cost of further moves after move i.
G	Value of achieving the goal or the event of successfully reaching the goal.
F	The event of failing to reach the goal.
D	Difference between current state and goal.
E	Effort spent so far.
B_n	Value of best plan generated in the first n tries.
I_n	The expected improvement by generating an nth plan after generating $n-1$.
z_n	Parameter for the exponential distribution of gains of the nth plan. See Equation 5-15.
Z_{n-1}	Expected value of move previous to the nth.

Densities and Bayesian Probabilities

$P(F)$	Prior proability that the goal being attemped is impossible. See Equation 5-5 in Table 5-3.
$\pi(S,x)$	Prior probability density for success with cost x. See Equation 5-6 in Table 5-3.
$G(x \vert v,b)$	Distribution of costs x, given a gamma distribution with parameters v and b. See Equation 5-7 in Table 5-3.
$\pi(D \vert F)$	The probability density describing the distribution of differences, D, between the current state and an achievable goal, conditional on the goal being impossible.
$\pi(D \vert S,c)$	Probability density of differences, D, between the current state and the goal, conditional on there being a cost, c, yet to expend before achieving the goal.
$P(F \vert D,E)$	Posterior probability of the problem not being solvable given that there is a difference, D, from the goal and an effort, E, expended so far.
$\pi(S,c \vert D,E)$	Posterior probability density for success with further cost, c, given that there is a difference, D, from the goal and an effort, E, expended so far.
$Z_n(x)$	Distribution of expected values of the nth plan generated.

(Continued)

TABLE 5-2 (*Continued*)

Parameters	
s	Probability of choosing a solvable goal. Set at .8 throughout chapter.
f	Proportion reduction in probability of success if a move fails to have its intended effect. Set at .5 throughout the chapter.
v,b	Parameters of the gamma distribution giving distributions of cost *c*. See Equation 5-7. Both are set at 2 throughout the chapter.
α	Parameter of the exponential distribution giving the difference between the current state and the goal when the goal cannot be reached. See Equation 5-8 in Table 5-3. Set at .2 throughout the chapter.
β	Parameter of the exponential distribution giving the difference between the current state and the goal when the goal can be reached. See Equation 5-9 in Table 5-3. Set at 1 throughout the chapter.
w	Satisficing level, cost of generating a plan.

ities, costs, and gains are directly manipulated. The answer is: usually, yes. For instance, people will prefer a 60% probability of getting $30 that costs them $10 over a 30% probability of getting $30 that costs them $8. However, there are many second-order complications on this general trend of rationality, which has left the field with the opinion that human decision making is, typically, irrational. Therefore, the remainder of this section considers these second-order effects.

Subjective Utility and Subjective Probability

The typical experiment in this field has involved presenting subjects with choices of gambles between various amounts of money. A typical example used to show deviation from rationality is the choice between the following two gambles:

a. A 100% chance of $240
b. A 25% chance of $1000

Subjects prefer the former, although one can show that the latter has a higher expected gain (.25 × $1000 = $250). As Kahneman and Tversky (1984) review, this result is typically explained by assuming that subjective utility and subjective probability are not linear with respect to objective utility and probability. Figs. 5-1 and 5-2 illustrate typical functions relating the subjective measures to the objective values. The preference for (a) is because of the nonlinearity value of money—$1000 is not valued 4 times greater than $250. Note, in Fig. 5-1, that the curve for losses is steeper than the curve for gains. This means that subjects prefer to avoid gambles that offer opportunities like a 50% chance of losing $100 and a 50% chance of gaining $100.

VALUE

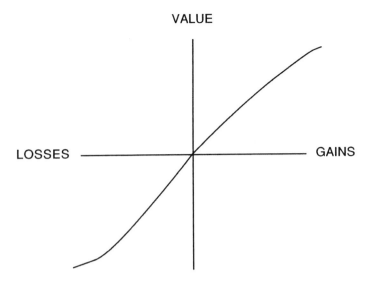

LOSSES ———————————————— GAINS

FIG. 5-1. A function that relates subjective value to magnitude of gain and loss.

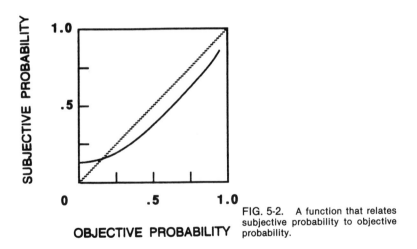

FIG. 5-2. A function that relates subjective probability to objective probability.

Note, also, that the curve for subjective probability in Fig. 5-2 is flattened. This means that subjects underestimate the extremity of probabilities. Thus, a subject might prefer a 1% chance of $200 to a 2% of $100, despite the general nonlinearity in the value of money.

Basically, a model based on subjective probability and subjective utility is no different than the rational model just described in this chapter. Such a model proposes that subjects respond to the product of probabilities and utilities. However, their model further asserts that the utilities and probabilities multiplied are subjective, rather than objective. This raises the question of whether the subjective forms in Figs. 5-1 and 5-2 are rational. Let us consider first the probability function and then the utility function.

Probability. Figure 5-2 represents the fact that people partially discount information about probability. It embodies a certain amount of regression towards the mean. This is a rational thing to do. One should discount any statements couched with certainty or near certainty—the Titanic could not sink; we were told there was a 1% chance of people testing positive for AIDS developing full-blown AIDS; my programmer tells me he is almost certain he will finish the program by the end of the week; and so on. Also, the models developed in the previous chapters for estimating probabilities from proportions in experience discounted the empirical proportions. Thus, if we observe m successes and n failures in experience, these models delivered to us expected mean probabilities of $(\alpha + m)/(\alpha + \beta + m + n)$ where α and β were parameters of a prior Beta distribution of probabilities. In effect, the parameters α and β are "inertia" factors that discount the proportion $m/(m + n)$ in experience.

Utility. In the extreme, subjective utility must be a negatively accelerated function of any objective property like money. In purely adaptive terms, there is a limit to how bad things can get (i.e., death and no offspring) and a less clear but no less real limit to how good things can get. Thus, the negatively accelerated utility curves are to be expected.

It is less clear that the curves for losses should be steeper than for gains. This depends on one's position in life. For me, a "true loss" (i.e., no bankruptcy court to blunt the blow) of $1,000,000 would spell ruin, whereas a gain of $1,000,000 would only be a fairly pleasant outcome. On the other hand, I have little objective reason to consider more negatively a loss of $10 than I would consider positively a gain of $10. Again, there is no difference for me between a loss of $1,000,000 and $1,000,000,000, because both are complete disasters, yet there are consequences to the difference between a gain of $1,000,000 and a gain of $1,000,000,000. Kahnemann and Tversky reported that individual utility functions are not all alike, and the one in Fig. 5-1 is only an average.

So, we can emerge from this discussion with the conclusion that the functions in Figs. 5-1 and 5-2 are fairly rational. Indeed, the predictions of rational analysis correspond basically to the prediction that one should combine subjective probability and subjective utility, as defined by Figs. 5-1 and 5-2, according to the standard economic logic. One can take the general success of the subjective probability and subjective utility formulation as evidence for the rationality of decision making.[2] The basic point is that the subjective functions are more adaptive than the objective functions. It is common to come to different conclusions about rationality, partly because these functions, in the hands of Kahnemann and Tversky's theory of outcome framing, can lead to some inconsistent behavior, which seems pretty irrational. In particular, it is claimed that people respond differently to the same objective choice depending on how it is framed. It is to consideration of these effects of problem framing that we now turn.

Problem Framing

Perhaps the most problematic demonstrations concern the effect of framing a problem. For instance, consider someone who has lost $140 at the racetrack and has the opportunity to bet $10 on a 15-1 shot. If the bettor views not making the bet as a certainty of losing $140 and making the bet as a good chance of losing $150 and a poor chance of breaking even, he or she is likely to make the bet. This reflects the negatively accelerated utility functions for money. On the other hand, if the bettor thinks of not making the bet as staying pat and making the bet as a good chance of losing $10 and a poor chance of making $140, he or she is likely to avoid it. This also reflects the negatively accelerated utility function. People tend to continue to bet, because they take the first perspective. However, as Dawes (1987) asserted, one should evaluate this decision with respect to his or her current situation and let go of the perspective of the initial situation.[3] As another example of frame of reference, Kahneman and Tversky asked us to consider the situation of someone who must purchase a $15 item and a $125 item. If another store offers a $5 discount on the $15 item, the person is likely to make the effort to go to the other store, whereas this is not the case if the same $5 discount is offered on the $125 item.

The interesting observation about these framing examples is that they take place in situations where not much is at stake in the choice. It is doubtful that much is contingent on the $5 or the trip in the Kahneman and Tversky example. As for the betting example, an individual who has lost a lot of money may be in a great deal of trouble, but losing one bet more is probably inconsequential, and the odds of winning the bet are sufficiently low to be inconsequential too.

---

[2]Indeed, I am not analyzing specific experiments in detail, because rational analysis says nothing that hasn't already been asserted in this theory of the combination of subjective probability and subjective utility.

[3]All this discussion ignores the rationality of gambling at all when the odds are in the house's favor. Presumably, much of gambling behavior, when rational, has to be understood in terms of its recreational value (whatever that means).

As an example that appears to be more consequential, consider this situation described by Kahneman and Tversky (1984):

Problem 1: Imagine that the U.S. is preparing for the outbreak of an unusual Asian disease, which is expected to kill 600 people. Two alternative programs to combat the disease have been proposed. Assume that the exact scientific estimates of the consequences of the programs are as follows:

If Program A is adopted, 200 people will be saved.

If Program B is adopted, there is a one-third probability that 600 people will be saved and a two-thirds probability that no people will be saved.

Which of the two programs would you favor? (p. 343)

Seventy-two percent of the subjects preferred Program A, which guarantees lives, over dealing with the risk of Program B. However, consider what happens when, rather than introducing the prospect of 600 deaths, the two programs are described as follows:

If Program C is adopted, 400 people will die.

If Program D is adopted, there is a one-third probability that nobody will die and a two-thirds probability that 600 people will die. (p. 343)

Now, only 22% preferred Program C, which the reader will recognize as equivalent to A (and D is equivalent to B). Both of these choices can be understood in terms of a negatively accelerated utility function for lives. In the first case, the subjective value of 600 lives saved is less than three times the subjective value of 200 lives saved, whereas, in the second case, the subjective value of 400 deaths is more than two-thirds the subjective value of 600 deaths.

Is it not the case here that how we frame the problem has substantial consequences? The answer is certainly not. Although losing 400 lives is a serious matter, the two programs do not differ in their expected loss, and so, in terms of difference in expected loss, there is no consequence to the choice. To be sure, it is a difficult decision and requires careful consideration of other things, such as political cost, besides objective expected loss of lives. However, there is just no rational model known for making the choice. One can hardly expect subjects to behave consistently in a situation where there is no known basis for behaving.[4]

---

[4]One might object that the same result would likely occur if we were to compare Program A, where 199 people will be saved, to Program B. Now, there is a real difference of one

Note that none of these comments denies the truth or value of Kahneman and Tversky's theory of problem framing, which nicely accounts for the phenomena at hand. The force of the arguments here is that these effects are not evidence against rationality in the adaptive sense. At best, they are evidence against rationality in the normative sense; that is, although it may not be normatively rational to be inconsistent, it is not adaptively irrational when there is little at stake or no basis for deciding what is at stake.

This completes the discussion of the simplest problem-solving situation. Human behavior is quite rational by the definition used in this book. This conclusion contrasts sharply with the typical evaluation of human decision making. As an interesting aside, this level of rationality does not seem to be unique to humans. Optimal foraging theory (Stephens & Krebs, 1986) uses just this kind of maximized expectation model to predict the foraging behavior of many species. The assumption often is that animals organize their foraging to maximize their expected caloric intake (although more complex nutritional goals have sometimes been used). The application of such models is not universally successful, but it often is.

COMBINING STEPS

The previous section considered problems where the goal could be achieved in a single step. A major complication can arise in trying to achieve a goal when there is no known step that will achieve it. Thus, in the Tower of Hanoi problem, no single allowable step will get me from the start state to the goal state. In a more everyday vein, no single step will get me from a child running wild in the house at 8:30 p.m. to a child asleep in bed at 9:15 p.m. In a more exotic vein, no one step will get me from Pittsburgh to Bora-Bora. In each of these cases, it is necessary to perform a sequence of steps.

There are logically more complex possibilities, but consider the situation of a pure serial structure of steps, such as in an eight puzzle[5] or moves to get from my office to a new lecture hall.[6] In these cases, each step causes a new

---

expected life. However, it remains far from obvious that B becomes the rational choice given that we have to factor in things like political cost. The point remains that there is no justified rational basis for making the decision one way or the other.

[5]The eight puzzle is the tile-moving game (see Anderson, in press a) where the problem solver is given a 3×3 matrix containing eight tiles and one open space. The problem solver can move the tiles into the free space. The goal is usually to achieve some target configuration of the tiles. See Fig. 5-4 on p. 208.

[6]Presumably, a "step" in going from the office to the lecture hall is not an actual physical step but some well-learned fragment of a route, such as getting from my office to the main hall.

state, which enables the next step and, finally, results in the goal. These steps are the causal links from the previous chapter.

The probability of any sequence of steps succeeding is the product of the probabilities of the individual steps. The cost is the sum of costs of all the steps. This suggests that such step combinations can be treated as single macrosteps, and one can choose among them with the same expected utility logic used for choosing single steps. In cases where such macrosteps are repeated sequences (as is the case for my getting to a lecture hall), these are, in fact, probably treated this way.

The major problem is discovering such sequences for the first time. This is the traditional domain of problem-solving search. In the traditional problem-solving literature, these causal links are called *operators*. The problem is searching the exponentially expanding space of operators leading from the current state. The problem is that one cannot always know which next operator is on the correct path, and one might have to search through all possible sequences of operators. If a operators can apply to each state, there are a^n chains of n operators extending from the start state.

Iterative Plan-and-Act Structure

The typical AI program searches through such sequences of steps using various heuristics, finds some sequence that leads to the goal state, and then executes that sequence. Thus, the typical scheme is to plan a complete solution and then act on it. There are two problems with transferring this scheme to the situation of humans solving human problems. The first concerns the probabilistic nature of these steps. That is, the planned sequence of steps will lead to the goal only with a certain probability. With a certain probability they will fail and lead elsewhere. It would not always be rational to plan a long sequence of steps if the sequence is going to diverge from the intended path at an early point. The second problem is that the memory span results imply that one cannot hold a long sequence of such steps in mind, let alone compare a large number of such sequences.

Thus, at best, one can plan a few steps before acting. This is, in fact, how human problem solving typically plays itself out. For instance, when I plan to go to a new location on campus, I plan to get to the building, and I postpone worrying about getting to the room. This can lead to impasses — I may not be able to get to the room by the door I have entered. However, this iterative plan-and-act structure is an inevitable consequence of the uncertainty of problem solving in these domains and the limited working memory.

It is an interesting observation that problem-solving theories seldom acknowledge this iterative plan-and-act structure to human problem solving. It is transparent in almost all situations. For instance, people trying to solve the eight puzzle will often plan short sequences of steps to get a piece in a desired position. Their problem-solving episodes consist of a pause when a plan of some sort is being hatched, a sequence of steps resulting in a piece in position, another pause, and so on.

One of the interesting consequences of this iterative plan-and-act structure is that, when faced with complex problems, it inevitably forces search to take place externally, in that we choose a short sequence of steps, execute it, see the results, and choose another. Thus, in games like the eight puzzle, the search is external, in the puzzle, not internal in a mental representation of the "problem space." A consequence of the external nature of search is that search must take place in a forward direction. That is, in the real world, causality can only move forward from the current state. One of the interesting events in the early development of problem-solving theory was Newell & Simon's exploration with the Logic Theorist (Newell, Shaw, & Simon, 1957). Operating with a computer that did not have a working-memory limitation in a domain like logic, where steps were characterized by certainty, they developed a system that reasoned backward from the goal. Backward reasoning was the thing to do given the structure of that domain and the lack of memory constraints. They found, however, that humans searched in a forward direction. This discovery was one of the stimuli for developing the General Problem Solver (Newell & Simon, 1961).

Choice of Partial Plans

In this chapter, we use the phrase *plan* or *partial plan* to refer to a plan for achieving a goal that involves a move (a sequence of one or more steps) followed by the intentions to try to complete the achievement of the goal after this move. An interesting question is how one chooses the partial plan to execute. One cannot use the criterion that the plan achieves the goal, because the plan does not get one all the way to the goal. People choose moves that promise to lead to the states that (a) they have not been to before—that is, they avoid returning to old states, and (b) that are more similar (by some criterion) to the goal.

Neither of these are absolutes. When one hits dead ends, one has no choice except to return to old states. Again, one can be in a situation where the only moves that do not involve a return to an old state are moves against the grain of increased similarity. Still, these characteristics (a and b) produce probably the most dominant features of human problem solving. The interesting question is to inquire as to their rational basis.

Figure 5-3 is an objective (i.e., not necessarily in the subject's head) analysis of the state of affairs with respect to evaluating a plan *i* involving a move of one or more steps and then the intention to reach the goal. The

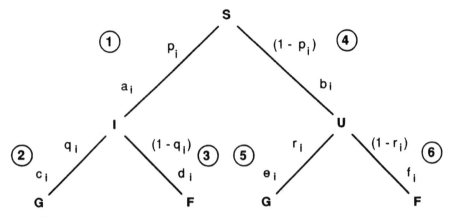

FIG. 5-3. The state of affairs with respect to evaluating a move, i. The first level in the tree represents whether the move achieves its intended state (I) or some unintended state (U). The second level reflects whether it is possible to get from these states to the goal (G) or not (F).

diagram starts at state S and branches off from there. Let us explain each branch in that diagram:

1. The move in plan i has some probability, p_i, of producing its intended state, I, and some cost, a_i, associated with that move.

2. Because I is not the goal state, there is some probability, q_i, that the goal state will be reached from I and a cost, c_i, with the moves along that path.

3. With probability $(1 - q_i)$, the goal state cannot be reached from I. There will be some cost, d_i, associated with the moves before the goal is abandoned.

4. With probability $(1 - p_i)$, the move in plan i does not produce its intended state, I, but some unintended state, U. There is a cost, b_i, associated with getting to U. Note that, in general, b_i need not be equal to a_i, because the same steps may not be made. One possibility is that, if the steps in a multistep move diverge early from intention, the system may abandon the effort early, producing $b_i < a_i$.

5. From state U, there is still some probability, r_i, that the goal can be achieved with cost e_i.

6. Finally, there is a probability $(1 - r_i)$ that the goal cannot be reached from state U and a cost, f_i, before the goal is abandoned.

The overall probability of success and cost associated with plan i is:

$$P_i = p_i q_i + (1 - p_i) r_i \qquad (5\text{-}1)$$

$$C_i = p_i(a_i + q_i c_i + (1 - q_i)d_i) + (1 - p_i)(b_i + r_i e_i + (1 - r_i)f_i) \quad (5\text{-}2)$$

Given this definition of P_i and C_i for a plan i, the system should choose among the plans just as it chose in the previous section when there was only one step to the goal. The logic for choosing among plans involves considering these plans mutually exclusive and choosing the one that maximizes $P_i G - C_i$, provided that quantity is positive. Indeed, multimove plans can be put into competition with a single-move plan to the goal, and a choice can be made among all of the possible plans according to this economic logic. In some cases, a multimove plan might be chosen over a single-move plan because the multimove plan is cheaper. For example, the Appendix to this chapter discusses an example of a case where I chose to go through an elaborate process of repairing a clothesline rather than simply calling a repairman because the latter, one-move possibility was more expensive.

Mathematical Simplifications

The problem with this resolution of multimove planning is that it leaves a lot of quantities undefined. The quantities p_i and a_i can be calculated from knowledge of the probabilities and costs associated with each step in move i. However, because we have not decided what else we will do after attempting move i, how do we estimate c_i, d_i, e_i, f_i, q_i, or r_i? I am going to offer some simplifications to the estimation problem that allow us to focus on estimating just c_i and q_i for the intended path and then offer a proposal for these. These simplifications are being done for analytic tractability. No claim is being made that these simplifications are optimal nor that the mind makes them. However, to the extent that they approximate what is optimal, it is possible to derive rational predictions about problem-solving behavior.

First, let's try to eliminate r_i, the probability of success should the move fail to produce its intended effect. One reasonable assumption is that the probability of success should be worse conditional on this than it was before this failure. Assume that the expected value of r_i is some fraction, f (less than 1), of P_i—that is, things always get worse when there is a failure.

$$r_i = fP_i$$

Then it is possible to solve for P_i from Equation 5-1 in terms of p_i, q_i, and f:

$$P_i = p_i q_i / (1 - (1 - p_i)f) \quad (5\text{-}3)$$

This makes P_i an increasing function of p_i and q_i, which is reasonable. We will assume that f is constant and does not depend on i. P_i has an interesting value when $p_i \approx 1$ — that is, one is nearly certain that the move will produce its intended effect: $P_i \approx q_i$. This simplification is unrealistic in many real-world situations, but much of the experimental research on problem-solving involves situations where $p_i = 1$ is a realistic assumption.

Now let us try to eliminate some of the cost values. As a radical approximation, let us assume that all costs at a particular level are equal. That is,

$$a_i = b_i$$

$$c_i = d_i = e_i = f_i$$

The $a_i = b_i$ can be roughly justified by noting that there may be either early abandonment (leading to lower cost) on the branch to U or unexpected obstacles leading to higher-than-anticipated costs. A similar reasoning can justify $c_i = d_i$ and $e_i = f_i$. The assumption that $c_i = e_i$ is truly problematical, and it might be more accurate to assume that $c_i < e_i$. However, the more dismal prospects in the U branch are already captured by the fact that $r_i < q_i$. With these simplifications, we can convert Equation 5-2 into a truly simple expression for C_i:

$$C_i = a_i + c_i \tag{5-4}$$

The upshot of these implications is to reduce the estimation problems to the problem of estimating p_i, the probability of the move in partial plan producing the intended state; q_i, the probability of getting from that state to the goal; a_i, the cost of the partial plan; and c_i, the remaining cost if it succeeds. The decision procedure becomes simply to choose i with maximum expected $P_i G - C_i$ (as defined by Equations 5-3 and 5-4) or to give up if there is no i such that $P_i G > C_i$.

Let us summarize where we are in the analysis of this iterative plan-and-act structure. It is necessary to estimate P_i, the probability of success of the partial plan, and C_i, the cost of the partial plan. Equation 5-3 identifies p_i and q_i as critical to the estimation of P_i. Equation 5-4 identifies a_i and c_i as critical to the estimation of C_i. The terms a_i and p_i can be estimated directly from knowledge of the steps in the move associated with the partial plan. The question becomes how to estimate q_i and c_i. There are a number of possible bases for their estimation, but this chapter analyzes two. One is the similarity between the goal and the state that the move is intended to result in. The second is the amount of effort spent so far.[7]

Use of Similarity

Although it is typical to speak of similarity, for many analytic purposes it makes sense to think about measuring the difference between the current state and the goal, and not the similarity. This is because we can simply add up differences. Consider a choice between move 1, which creates a state I_1 with difference d_1 from the goal, and move 2, which creates a state I_2 with difference d_2 from the goal. It is a fact about problem solving that on average, when $d_1 < d_2$, there will be a greater probability of success (i.e., $q_1 > q_2$) and less expected cost to achieve the goal (i.e., $c_1 < c_2$). Note that this is a probabilistic expectation. There clearly are specific cases where this expectation is violated. Puzzles that have played a major role in research on problem solving often violate this expectation. However, they are often puzzles just because they have this property.

The number of real-world domains where increasing similarity implies greater q_i and c_i are many. The most apparent is actual travel—usually, but not always, it is the case that when we get closer to our destination, our chances of reaching it go up and costs to reach it go down. Another domain is construction—usually (but not always) the more similar an artifact we are building is to its final intended form, the less we have to do to reach that form. Achieving a consensus in a social group is another example—the more people we have persuaded, the greater our probability of success and less distance we have to go. In all domains, it does not require much imagination to think of exceptions, but we should not let such flights of imagination blind us to the overwhelming truth of the statistical law "The closer in similarity we are to our goal the closer we are in number of steps."

There is a simple reason why there should be a correlation between difference (the d_i) and cost or effort of further problem solving (the c_i). If the differences are independent, it will add a certain amount to the problem-solving effort to eliminate each difference. Thus, if my goal is to tidy my desk, then as a first approximation each messy thing on my desk adds another difference from my goal and will add a further unit of work to my effort. Although exceptions abound, independence of the pieces of a problem is a good first approximation. This independence produces the

---

[7]Other possible bases include the history of past success with a method. Thus, if I have had a recent history of success with trying to repair things by hand, I will be more inclined to try to repair something myself rather than call a repair shop.

correlation between difference from the goal and effort. The correlation with probability of success also holds in the case of independent differences. Each difference adds another chance for an unsolvable subgoal to arise. The interesting feature about the correlation between difference on one hand and probability and cost on the other is that it partially relieves the system of the responsibility of incorporating probability and cost into its decision making. It can simply do hill climbing along the slope of steepest ascent and choose the move that minimizes the difference from the goal. However, this does not totally relieve the system of making its behavior contingent on probability and cost, because it has to know when to stop trying to solve the problem. Rationally, one should stop when the cost is high enough and the probability low enough to make the best plan unprofitable. Note that, in saying the behavior should depend on cost and probability, the claim is not that the system actually computes these quantities. Rather, the claim is that the system's computations should reflect these quantities.

An important question concerns how to measure difference from the goal. For example, consider the eight puzzle illustrated in Fig. 5-4. Novices will typically measure difference in terms of number of tiles out of position. Thus, in Fig. 5-4, they will rate positively the fact that the 1, 5, and 7 are in position. However, it proves to be more important to measure difference in terms of how many tiles are in sequence around the periphery. Thus, the fact that 3 and 4 are in correct sequence is most important, and one wants to preserve this in future moves.

A return to a previous state counts negatively against similarity. It is evidence that the superficial similarity is somewhat deceiving (the initial assessment did not know the best-appearing path would lead right back to the current state) in this case, and one needs to lower similarity. In our applications, we measure difference as a weighted sum of superficial differences plus number of returns to that state.

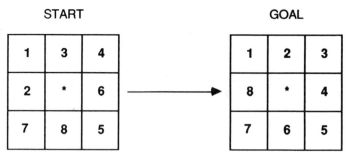

FIG. 5-4.   A typical eight-puzzle problem. The problem is to move the tiles in the start state so they achieve the configuration in the goal state.

Effort Spent So Far

The other factor that can be used in estimating q_i and c_i is the effort spent so far. The basic idea is that one has a notion of how much effort it takes to solve a problem. (As is argued later, it is necessary to conceive of this as a probability density over possible efforts.) Under some conditions, as we expend more effort we can conclude that we are closer to our goal. Under other conditions, as we expend more effort we can start to doubt whether we will ever achieve our goal.

Estimation of Probability and Cost

Equation 5-3 reduced the estimation of P_i, the probability of the move succeeding, to an estimation of p_i and q_i, probability of achieving the goal if the move succeeds. p_i can be estimated from knowledge of the probability of the steps involved. q_i requires a different estimation scheme. Similarly, Equation 5-4 reduced estimation of overall cost, C_i, to a quantity a_i, cost of the move, and c_i, cost of further effort after the move succeeds. The cost a_i can be gotten from knowledge of the steps required, but c_i requires a different estimation scheme. The problematical q_i and c_i can be estimated by a Bayesian scheme that starts with a prior distribution of probabilities and costs and uses conditional probabilities to update this prior distribution into a posterior distribution. These conditional probabilities will be based on difference from the goal and effort spent so far.

The mathematics of this estimation process is described in Table 5-3. It involves assuming the following prior model of problem structure:

1. There is some probability, s, of adopting a solvable problem.

2. Conditional on the problem being solvable, there is a gamma distribution, $G(x|v,b)$, of amount of effort to solve the problem. The mean of this gamma distribution is v/b with variance v/b^2. If $v = 1$, the distribution takes the form of a heavily skewed exponential. As v gets large, the distribution becomes more normal.

Then there are the following conditional probabilities:

3. If one is trying to solve an unsolvable problem, there is an exponential distribution of differences between the current state and goal state (see Equation 5-8). The mean of this distribution is $1/\alpha$. Note an exponential distribution is the standard noninformative Bayesian prior for a dimension that varies from 0 to infinity (Berger, 1985).

4. If one is solving a solvable problem, there is also an exponential distribution of differences with mean c/β where c is the amount of effort

Variables

q_i is the probability that we can achieve the goal if move i has its intended effect.

c_i is the further cost of achieving the goal if move i has its intended effect.

D_i is the difference between the intended state of move i and the goal.

E_i is the amount of effort expended so far plus move i.

Note: We suppress the i subscript in the derivations in this table.

Derivations

Let $P(F)$ be the prior probability of the goal not being solvable.

$$P(F) = 1 - s \qquad (5\text{-}5)$$

Let $\pi(S,x)$ be the prior probability for a success with cost x.

$$\pi(S,x) = sG(x|v,b) \qquad (5\text{-}6)$$

where $G(v,b)$ is the gamma distribution with parameters v and b:

$$G(x|v,b) = \frac{x^{v-1}b^v e^{-bx}}{\Gamma(v)} \qquad (5\text{-}7)$$

where $\Gamma(v) = (v-1)!$ Let $\pi(D|F)$ be the probability density describing the distribution of differences D in a failure state. We assume that this is the Bayesian noninformative exponential:

$$\pi(D|F) = \alpha e^{-\alpha D} \qquad (5\text{-}8)$$

Let $\pi(D|S,c)$ be the probability density of differences D in a success state with cost c yet to spend. Again, we assume a Bayesian noninformative exponential with mean proportional to the cost c.

$$\pi(D|S,c) = \beta/c \; e^{-\beta D/c} \qquad (5\text{-}9)$$

Then we can calculate the posteriori probability of a failure:

$$P(F|D,E) = \frac{P(F)\pi(D|F)}{P(F)\pi(D|F) + \int_0^\infty \pi(S,x+E)\pi(D|S,c)dx} \qquad (5\text{-}10)$$

Similarly, we can calculate the posteriori density of a success with cost c:

$$\pi(S,c|D,E) = \frac{\pi(S,c+E)\pi(D|S,c)}{P(F)\pi(D|F) + \int_0^\infty \pi(S,x+E)\pi(D|S,x)dx} \qquad (5\text{-}11)$$

Now we can calculate the desired quantities q and c:

$$q = 1 - P(F|D,E) \qquad (5\text{-}12)$$

$$c = \left(\int_0^\infty x\pi(S,x|D,E)dx\right)/(1-q) \qquad (5\text{-}13)$$

still required to solve the problem (see Equation 5-9). This has the reasonable consequence of making the mean difference proportional to c.

From these prior probabilities and conditional probabilities, Equations 5-10 through 5-13 derive posterior distributions for failure, success, and amount of further effort given an effort, E, spent so far and a difference, D, between the current state and the goal state. From these it is possible to calculate q_i and c_i.[8]

The parameters that control this estimation are v and b, which describe the gamma distribution of costs in success states; α and β, which describe the distribution of differences in failure and success states; and s, which describes the probability of success. The mean of the gamma distribution is v/b. Because the units in which costs are measured are arbitrary, we can define $v/b = 1.0$, which is the expected amount of effort on a problem. This means that there is only one non-arbitrary parameter for $G(x|v,b)$, which is v, and this determines the shape of the gamma distribution. Again, the metric of difference is arbitrary, so we can set $\beta = 1$, which means that there is a mean difference of 1 when we are 1 unit away from the goal. Thus, the real parameters are v, α, and s. In the applications that follow, s is arbitrarily set to .8, and $\alpha = .2$. It is of interest to consider how the values of c_i and q_i varied with v, because v influences the form of the distribution that represents the system's prior beliefs about problem-solving costs.

Figure 5-5 plots q_i, the probability of success, given various values of v, various amounts of effort expended so far, and differences from the goal. As can be seen, probability decreases systematically with either difference or effort expended so far. The function for effort $E = 0$ does not vary much as a function of the v parameter. However, as E gets larger, the functions are lower for higher v. This reflects the fact that with high value of v, a high effort spent so far is a sign that one is on a hopeless cause.

Figure 5-6 plots C_i, the mean expected future cost, given various values of v, various amounts of cost so far, and differences from the goal. As can be seen, these functions do not vary much as a function of cost spent so far, and in the case of $v = 1$ there is no variation. On the other hand, they grow quite dramatically as a function of difference from the goal.

In all of the modeling reported in this chapter, v was set to be 2.

With this discussion as background, it is possible to specify a rational algorithm for iterative planning and acting. We can now use Equations 5-3, 5-4, 5-12, and 5-13 to associate with each partial plan, i, a probability, P_i, of success and a cost, C_i. The basic strategy is to generate a number of partial plans that fit within the constraints of working memory and adopt

---

[8]Equations 5-10 through 5-13 do not have closed-form solutions and are solved in the applications in this chapter by numeric integration techniques.

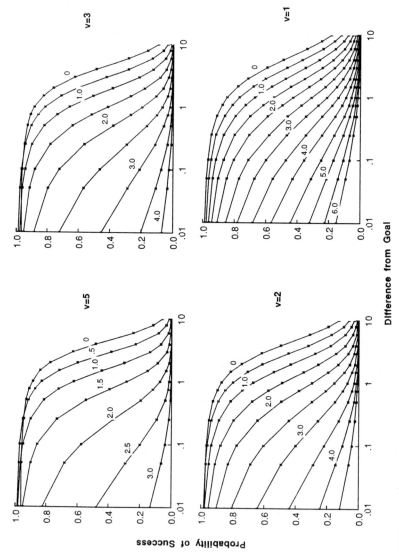

FIG. 5-5. Probability that a problem is solvable as a function of difference from goal (abscissa), amount of effort so far (different curves in a panel), and setting of the v parameter (different panels).

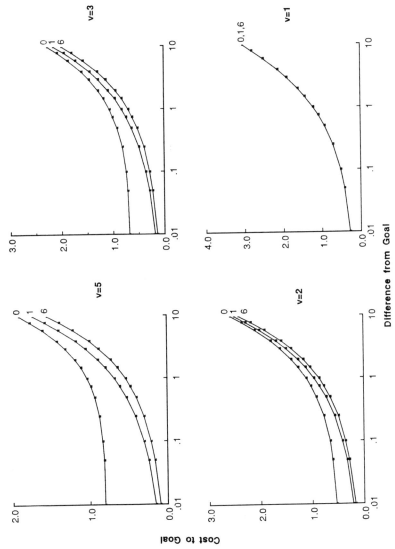

FIG. 5-6. Cost until goal can be achieved (for a successful goal) as a function of difference from goal (abscissa), amount of effort so far (different curves in a panel), and setting of the v parameter (different panels).

213

the one with maximal $P_iG - C_i$, provided that one exists with a value greater than 0.

Generation of Moves: Satisficing

The question of generating candidate moves is an interesting one. Presumably, the set of combinations of steps we can imagine is often very large, if not infinite. We clearly do not consider all possible moves. Duffers at chess miss mate in one step. In general, it is not rational to consider all possible moves. In Simon's (1955) terminology, we consider moves until we find one that satisfices.

I assume that the generation of moves is basically a function of the memory processes discussed in the second chapter. That is to say, generating a step depends on retrieving causal links to map into the current situation. Thus, the factors discussed in chapter 2 produce an ordering on moves. As discussed in chapter 2, these factors were designed to order memories in terms of their usefulness.

What determines when we stop generating candidate partial plans? Rationally, we should stop when the cost of generating a partial plan exceeds the potential gain of considering it. Let w be the cost of generating a partial plan. This will largely reflect the time in generating and combining a sequence of steps. The gain in generating a partial plan will be the possibility that it will be better than the previous best. This is to be measured by the probability of generating a better plan times how much better it is.

The value of any plan i is to be measured as $P_iG - C_i$. This is a quantity that can have a maximum value of G in the case $P_i = 1$ and $C_i = 0$ and can have unbounded negative value (of course, the plan should not be executed if it has negative expected value). Let B_{n-1} denote the best plan generated of the first $n - 1$. One should generate an nth plan to the extent that one expects the value of another plan to be better than B_{n-1}. Before generating the next plan, we cannot know how good it will be. All we can have is an expectation of a certain distribution of goodness of plans. Let $Z_n(x)$ be such a distribution. It is indexed by n to allow for the possibility that later plans are less likely to be as good as earlier plans (because memory tends to deliver better plans earlier). The following expresses the expected improvement I_n over B_{n-1} if we consider an nth plan:

$$I_n = \int_{B_{n-1}}^{G} (x - B_{n-1}) \, Z_n(x) dx \tag{5-14}$$

This equation considers all cases when the nth plan is better than B_{n-1} (when the variable x is in the range B_{n-1} to G) and multiplies the amount of improvement, $(x - B_{n-1})$, by the probability of that improvement, $Z_n(x)$.

We will stop sampling when I_n is less than the cost, w, of generating the next partial plan. Thus, satisficing (Simon, 1955) becomes getting a partial plan that is good enough so that further effort is not worth it.[9]

This produces satisficing behavior with the following properties:

1. The satisficing level drops as one extends the search because one's expectation of significantly improving on the best is decreased.
2. The poorer the current best is, the more one searches.
3. The larger the value of G is, the more plans one generates before acting.

These three predictions seem intuitively right, although I know of no relevant data.

This completes the theory except for specifying the form of $Z_n(x)$, the density function for the expected values of the nth plan. As a first-order approximation, I have assumed that the expected gains were distributed according to the Bayesian noninformative exponential distribution:

$$Z_n(x) = z_n e^{-z_n(G-x)} \tag{5-15}$$

where $z_n = 1/n(G - Z_{n-1})$, and Z_{n-1} is the expected value associated with the previous move actually performed (not the previous move considered).[10] This distribution has mean $G - n(G - Z_{n-1})$, which decreases linearly with the number (n) of moves considered.

STUDIES OF HILL CLIMBING

There has been a fair amount of research that has looked at subjects' problem-solving behavior in situations where the only variables to guide them are effort so far and similarity. The model developed in this section is applied to a couple of these studies.

Jeffries, Polson, Razran, & Atwood

The experiment by Jeffries, Polson, Razran, & Atwood (1977) on the missionaries and cannibals problem is fairly representative. Figure 5-7

---

[9]This basic idea was introduced into economics by Stigler (1961), in his paper on the cost of search.

[10]In the case of the first move in a problem-solving series, the value of Z_0 is set at 0.

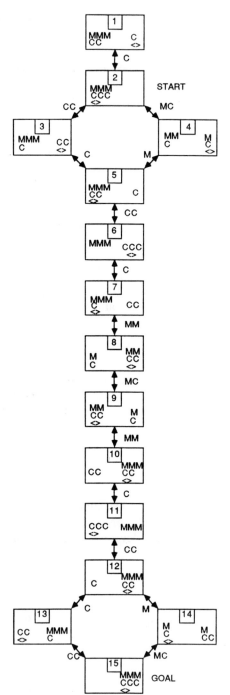

FIG. 5-7. The problem space for the missionaries and cannibals problem studied by Jeffries et al. (1977). Each state is represented by the position of the three missionaries (M), the three cannibals (C), and the boat (< >). Arrows indicate legal transitions among states.

shows the state space for this problem. Subjects start out on State 2, where the boat, three missionaries, and three cannibals are on one side of the river. They want to cross the river, and they have a boat, but the boat can hold only two individuals. In addition, if cannibals outnumber missionaries on either side of the river, the cannibals will eat the missionaries. Steps that lead to such configurations are illegal. Jeffries and her colleagues created a computer system that recorded the steps that subjects made and prohibited illegal steps. Subjects required an average of 19.1 moves to solve the problem, although the minimum is only 11. Figure 5-8 describes their behavior in terms of mean number of visitations to the various states.

Figure 5-8 also illustrates the predictions of the theory in terms of number of visitations to states. To apply this theory, a number of simplifying assumptions were made. It was assumed that subjects just planned one-step moves. The probability of getting the intended state from a step (i.e., p_i) was set at 1.[11] The cost of a step was set at 1/12. With these assumptions, it was possible to calculate q_i and c_i according to Equations 5-12 and 5-13. This required conditionalizing on past effort and difference. Past effort was measured as $n/12$ where n is the number of past steps. Difference was measured in terms of the number of missionaries and cannibals still on the left bank. Using the recommendation of Jeffries and colleagues, missionaries were weighted three times as much as cannibals. Then the metric of difference was $(3M + C)/4.0$ where M was the number of missionaries on the left bank and C was the number of cannibals. This difference measure was incremented by 1 for every repeat visit to a state. Legal moves were randomly generated with replacement.

A criterion is needed for stopping the consideration of moves and actually making a move. This involved calculating I_n from Equation 5-14 and comparing it to a satisficing level, w, which was set to 2.50 for this experiment. It is also necessary to set a value of G, the goal, which we set to 20. If I_n was greater than w, another move was generated, because the expected gain from that move exceeded the cost, w, of generating it.

Moves were randomly generated with replacement. One hundred computer simulations were run to get the number in Fig. 5-8. The mean number of moves was 20.05, which is close to what the Jeffries group observed. The correlation between the model and the theory for number of visits per state was .92. Thus, the theory generally matched the data.

----

[11]This means that $P_i = q_i$, and we do not have to assign a value to f—see Equation 5-3. As noted earlier, this assumption is reasonable in many experimental situations if not in many real-world problem-solving tasks.

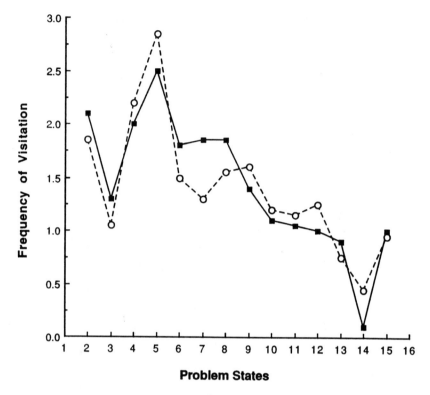

FIG. 5-8.   Frequency of visitation to the various states of the problem space in Fig. 5-7 by subjects (solid lines) or by simulation (dotted lines).

Atwood & Polson

The model was also applied to the experiment of Atwood and Polson (1976) on the water jug problem. Figure 5-9 shows the state space for their first experiment. Subjects have three waterjugs of capacities 8, 5, and 3 units. They have the first jug full and the others empty; thus, the initial state can be denoted (8, 0, 0). The goal is to get the water evenly distributed between the first two jugs. This goal state can be denoted (4, 4, 0). Water can be poured between jugs with the constraint that when one pours between jugs A and B, one must continue until either A is empty or B is full.

Our model was run on this task using the same parameters as in the river-crossing experiment (except $w = 2.0$) but using the metric that Atwood and Polson suggested, which is $|C(1) - 4| + |C(2) - 4|$ where $C(X)$ refers to the contents of jug X.

Figure 5-10 compares the model with the results of the experiment. The correlation was .94. Atwood and Polson reported the results from four

WATER JUG PROBLEMS

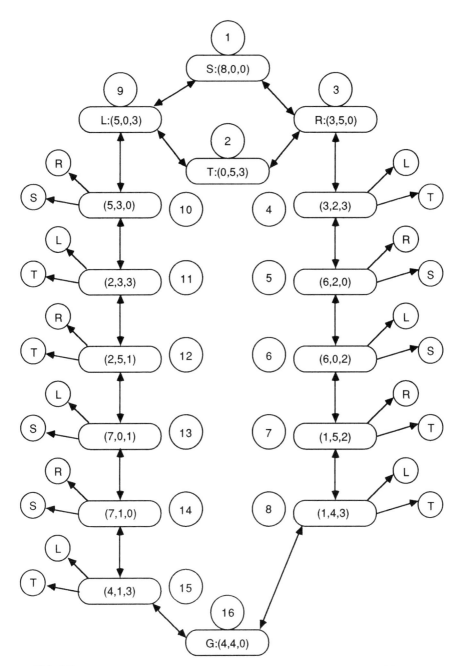

FIG. 5-9.   The problem space for the water jug problem studied by Atwood & Polson (1976). Each state is represented by the quantity of water in each of the three jugs. Arrows indicate legal transitions among states.

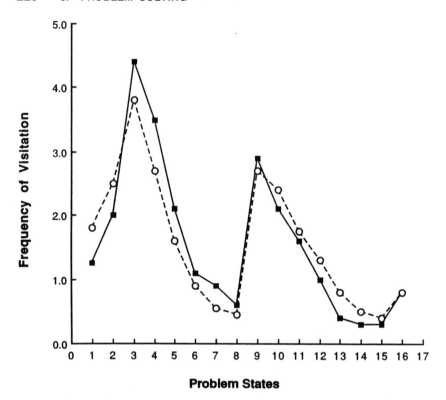

FIG. 5-10.   Frequency of visitation of various states in the problem space of Fig. 5.9 by subjects (solid lines) and by simulation (dotted lines).

other, different water jug problems. The correlations between prediction and theory for these were .72, .95, .85, and .89. These were fit without any extensive parameter search. We simply looked for a value of w that produced a number of steps that matched the overall total. By increasing w, the subject deliberates less in choosing a move and so takes longer in terms of overt steps to complete the task. Recall that the parameter w reflects the cost of considering another move relative to the cost of actually executing a move.

The two papers by Jeffries and colleagues and Atwood & Polson describe essentially the same mechanistic model to account for the data. They proposed that a subject may go through up to three stages in choosing a problem-solving move. First, the subject restricts consideration to steps that lead to states that are not recognized as old and that are more similar to the target state. If this fails (because all moves lead to old states or are against the grain of similarity), subjects weaken their criteria to consider any move to a new state. If this fails, subjects select the move that leads to a state that is more similar to the goal. Their model is probabilistic, in that subjects sometimes fail to consider a move at a stage and that memory for old states is not perfect. Their models provide somewhat better fits to the data than the rational model, but their fits are the result of extensive parameter searches. The similarity between the predictions of the rational model and the predictions of their models is another case of convergence of mechanistic models induced from data and prescriptive models derived from rational considerations. The rational model used a combined difference metric that weighted both physical difference and whether the state was an old state. This difference metric was mapped into an expectation about probability of success and cost by Equations 5-12 and 5-13. Thus, this rational model is like that of Atwood & Polson and Jeffries and colleagues in that it responds to similarity. The only essential difference is that, rather than responding directly to similarity in its choices of what to do, it mapped difference onto expectations about success and cost. Thus, it identifies the rational basis for the computations performed by the models of Atwood & Polson and Jeffries and colleagues. Said another way, it does not challenge their computations; rather, it justifies them.

MEANS-ENDS ANALYSIS

A major simplification in the discussion to this point is that the analysis has ignored the fact that moves can have preconditions on their applicability. To use the classic Newell & Simon (1972) example, I know that driving my son will get him to nursery school, but a precondition of a functioning battery for my car is not satisfied. Rather than look for some other move, I can set as a new goal to remove the blocking precondition. This is what gives rise to means-ends problem solving where the means becomes an end in itself. It is fairly straightforward to extend our economic analysis to this situation. The probability, p_i, of the move succeeding must be reduced to reflect the probability of satisfying the precondition. That is, let p_i' be the probability that a move will produce its intended state and p_i'' be the probability that its precondition will be satisfied. Then, the p_i in the prior analysis becomes $p_i'p_i''$. Similarly, it is necessary to estimate a_i as $a_i' + a_i''$, where a_i' is the cost of the move and a_i'' is the cost of satisfying the precondition.[12]

The critical issue is how to estimate p_i'', the probability of satisfying the precondition and how to estimate a_i'', the cost of satisfying the precondition. How do I estimate a probability of fixing the battery in my car to get

---

[12]One of the peculiar issues that this analysis ignores is the issue of the certainty with which the precondition holds. Thus, I might think I have to get a key to unlock a door, but it is always worth a try to see if the door is actually locked.

my son to nursery school? Presumably, this can be estimated on the same basis that the probability is judged of getting from any state to a goal state. It is just that the goal state becomes satisfying the conditions for the move rather than the original goal. It is also possible to estimate a_i'', the cost, by similar means. Thus, the p_i'' and a_i'' are to be estimated by Equations 5-12 and 5-13, just as the q_i and c_i were. That is to say, they are to be estimated from the difference between the current state and the subgoal and from how much effort has been put into achieving the subgoal so far.

Means–ends analysis is potentially recursive, in that one can wind up subgoaling the means to achieve the means. In the Newell & Simon example, I can use a repair shop to replace my battery, but I need to get the car and repair shop together. This now becomes the goal in service of an operating battery, which is a goal in service of driving my son to nursery school.

There is the issue of how much value to give to achieving a subgoal. This becomes important in deciding when to abandon pursuing a subgoal. This can be quite complex, because it depends on judging the relative prospects if the goal is abandoned or not. In the model, I took a radical approximation to dealing with this. I assigned the subgoal a value that depended on the value, G, of the supergoal, the value, P_i, of success along that path, and the cost, C_i, along that path. $P_iG - C_i$ is the expected value of that path. I made this the value of the subgoal, reasoning that the subgoal should not cost more than the value of the path. With this subgoal value set, I then assumed that it was pursued with the same logic as a top goal.

Maintaining such a stock of subgoals causes difficulty because of short-term memory limitations. However, the important observation is that we often do not need to maintain this stock because the world does it for us. Even if I forget why I wanted to repair my car, the presence of my son will soon remind me.

Thus, means–ends analysis can be quite effective, despite its goal recursing. All that is required is that we remember our current goal. It is true that we can occasionally fail to reconstruct why we are doing something. This is particularly likely when we are following an unusual path of solution in novel domains. When we try to reconstruct our reasoning, we might choose different steps and so not arrive at the same spot.

Tower of Hanoi

A classic domain where means–ends analysis is applicable is the Tower of Hanoi puzzle. Novice subjects have trouble executing the means–ends strategy and other strategies that require recursive subgoals. For people like myself, who have been exposed to the puzzle for years, there is no difficulty in executing this strategy—not because I can maintain the goal stack, but

TABLE 5-4

The Monster Move Isomorph of the Tower of Hanoi Problem

Three five-headed extraterrestial monsters were holding three crystal globes. Because of the quantum-mechanical peculiarities of their neighborhood, both monsters and globes come in exactly three sizes with no other permitted: small, medium, and large. The small monster was holding the large globe; the medium-sized monster was holding the small globe; and the large monster was holding the medium-sized globe. Because this situation offended their keenly developed sense of symmetry, they proceeded to transfer globes from one monster to another so that each monster would have a globe that was proportionate to its own size.

Monster etiquette complicated the solution of the problem, because it requires that:
1. Only one globe may be transferred at a time;
2. If a monster is holding two globes, only the larger of the two may be transferred; and,
3. A globe may not be transferred to a monster who is holding a larger globe.

By what sequence of transfers could the monsters have solved this problem?

because my thinking about the domain has become so reliable that I can reconstruct the stack at any time.

There has been a fair amount of research on the Tower of Hanoi problem (Anzai & Simon, 1979; Cohen & Corkin, 1981; Hayes & Simon, 1974, 1977; Karat, 1982; Kotovsky & Fallside, 1988; Kotovsky, Hayes, & Simon, 1985; Newell & Simon, 1972; Simon & Hayes, 1976), although relatively little of it has been focused on predicting the actual sequences of steps that novices make when solving the problem for the first time. Much of this research is concerned with situations where subjects are transferring solutions from earlier problems to later problems, and much of this research is concerned with isomorphs of the Tower of Hanoi problem, such as one presented in Table 5-4. Although interesting, such transfer data are beyond the scope of this chapter.

Probably the best systematic investigation of novice steps in Tower of Hanoi is one reported by Kotovsky, Hayes, & Simon (1985) in which they looked at student solutions of problems like the one in Table 5-4 and other isomorphs, including the original Tower of Hanoi problem. They found an interesting characteristic to subjects' first attempts to solve such problems. Subjects appeared to wander around in the problem space almost randomly at first and were often as far away from a solution as they were at the beginning. Then, suddenly, subjects would execute a sequence of steps that brought them to the goal. This could be characterized as discovering means–ends analysis in the middle of the solution of the first problem.

It is possible to map the preceding general discussion of means–ends analysis to a model for Tower of Hanoi. Thus, suppose there is a standard three-peg configuration with disks 1, 2, and 3 on peg A (see Fig. 5-11). There are the direct moves of moving disk 1 to peg B or C. There are also the possibilities of subgoaling moving disks 2 or 3 to pegs B or C. Consider the subgoal of moving disk 3 to peg C. This involves getting disks 1 and 2 to peg B and disk 3 to peg C. Thus, in terms of the preceding discussion:

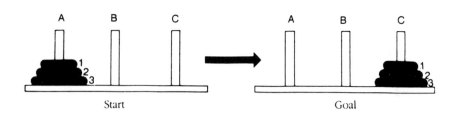

FIG. 5-11. The three-disk version of the Tower of Hanoi problem.

p_i'' is the probability of getting disks 1 and 2 to peg B;

p_i' is the probability of getting disk 3 to peg C if disks 1 and 2 go to peg B;

a_i'' is the cost of getting disks 1 and 2 to peg B;

a_i' is the cost of getting disk 3 to peg C if disks 1 and 2 go to peg C.

Modeling Kotovsky, Hayes, & Simon

I decided to see if this Tower of Hanoi model would reproduce the Kotovsky, Hayes, and Simon data. As in the previous modeling of hill climbing, all one-step moves were assumed to have a fixed cost (set at .1 in modeling this experiment) and a probability of 1—that is, $p_i' = 1$ and $a_i' = .1$. The quantities p_i'' and a_i'' were estimated, as described earlier, from the difference between the current state and the desired precondition subgoal and from the amount of effort expended in trying to achieve the subgoal. This model differed from the one used for Atwood and Polson and Jeffries and colleagues in that the probability, p_i, of the planned move was not always 1. Although we can continue to assume that the probability of successfully making a move is 1 should the precondition be satisfied, we cannot assume that the probability of satisfying the precondition is 1. Thus, $p_i' = 1$, but $p_i'' < 1$ and, hence, $p_i = p_i'p_i'' = p_i'' < 1$. Because p_i is less than 1, it is necessary to specify f to combine p_i and q_i to calculate P_i for Equation 5-3. The parameter, f, represents the proportion reduction in probability that the goal can be achieved should the current operation fail. This was set somewhat arbitrarily at .5.

The same values were used for all the parameters that were fixed in the modeling of the Atwood and Polson experiments and the Jeffries, Polson, Razran, and Atwood experiment. The variable parameter in those models was the satisficing level, w, and this was set at .5 for the Tower of Hanoi model. Differences were measured as the average of the sizes of the disks out of place. So, the start state in Fig. 5-11 is $(3 + 2 + 1) / 3 = 2.0$ units from the goal.

This has a rather peculiar mapping onto an isomorph like the one in Table 5-4, because the large disk becomes the small globe. The small globe is the most restricted in its moves, and it was assumed that it would be recognized as most critical and given a weight of 3.[13] In the case of the isomorph in Table 5-4, subjects also appear to have an affinity for preserving an even distribution of globes among monsters, as is required in the goal state. This is modeled by measuring difference as $(D_1 + D_2)/4$ where D_1 is measured as the sum of the values of globes out of position, and D_2 is measured as the sum of absolute differences between the number of globes per monster and the ideal of one per monster in the goal state.

Somewhat to my surprise, I found that this system reproduced the behavior noted by Kotovsky, Hayes, and Simon. This is that its moves were initially dominated by simple local hill climbing that tried to maximize similarity to the goal state. This leads to flailing in the problems that Kotovsky and his colleagues presented to their subjects. Later, the program switched to subgoaling and quickly solved the problem. It turns out that the reason for this is quite rational and does not depend on the rather arbitrary details assumed to apply the model. Generally speaking, choosing to achieve a means–ends subgoal rather than the goal itself has an advantage and a disadvantage. If the subgoal is well chosen, it will be relatively similar to the current state. Moreover, the goal state will be relatively similar to the state that would arise if the subgoaled action could be performed. This tends to lead to a higher estimated probability of achieving the main goal by way of the subgoal. Logically, however, the minimum number of steps going through the subgoal cannot be less than the number of steps on the best path to goal and may be more. Thus, the estimated amount of effort is greater for subgoaling. In summary, maximizing probability votes for subgoaling, whereas minimizing effort votes for hill climbing.

Initially, the estimates of probability of success are high, and effort considerations dominate, so hill climbing is tried. However, consider what happens when hill climbing does not succeed. As Figs. 5-5 and 5-6 illustrate, amount of past effort seriously impacts on estimate of probability (Fig. 5-5) but not estimate of future effort (Fig. 5-6). Thus, as one gets nowhere by

---

[13]Inspecting some protocols that Ken Kotovsky generously shared with me, this does seem a reasonable assumption. That is, subjects appear to realize that it is most important to move the small globe.

hill climbing, estimates of eventual success become more and more pessimistic. This means that measures that boost estimated probability begin to look more attractive, and means–ends analysis crosses the threshold as the best method.

In summary, in a novel domain, hill climbing is a reasonable first approach, as it promises to minimize effort. If it does not succeed, then it is reasonable to back up to more effortful problem-solving strategies that promise greater probability of success.

The strongest data that Kotovsky and his colleagues have offered for this switch comes from solving the monster isomorph in Table 5-4. That problem starts out five steps from the goal. Subjects spent 14.5 steps, on average, to solve this problem. They typically wandered around the problem space and would wind up in some problem state still five steps from the goal. Kotovsky, Hayes, and Simon broke up the step sequences into a first phase that ended the last time subjects were five steps from the goal and a second phase, which was the remaining steps. They averaged 9 steps in the first phase and only 5.5 in the final phase (minimum would be 5). I ran a simulation of the rational model in the same way I had for the other experiments (Atwood & Polson and Jeffries et al.). The simulation averaged 8.3 steps in the first phase and 5.7 steps in the final phase. In the model, this final spurt to the goal always occurred when the program set the subgoal to get the most constraining globe (disk) into position.

Another interesting statistic is the time per step in the first phase and in the second. Kotovsky, Hayes, and Simon reported 23 seconds per step in the first phase and 15 seconds per step in the final phase. With respect to the rational model, the statistic that corresponds to time is the number of iterations before the model settled on a candidate move (see the discussion surrounding Equation 5-14). There was an average of 11 such iterations on average in the first phase and only 7 in the final phase. It is much easier for the program to satisfy itself that it has a good move in the final phase, because it has broken the problem down into subgoals that are easier to obtain.

Kotovsky also shared with me some more detailed data from a subsequent, unpublished experiment using the problem in Table 5-4. These data are actually the combined results from 20 subjects in one experiment and another 50 in a second experiment. From these data it is possible to calculate how often subjects make each state-to-state transition in the problem. There are 27 possible states and 75 state-to-state transitions. Subjects average about .22 uses of each state-to-state transition with the mean for different state-to-state transitions varying from 0 to .91. Individual subjects may repeat a particular state-to-state transition a number of times. We ran 100 simulation runs to get some comparable numbers. The simulation shows a similar mean and range (mean = .16 and range from 0 to 1.00) with similar variability across runs. The critical issue was the correlation between the state-to-state transitions of the data and the subject. This correlation was a high .84. To get a standard of comparison, the correlation between the data from the two subexperiments was .81. This quality of fit to this detail of data is unknown in the problem-solving literature.

Comparisons with the Kotovsky, Hayes, & Simon Model

Kotovsky and his colleagues proposed a memory-load explanation of the phenomenon. They proposed that subjects initially cannot construct plans that involve subgoals, but, as they become more practiced in moves, they are able to see far enough ahead to plan by means-end analysis. This depends on automating the move rules with practice. There are two pieces of data that support this memory-load explanation. First, they looked at the effect of a hint at the beginning of the problem. For the monster move problem in Table 5-4, this hint was "Your first goal should be to take care of the small monster (i.e., to get him the right-sized globe)." If subjects could have followed this hint, they would have been only three steps away from the goal. However, subjects were systematically unable to use this hint. Second, they looked at transfer to a new problem that does not overlap in the step sequence. They found that subjects much more readily subgoaled in this second problem, suggesting that they could then use a subgoal strategy. This is what would be expected if they had automated move operators for the first problem, which would enable subgoals to be immediately tried in the second problem.

It is hard to be certain how subjects interpreted the hint. If they interpreted it as simply "It is most important to get the small globe to the small monster," then we would not expect the hint to have any effect, because the difference metric already places greatest weight on getting the small globe to the small monster. If they interpreted it as "You should move the large globe from the small monster so you can move the small globe to the small monster," then this would be means-ends subgoaling and would produce a large benefit. Presumably, subjects did not interpret the hint in this second sense, because that is not what they did.

The transfer phenomenon that Kotovsky, Hayes, and Simon reported is more interesting from a rational analysis than the noneffect of the hint. It can be interpreted as subjects adjusting the probability of success and estimated cost of types of moves. In particular, they should associate a higher probability of success with subgoaling as a consequence of experience with the first problem. This is something very much in keeping with the causal estimation scheme of the previous chapter but not something that is modeled here.

Are the rational analysis and the memory-load explanations competing hypotheses? The glib answer given to this sort of question throughout the book has been that the mechanistic model is just implementing the prescription of the rational model. This answer certainly applies in the current case. By making means–ends analysis impossible early in a task domain, the memory-load mechanism forces the system to first consider hill climbing, which is usually the better choice.

However, this analysis hides an issue about rationality. By not initially automating the search operators, the memory-load mechanism is not only putting a rational ordering on hill climbing versus means–ends analysis; it is also avoiding an initial cost in creating automated means–ends rules. The rational model has not factored in creation costs for rules, but it certainly seems like something the mind should do if it were operating optimally. The final section on implementation returns to this issue of creation costs for problem-solving rules.

INSTANTIATION OF INDEFINITE OBJECTS

As was noted in chapter 4, causal links will often involve objects that occur in just the cause or the effect. For instance, if we infer the causal rule "When the switch is flipped, the light comes on: *switch* only occurs in the cause, and *light* only occurs in the effect. When we try to generalize such links, we create predictions about indefinite objects. For instance, when we flip a new switch, we may not know which light will come on. In problem-solving cases where we reason from desired effect to necessary cause, indefinite objects can occur in our prescription of the cause (e.g., we are looking for some switch). This creates a serious obstacle to achieving the goal. If I want to get a new light to turn on, I need to know which switch to flip, not just that some switch must be flipped.

A somewhat better situation is when we have induced a relational link binding the indefinite object in the cause to something in the effect. Thus, if we observe that the switch is found on the lamp that holds the light, we are in a better position to select the correct switch in a future situation—it must satisfy the relation "attached to the lamp." Again, the analysis from the previous chapter can be called on to assign a confidence to this generalization.

The most interesting case is when there is no object available to satisfy the indefinite object. Then, we have the option of subgoaling the creation of such an object. Thus, if I am trying to use an example of creating an arrow, and I have no feathers for the shaft, I can create the subgoal of obtaining the feathers. Such subgoaling is very common in creation of artifacts in modern society, which can require that we obtain screws, hammers, batteries, and so on. It is also very characteristic of problem solving in a domain that I have studied quite extensively: computer programming. A typical problem might be to write a program that calculates the factorial of n (i.e., the product of all the digits from 1 to n). Part of that program may require specifying the factorial when $n = 0$. This creates the subgoal of finding the factorial of 0.

I have not done a detailed rational analysis of this kind of problem-solving situation, let alone any experimental comparisons. However, such problem solving can be analyzed as a special case of means–ends analysis where creation of the indefinite object is the precondition on making the problem-solving move. Its probability of success and cost can be measured from the difference between the current state and the goal state of having such an object.

CONCLUSIONS ON RATIONAL ANALYSIS OF PROBLEM SOLVING

The basic goal of this chapter has been to sketch a rational framework within which to understand problem solving. An effort has been made to look at a wide variety of problem-solving activities and indicate how they are to be understood. Sometimes, the discussions were quite general. In other cases, assumptions were quite arbitrary and were made in order to show that the analysis could be pushed through. With respect to Figs. 5-7 through 5-10 and the Tower of Hanoi task, these analyses were brought all the way to experimental predictions. Thus, there are not problems of incompleteness or inconsistency hiding in the mathematical discussions.

The empirical evidence for the rational analysis of problem solving is much weaker than in the case of the domains analyzed in previous chapters. This is more a comment on the state of the literature on problem solving than on the theory. There is essentially no literature that deals with problem solving that involves uncertainty, real costs and gains, and complex problem-solving structure. There are the decision-making tasks that involve uncertainty and real costs and gains. Unfortunately, they focus on simple one-step problems. There are the problem-solving tasks that have a complex combinatorial structure but involve steps whose outcome is certain with unclear costs and gains. The model developed in this chapter applies to these two types of tasks in a rather degenerate way.

In the case of decision making, the issue of managing search does not arise. The issue is how gradations in subjects' choice behaviors vary with gradations in the choice sets. In contrast, the problem-solving literature tends to treat the subject as totally deterministic, making all-or-none choices. There is no way to conceptualize the fact that subjects make different choices except to put a random function in the simulation. As a consequence, the typical problem-solving theories (including previous theories of my own) have great difficulty dealing with the statistics of group behavior and are content to simulate single subjects. They choose unimportant tasks with deterministic structure, like Tower of Hanoi, because this is all they can deal with.

I contend, however, that most everyday problem solving has a structure that is more complex than that studied in either the decision-making or problem-solving literature. A paradigm example is route finding, where the maze of potential paths creates a very concrete search space, where the uncertainties of passage cause real variability, and where time and money mean real costs. Presumably, it should not be hard to study such tasks in the laboratory. People's behavior in such tasks would justify the complexities of the problem-solving theory introduced in this chapter. The Appendix to this chapter presents an analysis of such an everyday problem-solving task.

IMPLEMENTATION IN ACT

The problem-solving steps that have been the focus of analysis in this chapter map onto production rules in an ACT architecture. Let us consider a simple production rule that might implement the hill climbing strategy for Tower of Hanoi:

IF the goal involves getting disk 1 to peg A,
    and disk 1 is on top of peg B,
    and there is no disk smaller than disk 1 on peg A,
THEN move disk 1 to peg A.

The first question to ask is "When is such a production rule created?". The implication of the rational analysis seems to be that this rule is created immediately upon receipt of the task instructions. However, there is good data from latency and other analyses that such rules are not created immediately upon instruction but are learned in the process of problem solving (Anderson, Conrad, & Corbett, in press; Kotovsky, Hayes, & Simon, 1985).

Singley and Anderson (1989), in their analysis of transfer, have argued that the knowledge underlying such a rule is first encoded in declarative form and converted to procedural form only when used. For instance, ˙⸗ (1988) has shown that subjects could be trained to be excellent ˙ ⸗ ISP code without this transferring to other uses of LISP ⁄neration or code debugging; for similar data, see McKen- ⁄n, 1987). This is interpreted as subjects creating productions to embody the knowledge for one problem-solving task (e.g., evaluation) that are separate from productions for another problem-solving task (e.g., generation).

This can be viewed as rational behavior of the system's part if there is a real cost associated with creating such a production rule. If there were, there would be no point to creating such rules until there was evidence that they would be needed. Such a creation cost was not part of the theory of memory, which only assumed a search cost.

Production rules, presumably, also have a search cost, and they should be ordered such that the most likely is the first to be tried. This is what production strength does in the ACT system.

Conflict Resolution

A major issue in any production system implementation is specifying the rules of conflict resolution. There are many competing production rules in the system, and the issue becomes one of determining which production rule is actually going to fire. The rational analysis in this chapter provided us with fairly direct guidance as to how to design such a conflict-resolution scheme. According to the analysis, the relevant factors are:

1. The probability that the production rule will produce its intended effect. This is p_i in the analysis.
2. The cost of executing that rule. This is a_i in the analysis.
3. The difference, d_i, between the resulting state and the goal state.
4. The amount of effort, E, spent so far.
5. A satisficing level, w.
6. A value of the goal, G.

Although working out the computational details is undoubtedly a major research project, I think this could be achieved in something very much like the ACT* conflict-resolution scheme. In the ACT* system, productions compete among themselves to determine who gets to match to goal elements and other data elements. This competition is implemented by activation-based computations. Activation from the data elements is divided up among production rules, and inhibitory links cause the production system to relax into a state in which one production takes all the activation. The winning production is determined both by the production's strength and by the amount of activation that comes from the data elements it matched.

Factors 1-3 in the preceding list could be mapped into a measure of production strength. The value of the goal (Factor 6) could be mapped onto the level of activation of the goal element. Factors 4 and 5 could be mapped onto how slowly the system relaxed to identify a winning production.

APPENDIX:
PROBLEM SOLVING AND CLOTHESLINES

An important personal event in the development of this theory occurred one day while I was living in Mary Luszcz's house in Adelaide. The clothesline in the backyard broke, and I tried to fix it. It just so happened that this was at a time when I was trying to draft a problem-solving chapter for this book. After fixing the clothesline and getting to my office, it suddenly struck me that solving the clothesline problem had nothing to do with the problem solving that I was writing about. It seemed that everyday problem solving, which is presumably what we are adapted for, does not at all fit the received conception of problem solving in cognitive science. I struggled for a long time, trying to characterize to myself how it is different, and, truth be told, I am still struggling with this problem. I swore to myself that I would not publish this book until I was able to apply the theory to the clothesline problem-solving episode. Because it is so highly personal and the data collection is anything but rigorous, I have confined its discussion to an appendix so readers can ignore it if they are offended by such things; however, I still think it is a very important protocol to be able to capture.

The Clothesline Scenario

The basic facts were as follows:

1. There were four lines to the clothesline. They were attached to the house at one end and to a bar supported by a pole on the other end. The pole and bar made basically a T configuration.
2. One of the lines had previously broken. When I came upon the broken clothesline, the crossbar was dangling from the pole rather loosely, and the clothes on the line were on the ground because one end of the bar was near the ground. I considered calling a handyman whom we had been using but decided to try fixing it myself first because the handyman would be somewhat expensive.
3. My first assumption was that the bar must be screwed to the pole and that the screw had come loose or had broken.
4. I decided to find the screwing mechanism and try to rescrew it. Unfortunately, no such mechanism was to be found.
5. Looking at where the bar and the pole met, it seemed to me that the bar must clamp onto the pole in some way.
6. I removed the clothes from the line so I could more easily lift the bar, and I spent some amount of time trying to force the bar into a clamped position. It was physically exhausting and unsuccessful.

7. I noticed that a second line was broken and that both of the broken lines were on the same side of the bar. This led to the conjecture that the bar was held in place by having clotheslines pull on both sides of the bar in a balancing action just like guy lines hold a pole in position. The problem was that there were no functioning lines on one side of the bar.

8. I set as my goal to make at least one of the lines functional. I thought about going to a local store to buy some line, but I decided to try to retie it.

9. Unfortunately, I found out that the two ends of the snapped line were not long enough to be retied.

10. I looked at where the line was tied to the house and noticed that there was some excess line. I decided to try to untie the line and retie it with more line available.

11. I tried to untie the line. It was a wire, and it was sufficiently unpliable that I was not able to unbend it.

12. I decided to get a pair of pliers in order to unbend the line and found one where Mary kept her tools.

13. With the aid of the pliers, I undid where the line was attached to the house.

14. I decided to tie the two ends of the line together first, so I would know how much slack to give myself. I accomplished that with the aid of the pliers that I had retrieved for the other purpose.

15. I decided to put the bar back on the pole so that when I tied it to the house there would be enough tension on the bar to keep it in place.

16. I then pulled the line tightly through the hook where it attached to the house and tied it again, using the pliers I had with me.

17. I hung the clothes back on the line.

Contrasts with the Received Model of Problem Solving

There are a number of features that this episode has in common with the received conception of problem solving (i.e., Newell & Simon, 1972):

1. I was clearly applying operators in the standard problem-solving sense to produce changes in the state of the world.
2. I was responding to relatively well-defined goals.
3. I was engaged in search.
4. I was setting subgoals in a means–end spirit.

The differences, however seem more striking:

1. There is no real sense of a problem space (specification of a set of possible states and operators) in which I was searching. It was not part of

my initial conception that pole balancing was a possible operator or unpliable wire was a possible state.

2. In no sense are there any states of the world being represented internally. The state of the world is held externally. What I am doing mentally is evaluating the **changes** various operators would make in the world.

3. At no point in time is it apparent what my set of operators are. They are whatever steps occur to me at the moment. They are determined by whatever cues the current situation provides me for access of long-term memory.

4. The search is taking place externally. I am not imagining various sequences of problem states; I am experiencing the sequence.

5. I am not stacking subgoals. When I achieve a subgoal, what I do next is controlled by the environment. Thus, when I started to untie the line, I did not intend to balance the bar next. When I took the clothes off the line, I had no intention of putting them back.

6. I have no strong assumption that my operators will succeed. I was not greatly surprised when I could not untie the line by hand, although I had not anticipated this difficulty.

7. I was considering cost of operators. I chose not to call a repair person. I chose to try to retie the snapped line rather than to just buy another. In the first case, I was concerned about financial cost. In the second case, I was worried about time.

Simulation of the Clothesline Scenario

Now the challenge becomes whether I can reproduce this sequence of problem-solving steps in the simulation I have developed for modeling the various experiments in this chapter. That simulation requires a model of the availability of various problem-solving steps and what their anticipated outcomes are. It then applies its satisficing logic to select problem-solving steps. In the simulation in the chapter, a formal model was developed of the steps and their outcomes in domains like Tower of Hanoi. Given the rather unbounded character of this task, I simply provided it with the possible steps and left the simulation task of choosing the problem-solving step. As is the case in any attempt to assume operators to simulate the problem-solving protocol of a single subject, it is always possible to reproduce the protocol. The critical issue becomes the plausibility of that reproduction. If plausible, we feel we have real insight into the problem-solving episode. Stronger experimental tests require that we formally model step availability and apply it to group data, which is why situations like Tower of Hanoi are better, experimentally.

Table 5-5 provides the protocol of the model solving this problem. It

TABLE 5-5

Protocol of Model Solving Clothesline Problem
(The Input to the Simulation Is in Bold)

The value of the goal FIXED-CLOTHESLINE is 20.
The current state is BROKEN-CLOTHESLINE.
Does BROKEN-CLOTHESLINE satisfy FIXED-CLOTHESLINE?
Respond t or nil. **nil**

What move comes to mind? **use-a-repair-man**
What is its cost? **12**
What is its probability of success? **.95**
What is the difference from the goal if you succeed? **.01**
The probability of USE-A-REPAIR-MAN is 0.948, and its effort is 12.529, and its value is 6.431.

What move comes to mind? **look-around**
What is its cost? **.2**
What is its probability of success? **.5**
What is the difference from the goal if you succeed? **2**
The probability of LOOK-AROUND is 0.499, and its effort is 1,591, and its value is 8.390.

What move comes to mind? **screw-the-bar-to-the-pole**
What is its cost? **1**
What is its probability of success? **.8**
What is the difference from the goal if you succeed? **.01**
The probability of SCREW-THE-BAR-TO-THE-POLE is 0.864, and its effort is 1.529, and its value is 15.767.

What move comes to mind? **nil**

I have decided to try action SCREW-THE-BAR-TO-THE-POLE. What happened? **There-was-no-screw**

The current state is THERE-WAS-NO-SCREW.
Does THERE-WAS-NO-SCREW satisfy FIXED-CLOTHESLINE?
Respond t or nil. **nil**

What move comes to mind? **use-a-repair-man**
What is its cost? **12**
What is its probability of success? **.95**
What is the difference from the goal if you succeed? **.01**
The probability of USE-A-REPAIR-MAN is 0.950, and its effort is 12.457, and its value is 6.557.

What move comes to mind? **(goal clamp-the-bar-to-the-pole)**
What is its cost? **2**
What is its probability of success? **.7**
What is the difference from the goal if you succeed? **.01**
The probability of (GOAL CLAMP-THE-BAR-TO-THE-POLE) is 0.803, and its effort is 2.457, and its value is 13.613.

TABLE 5-5 *(continued)*

What move comes to mind? **look-around**
What is its cost? **.2**
What is its probability of success? **.5**
What is the difference from the goal if you succeed? **2**
The probability of LOOK-AROUND is 0.481, and its effort is 1.574, and its value is 8.045.

What move comes to mind? **nil**

subgoal CLAMP-THE-BAR-TO-THE-POLE

The value of the goal CLAMP-THE-BAR-TO-THE-POLE is 13.613.
The current state is THERE-WAS-NO-SCREW.
Does THERE-WAS-NO-SCREW satisfy CLAMP-THE-BAR-TO-THE-POLE?
Respond t or nil. **nil**

What move comes to mind? **try-clamping-it**
What is its cost? **3**
What is its probability of success? **.5**
What is the difference from the goal if you succeed? **.01**
The probability of TRY-CLAMPING-IT is 0.648, and its effort is 3.529, and its value is
  5.300.

What move comes to mind? **get-clothes-off-the-line**
What is its cost? **.5**
What is its probability of success? **.95**
What is the difference from the goal if you succeed? **1.5**
The probability of GET-THE-CLOTHES-OFF-THE-LINE is 0.791, and its effort is 1.760,
  and its value is 9.017.

What move comes to mind? **nil**

I have decided to try action GET-CLOTHES-OFF-THE-LINE. What happened? **Clothes-
are-off-the-line**

The current state is CLOTHES-ARE-OFF-THE-LINE.
The value of the goal CLAMP-THE-BAR-TO-THE-POLE is 13.613.
Does CLOTHES-ARE-OFF-THE-LINE satisfy CLAMP-THE-BAR-TO-THE-POLE?
Respond t or nil. **nil**

What move comes to mind? **try-clamping-it**
What is its cost? **1.5**
What is its probability os success? **.7**
What is the difference from the goal if you succeed? **.01**
The probability of TRY-CLAMPING-IT is 0.803, and its effort is 1.957, and its value is
  8.981.

What move comes to mind? **nil**

I have decided to try action TRY-CLAMPING-IT. What happened?
It-would-not-seem-to-clamp

236

TABLE 5-5 *(continued)*

The current state is IT-WOULD-NOT-SEEM-TO-CLAMP.
Does IT-WOULD-NOT-SEEM-TO-CLAMP satisfy CLAMP-THE-BAR-TO-THE-POLE?
Respond t or nil. **nil**

What move comes to mind? **nil**

I quit the subgoal.

The value of the goal FIXED-CLOTHESLINE is 20.
The current state is IT-WOULD-NOT-SEEM-TO-CLAMP.
Does IT-WOULD-NOT-SEEM-TO-CLAMP satisfy FIXED-CLOTHESLINE?
Respond t or nil.**nil**

What move comes to mind? **look-around**
What is its cost? **.2**
What is its probability of success? **.5**
What is the difference from the goal if you succeed? **2**
The probability of LOOK-AROUND is 0.444, and its effort is 1.540, and its value is
7.357.

What move comes to mind? **use-a-repair-man**
What is its cost? **12**
What is its probability of success? **.95**
What is the difference from the goal if you succeed? **.01**
The probability of USE-A-REPAIR-MAN is 0.956, and its effort is 12.314, and its value is
6.809.

What move comes to mind? **nil**

I have decided to try action LOOK-AROUND. What happened? **There-are-two-snapped-lines-on-one-side**

The current state is THERE-ARE-TWO-SNAPPED-LINES-ON-ONE-SIDE.
Does THERE-ARE-TWO-SNAPPED-LINES-ON-ONE-SIDE satisfy
FIXED-CLOTHESLINE?
Respond t or nil. **nil**

What move comes to mind? **(goal balance-the-bar-against-the-pole)**
What is its cost? **2**
What is its probability of success? **.7**
What is the difference from the goal if you succeed? **.01**
The probability of (GOAL BALANCE-THE-BAR-AGAINST-THE-POLE) is 0.810, and its
effort is 2.242, and its value is 13.966.

What move comes to mind? **use-a-repair-man**
What is its cost? **12**
What is its probability of success? **.95**
What is the difference from the goal if you succeed? **.01**
The probability of USE-A-REPAIR-MAN is 0.958, and its effort is 12.242, and its value is
6.935

TABLE 5-5 *(continued)*

What move comes to mind? **nil**

subgoal BALANCE-THE-BAR-AGAINST-THE-POLE

The value of the goal BALANCE-THE-BAR-AGAINST-THE-POLE is 13.966.
The current state is THERE-ARE-TWO-SNAPPED-LINES-ON-ONE-SIDE.
Does THERE-ARE-TWO-SNAPPED-LINES-ON-ONE-SIDE satisfy
  BALANCE-THE-BAR-AGAINST-THE-POLE?
Respond t or nil. **nil**

What move comes to mind? **(goal replace-one-line)**
What is its cost? **1**
What is its probability of success? **.9**
What is the difference from the goal if you succeed? **1**
The probability of (GOAL REPLACE-ONE-LINE) is 0.826, and its effort is 2.107, and its value is 9.430.

What move comes to mind? **nil**

subgoal REPLACE-ONE-LINE

The value of the goal REPLACE-ONE-LINE is 9.430.
The current state is THERE-ARE-TWO-SNAPPED-LINES-ON-ONE-SIDE.
Does THERE-ARE-TWO-SNAPPED-LINES-ON-ONE-SIDE satisfy
  REPLACE-ONE-LINE?
Respond t or nil. **nil**

What move comes to mind? **buy-some-line**
What is its cost? **2**
What is its probability of success? **.9**
What is the difference from the goal if you succeed? **.5**
The probability of BUY-SOME-LINE is 0.875, and its effort is 2.915, and its value is 5.342.

What move comes to mind? **(goal tie-line-back)**
What is its cost? **.8**
What is its probability of success? **.8**
What is the difference from the goal if you succeed? **.5**
The probability of (GOAL TIE-LINE-BACK) is 0.821, and its effort is 1.715, and its value is 6.032.

What move comes to mind? **nil**

subgoal TIE-LINE-BACK

The value of the goal TIE-LINE-BACK is 6.032
The current state is THERE-ARE-TWO-SNAPPED-LINES-ON-ONE-SIDE.
Does THERE-ARE-TWO-SNAPPED-LINES-ON-ONE-SIDE satisfy TIE-LINE-BACK?
Respond t or nil. **nil**

TABLE 5-5 *(continued)*

What move comes to mind? **tie-the-line**
What is its cost? **.5**
What is its probability of success? **.7**
What is the difference from the goal if you succeed? **.01**
The probability of TIE-THE-LINE is 0.801, and its effort is 1.029, and its value is 3.803.

What move comes to mind? **nil**

I have deciced to try action TIE-THE-LINE. What happened?
  The-line-was-not-long-enough

The current state is THE-LINE-WAS-NOT-LONG-ENOUGH.
Does THE-LINE-WAS-NOT-LONG-ENOUGH satisfy TIE-LINE-BACK?
Respond t or nil. **nil**

What move comes to mind? **(goal lengthen-the-line)**
What is its cost? **1**
What is its probability of success? **.7**
What is the difference from the goal if you succeed? **.8**
The probability of (GOAL LENGTHEN-THE-LINE) is 0.725, and its effort is 2.008, and its value is 2.371.

What move comes to mind? **nil**
subgoal LENGTHEN-THE-LINE

The value of the goal LENGTHEN-THE-LINE is 2.371.
The current state is THE-LINE-WAS-NOT-LONG-ENOUGH.
Does THE-LINE-WAS-NOT-LONG-ENOUGH satisfy LENGTHEN-THE-LINE?
Respond t or nil. **nil**

What move comes to mind? **untie the-line-at-the-house**
What is its cost? **.5**
What is its probability of success? **.8**
What is the difference from the goal if you succeed? **.5**
The probability of UNTIE-THE-LINE-AT-THE-HOUSE is 0.821, and its effort is 1.415, and its value is 0.532.

What move comes to mind? **nil**

I have decided to try action UNTIE-THE-LINE-AT-THE-HOUSE. What happened?
  The-line-was-not-pliable-enough

The current state is THE-LINE-WAS-NOT-PLIABLE-ENOUGH.
Does THE-LINE-WAS-NOT-PLIABLE-ENOUGH satisfy LENGTHEN-THE-LINE?
Respond t or nil. **nil**

What move comes to mind? **(goal get-some-pliers)**
What is its cost? **.2**
What is its probability of success? **.9**
What is the difference from the goal if you succeed? **.5**
The probability of (GOAL GET-SOME-PLIERS) is 0.868, and its effort is 1.091, and its value is 0.969.

TABLE 5-5 *(continued)*

What move comes to mind? **untie-the-line-by-hand**
What is its cost? **1**
What is its probability of success? **.3**
What is the difference from the goal if you succeed? **.01**
The probability of UNTIE-THE-LINE-BY-HAND is 0.450, and its effort is 1.457, and its value is −0.390.

What move comes to mind? **nil**
subgoal GET-SOME-PLIERS

The value of the goal GET-SOME-PLIERS is 0.969.
The current state is THE-LINE-WAS-NOT-PLIABLE-ENOUGH
Does THE-LINE-WAS-NOT-PLIABLE-ENOUGH satisfy GET-SOME-PLIERS?
Respond t or nil. **nil**

What move comes to mind? **buy-a-plier**
What is its cost? **2**
What is its probability of success? **.95**
What is the difference from the goal if you succeed? **.01**
The probability of BUY-A-PLIER is 0.948, and its effort is 2.529, and its value is −1.610.

What move comes to mind? **go-to-the-tools**
What is its cost? **.1**
What is its probability of success? **.99**
What is the difference from the goal if you succeed? **.2**
The probability of GO-TO-THE-TOOLS is 0.949, and its effort is 0.779, and its value is 0.140.

What move comes to mind? **nil**

I have decided to try action GO-TO-THE-TOOLS. What happened? **At-the-tools**

The current state is AT-THE-TOOLS
Does AT-THE-TOOLS satisfy GET-SOME-PLIERS?
Respond t or nil. **nil**

What move comes to mind? **search-for-the-pliers**
What is its cost? **.2**
What is its probability of success? **.9**
What is the difference from the goal if you succeed? **.01**
The probability of SEARCH-FOR-THE-PLIERS is 0.924, and its effort is 0.657, and its value is 0.238.

What move comes to mind? **nil**

I have deciced to try action SEARCH-FOR-THE-PLIERS. What happened? **The-pliers-are-found**

The current state is THE-PLIERS-ARE-FOUND.
Does THE-PLIERS-ARE-FOUND satisfy GET-SOME-PLIERS?
Respond t or nil. **t**
I succeed at the subgoal

TABLE 5-5 (continued)

The value of the goal LENGTHEN-THE-LINE is 2.371
The current state is THE-PLIERS-ARE-FOUND.
Does THE-PLIERS-ARE-FOUND satisfy LENGTHEN-THE-LINE?
Respond t or nil. **nil**

What move comes to mind? **untie-the-line-with-pliers**
What is its cost? **.5**
What is its probability of success? **.8**
What is the difference from the goal if you succeed? **.5**
The probability of UNTIE-THE-LINE-WITH-PLIERS is 0.802, and its effort is 1.341, and its value is 0.562.

What move comes to mind? **untie-the-line-by-hand**
What is its cost? **1.0**
What is its probability of success? **.3**
What is the difference from the goal if you succeed? **.5**
The probability of UNTIE-THE-LINE-BY-HAND is 0.416, and its effort is 1.841, and its value is −0.853.

What move comes to mind? **nil**

I have decided to try action UNTIE-THE-LINE-WITH-PLIERS. What happened?
The-line-is-untied

The current state is THE-LINE-IS-UNTIED.
Does THE-LINE-IS-UNTIED satisfy LENGTHEN-THE-LINE?
Respond t or nil. **nil**

What move comes to mind? **tie-the-line-by-hand**
What is its cost? **1**
What is its probability of success? **.5**
What is the difference from the goal if you succeed? **.01**
The probability of TIE-THE-LINE-BY-HAND is 0.656, and its effort is 1.242, and its value is 0.313.

What move comes to mind? **tie-the-line-with-the-pliers**
What is its cost? **.5**
What is its probability of success? **.8**
What is the difference from the goal if you succeed? **.01**
The probability of TIE-THE-LINE-WITH-THE-PLIERS is 0.874, and its effort is 0.742, and its value is 1.331.

What move comes to mind? **nil**

I have decided to try action TIE-THE-LINE-WITH-THE-PLIERS. What happened? **The-line-is-tied-together**

The current state is THE-LINE-IS-TIED-TOGETHER.
Does THE-LINE-IS-TIED-TOGETHER satisfy LENGTHEN-THE-LINE?
Respond t or nil. **t**
I succeed at the subgoal.

241

TABLE 5-5 *(continued)*

The value of the goal TIE-LINE-BACK is 6.032
The current state is THE-LINE-IS-TIED-TOGETHER.
Does THE-LINE-IS-TIED-TOGETHER satisfy TIE-LINE-BACK?
Respond t or nil. **t**
I succeed at the subgoal.

The value of the goal REPLACE-ONE-LINE is 9.430.
The current state is THE-LINE-IS-TIED-TOGETHER.
Does THE-LINE-IS-TIED-TOGETHER satisfy REPLACE-ONE-LINE?
Respond t or nil. **nil**

What move comes to mind? **put-the-bar-back**
What is its cost? **.8**
What is its probability of success? **.7**
What is the difference from the goal if you succeed? **.8**
The probability of PUT-THE-BAR-BACK is 0.670, and its effort is 1.708, and its value is 4.614.

What move comes to mind? **tie-the-line-at-the-house**
What is its cost? **.5**
What is its probability of success? **.8**
What is the difference from the goal if you succeed? **2.0**
The probability of TIE-THE-LINE-AT-THE-HOUSE is 0.513, and its effort is 1.798, and its value is 3.040.

What move comes to mind? **nil**

I have decided to try action PUT-THE-BAR-BACK. What happened? **The-bar-is-back-on-the-pole.**

The current state is THE-BAR-IS-BACK-ON-THE-POLE.
Does THE-BAR-IS-BACK-ON-THE-POLE satisfy REPLACE-ONE-LINE?
Respond t or nil. **nil**

What move comes to mind? **tie-the-line-at-the-house**
What is its cost? **.8**
What is its probability of success? **.7**
What is the difference from the goal if you succeed? **.01**
The probability of TIE-THE-LINE-AT-THE-HOUSE is 0.810, and its effort is 0.958, and its value is 6.685.

What move comes to mind? **nil**

I have decided to try action TIE-THE-LINE-AT-THE-HOUSE. What happened? **The-line-is-tied-at-the-house.**

The current state is THE-LINE-IS-TIED-AT-THE-HOUSE.
Does THE-LINE-IS-TIED-AT-THE-HOUSE satisfy REPLACE-ONE-LINE?
Respond t or nil. **t**
I succeed at the subgoal.

The value of the goal BALANCE-THE-BAR-AGAINST-THE-POLE is 13.966.
The current state is THE-LINE-IS-TIED-AT-THE-HOUSE.

TABLE 5-5 *(continued)*

Does THE-LINE-IS-TIED-AT-THE-HOUSE satisfy BALANCE-THE-BAR-AGAINST-
THE-POLE?
Respond t or nil. **t**
I succeed at the subgoal

The value of the goal FIXED-CLOTHESLINE is 20.
The current state is THE-LINE-IS-TIED-AT-THE-HOUSE.
Does THE-LINE-IS-TIED-AT-THE-HOUSE satisfy FIXED-CLOTHESLINE?
Respond t or nil. **nil**

What move comes to mind? **put-the-clothes-back-on-the-line**
What is its cost? **.5**
What is its probability of success? **.99**
What is the difference from the goal if you succeed? **.01**
The probability of PUT-THE-CLOTHES-BACK-ON-THE-LINE is 0.968, and its effort is
0.635, and its value is 18.742.

What move comes to mind? **nil**

I have decided to try action PUT-THE-CLOTHES-BACK-ON-THE-LINE. What
happened? **The-clothes-are-back-on-the-line**

The current state is THE-CLOTHES-ARE-BACK-ON-THE-LINE.
The value of the goal FIXED-CLOTHESLINE is 20.
Does THE-CLOTHES-ARE-BACK-ON-THE-LINE satisfy FIXED-CLOTHESLINE?
Respond t or nil. **t**
I succeed at the goal.

---

starts with the goal of fixing the clothesline worth 20 of its internal value
points. I provide it with various moves, their expected cost (the a_j), their
expected probability of success (the p_j), and the anticipated difference
between their results and the goal (the D_j). The goal units, effort units, and
difference units are somewhat arbitrary, but the reader can keep in mind
that the significance of 1 unit on any of these three dimensions is roughly
equal to the significance of 1 unit on any other. What the program does is
estimate probability of eventual success if the plan involving the move is
adopted (the P_j); total cost, including move cost (the C_j); and the net worth
of that plan ($P_j G - C_j$). It chooses the best plan and tries it. This can either
involve setting a subgoal or taking an action. If it takes an action, I inform
it of the resulting state. I also inform it when a state satisfies a goal.

As can be seen, the program is sorting among alternatives according to an
economic logic and subgoaling. It matches my protocol and does so, I
think, in a reasonable way. Many of the unitary actions reported here are
better thought of as a set of actions organized under a subgoal. However,
as I no longer have memory of such details and this simulation is too long
already, I just summarized these with single actions.

In summary, we have a weak sort of existence proof that the theory in this
chapter can extend to a case of "real-world" problem solving.

6 Retrospective

Contents
Preliminaries 244
Twelve Questions About Rational Analysis 246
  1. Satisfactory Versus Optimal Solutions 246
  2. The Empirical Status of the Principle of Rationality 248
  3. Satisficing and Bounded Rationality 249
  4. Demonstrations of Human Irrationality 250
  5. Computational Requirements of the Rational Analysis 251
  6. Learning and Optimization 251
  7. Unified Theories of Cognition 252
  8. Other Cognitive Abilities 252
  9. Relationship to ACT* 253
  10. Individual Differences 254
  11. Role of Experimentation 255
  12. Implications for Practice 256

PRELIMINARIES

The preceding chapters applied a rational analysis to a large number of phenomena in cognitive psychology. Each chapter has taken an aspect of cognition and showed that it reflected an optimal performance, in a Bayesian sense, in an uncertain environment. Rational analysis, as practiced in this book, involves three kinds of assumptions: assumptions about the goals of a certain aspect of human cognition, assumptions about the structure of the environment relevant to achieving these goals, and assumptions about costs. Optimal behavior can be predicted by assuming that the system maximizes its goals while it minimizes its costs.

Table 6-1 provides a summary of the rational analysis for the four aspects of cognition covered in this book. The table states the assumptions about the goal, the structure of the environment, and the cost. In the case of memory, the goal was to get access to needed experiences from the past (my standard example is finding where I parked the car in the airport parking lot); the structure of the environment was based on observations of how need for information tends to repeat itself in information-retrieval systems;

244

TABLE 6-1
Summary of Rational Analyses in Chapters 2-5

	Memory	*Categorization*	*Casual Analysis*	*Problem Solving*
Goal	Get access to needed experiences from past	Predict features of new objects	Predict future events	Achieve certain states in external world
Structure of the Environment	Patterns by which need for information repeats	How features cluster together	Statistical models of causal structure	How problems vary in difficulty, how similarity to goal is related to distance goal
Cost	Retrieving a memory	Hypothesis formation	Hypothesis formation	External effort, internal effort to generate plans

and the simple cost function was that it cost something to retrieve a memory. In the case of categorization, the goal was to predict new features of an object (my favorite example is predicting whether the creature approaching me is dangerous); the relevant structure of the environment was described by a set of assumptions based on how the genetic phenomenon of species produces a disjoint partitioning of natural objects; and the one cost was hypothesis formation. In the case of causal inference, the goal was to predict future events (my favorite example is whether my back will ache after jogging); the relevant structure is described by general statistical models justified by current scientific understanding; and the one cost was, again, hypothesis formation. In the case of problem solving, the goal was to achieve certain external states of affair (my favorite example is repairing a clothesline); the relevant structure concerns assumptions about distributions of problems in terms of their difficulty and assumptions about the relationship between similarity of the current state to the goal and distance to the goal; and the costs were both external effort and internal effort in generating various problem-solving plans.

In each case, the explanation of human behavior was to be found in the assumptions about the environment and not the conjectured structure of the mind. These chapters do not constitute final and definitive proof of the value of a rational approach; nonetheless, they make the case that it is worth looking outside of the head as well as inside the head in trying to understand cognition. What is at issue here is more than the platitude that the environment is important; rather, it is the possibility that the mind might be optimized to the environment in a specific sense which, if true, enables us to approach cognition with a powerful set of analytic tools.

How could it be that I have found so much evidence for rationality in these fields when the received wisdom was irrationality? Naturally, I choose to blame the received wisdom. In each case, this received wisdom rests on what are, when they are exposed, bizarre assumptions about the situation facing human cognition. There are many such assumptions that can be exposed, but one stands out in each domain, and they bear repeating here: Human memory appears optimal when we let go of the idea that memory evolved to deliver optimal performance in laboratory experiments and view it rather as trying to optimize information retrieval in a much more complex environment. Categorization appears optimal if we view its goal not as inducing categories that correspond to linguistic labeling conventions but rather as trying to maximize accuracy of predictions about objects. Causal inference appears optimal when we abandon the assumption that it uses priors about the world whose only virtue is their parsimony and, rather, assume that the priors reflect the way the world actually is. Problem solving appears optimal if we recognize that people normally do not solve problems in bounded situations of certain information. Essentially, what has happened in each case is that the received wisdom has made the fallacy of assuming the laboratory task represented the real world. Laboratory experiments are fine for telling us how the mind works; they are not fine for telling us what the world is like. It is obvious when said, but so easy to ignore.

The real strength of this book lies in the detailed analysis of the previous four chapters and how far these were able to go in explaining behavior; the real weakness lies in the fact that these analyses did not go even further. However, I have been urged to end with some general discussion of rational analysis and, as this chapter gives witness, I have gone along with these urgings. In the epilogue to his book, Marr (1982) used a curious but highly informative format. He presented a hypothetical interview between him and a reporter. What is so effective about this is that it gave him an opportunity to say things that just did not fit in with the text exposition but that were critical to expressing his point of view. I did not feel I quite had the license to do this chapter as an interview with a reporter; however, there are some questions that are often asked about a rational analysis that I feel need to be stated in print and answered in print. Therefore, this chapter consists of these questions and their answers.

TWELVE QUESTIONS ABOUT RATIONAL ANALYSIS

1. Satisfactory Versus Optimal Solutions

Rational analysis depends on the assumption that the mind is optimized but, isn't it really the case that evolution produces satisfactory solutions and not optimal solutions?

I have been asked this question many times and really do not understand it. Evolution selects locally optimal variations just in the sense discussed in the first chapter. One sense of "satisfactory" might be "locally optimized." Specifying the computational constraints essentially amounts to defining the locality over which the optimization is defined. It is possible that the real theory will come from these computational constraints and not from the structure of the environment. This was not the case in the work of the prior four chapters, although the analysis of problem solving came closest to this.

A second sense of satisfactory rests on the belief that a species has only to be good enough to fend off other competing species and so preserve its niche. In my limited understanding, this is a fallacy. The real evolutionary pressure comes not from between-species competition but from within-species competition. If one member of the species has some advantage over the rest, it and its offspring will drive out the other members from the niche. It is this competition that guarantees that the species will climb to the local optimum.

A third sense of satisfactory relates it to Simon's sense of satisficing. It is addressed under Question 3 in this section, which is concerned with satisficing.

I raise this point first not so much to refute it as to decry this general type of question. The thesis in this book is not a thesis about evolution; it is a behavioral thesis about human cognition. The thesis is that cognition is optimized to the environment. It would be a shame if the response to this thesis were to degenerate into evolutionary arguments. The appropriate response should be to seek precision about what the environment is, what the constraints on optimization are, and whether behavior is really optimized. Right now we have only one precise predicate to describe the possible relationship between behavior and the environment — "optimal." If "satisfactory" or some other predicate can be defined and shown to be different than "optimal," it becomes an interesting question to explore which, if any, is the accurate predicate.

Of course, the rationality thesis of this book has to have some relation to evolution. It is hard (but not impossible) to conceive why it would be true except for evolutionary reasons. As we discover where human cognition is optimal and where it is not (perhaps "satisfactory" under some precise definition), this will have implications for evolutionary considerations, and evolutionary considerations will help us understand the constraints under which cognition is optimal. However, such considerations are premature. Right now we need to focus on understanding the environment and its relationship to cognition. Once this is understood better, we will be in a position to make connections to evolutionary theory.

2. The Empirical Status of the
Principle of Rationality

Isn't any behavior optimal in some imaginable environment? If so, isn't the rational approach invulnerable from empirical disproof because one can always derive the behavior from some environmental assumptions?
This is **the** criticism of all adaptionist approaches. Simon, in his paper (Simon, in press), commenting on an early report of mine (Anderson, in pressb), made this as his central point. It was already addressed in the introductory chapter but is such a frequent criticism that an answer to it bears repeating. There are three parts to the answer.

First, it is also the case that for any well-specified behavior there is a mechanism (in fact, infinitely many) that is (are) capable of producing the behavior. So, the rational approach is at no disadvantage here. The fact that one is, in principle, guaranteed that environmental or mechanistic theories exist does not mean that it is a trivial intellectual feat to come up with one. However, the mere fact one has produced a set of mechanisms or environmental descriptions from which the behavior can be derived is no guarantee that it has anything to do with what is actually happening. In both cases, one has to consider the plausibility of the mechanistic and environmental assumptions. That is, one either has to seek evidence about whether the brain is the way the mechanistic theory assumes or the environment is the way the rational theory assumes.

Second, although it is not trivial to confirm one's assumptions about the environment, one is in a lot better position because of the externally observable nature of the environment. Converging tests of an environmental theory are much easier than converging tests of a mechanistic theory. That is, it is a lot easier to observe what is out there in the environment than what is in there in the brain. One implication is that it is just as important to fund studies of the information-processing demands imposed by the environment as it is to fund studies of the information-processing characteristics of the brain. This does not sit well at first blush with cognitive psychologists, because physiological psychology is an accepted field, whereas study of the information-processing demands of the environment is not. It is purely a matter of that distrust of what is foreign that gives unfortunate parochial character to all academic fields.[1]

Third, let us consider what would happen if we did our converging test and found out that the environment specified in our theory is not, in some way, the environment that we actually face. The rational theory would still

---

[1]From my point of view, the greatest weakness in this book derives from the paucity of our knowledge about what the environment is really like. This makes such studies especially critical.

be useful in a number of ways. First, the rational characterization of the phenomenon would still be a legitimate and potentially powerful way of describing the behavior, just as is a biologically wrong mechanistic theory that predicts the behavioral phenomena. Second, knowing the environment under which the phenomena would be optimal could be of considerable applied value in doing things like designing educational environments. Third, and perhaps most important, this result could have substantial impact on our understanding of human nature. It might lend support to those who argue that human evolution is largely not an optimizing process. More likely, it might be evidence that there are important constraints on the optimization that we had not anticipated.

A final point should be made about the mechanistic versus rational approaches to understanding human cognition. There is much less doubt that the human cognition is implemented in some mechanistic system (i.e., the brain) than there is that human cognition is optimized. This probably is one reason that people tend to seek mechanistic explanations. However, it also means that discovering a mechanistic explanation has less impact on our prior beliefs than discovering a rational explanation. It would be a truly important discovery if we could say that human cognition (or some aspect of it) was optimal. Thus, seeking a rational explanation is, in a certain sense, a more high-risk, high-gain proposition than seeking a mechanistic explanation. However, the greater guidance that the rational approach offers in hypothesis generation more than compensates for the high risk. It is of little comfort to know that a mechanistic explanation exists if it hides like a needle in a haystack.

3. Satisficing and Bounded Rationality

Herbert Simon has argued that people do not adopt optimal solutions; they only satisfice. This has led to his model of bounded rationality. Doesn't this contradict your theory?

Simon's basic thesis about bounded rationality is that computational limitations and limits on knowledge prevent humans from taking the globally optimal solution. This book has been concerned with deriving locally optimal solutions within the constraints of computational limitations and uncertainty about the environment (represented as diffuse Bayesian prior distributions). In other words, this book can be viewed as an attempt to give bounded rationality a precise implementation rather than a broad programmatic statement. Simon does not see it this way. There are two points of disagreement:

First, he does not think that enough play has been given to computational constraints. It is the goal of this book to get as much as possible out of as weak assumptions about the mind as possible. This does not seem very different from his position in the Sciences of the Artificial (Simon, 1981), where he wrote: "A man, viewed as a behaving system, is quite simple. The apparent complexity of his behavior over time is largely a reflection of the environment in which he finds himself" (p. 65). In the book, Simon argued that one only needs to make assumptions about the rate of encoding information and about short-term memory size to understand much of human behavior. The rational memory model has replaced his two parameters by one — cost of search — but this does not seem like a fundamental difference in emphasis on computational constraints.

Second, Simon thinks that the rational analyses contradict his theory of satisficing (Simon, 1955). His theory holds that the organism does not have enough information or capacity to select the optimal choice. Rather, the organism sets a satisficing criterion and will select whatever first meets that. The chapter on problem solving involves computation of a satisficing threshold based on considerations of uncertainty in alternatives and computational cost. As noted there, this is very much like the ideas started by Stigler (1961) in economics. Simon anticipated this in his 1955 article and is critical of these attempts to produce a precise calculation of a satisficing threshold and seems to prefer to leave the satisficing threshold to be a free parameter that can be set arbitrarily for any situation. He feels that it is unrealistic to assume that people have information about distribution of possible payoffs or can perform the kinds of calculations described in chapter 5. The issue of the calculations is addressed under Question 5 in this section. As for information about the distributions, the brain is a wonderful associator and could easily store from experience what the distribution of payoffs were in the past.

In summary, this book is just an attempt to make more precise what Simon proposed in his theories of bounded rationality and satisficing. If there are differences, they are differences of emphasis.[2]

4. Demonstrations of Human Irrationality

Don't all of the demonstrations of irrationality in human cognition conclusively disprove your theory?
This is another very frequent criticism. It was dealt with at great length in the introductory chapter and elsewhere in the book; however, it is such a frequent criticism that the basic outline of the answer bears repeating here. The criticism reflects a confusion of two senses of rationality. There is the normative sense, as used in philosophy, in which human behavior is matched against some model that is supposed to represent sound reasoning. This is the sense in which human cognition is claimed to be irrational. Then

---

[2]Although he remains adamant that there are fundamental differences.

there is the adaptive sense, as used in economics, in which the behavior is said to be optimized with respect to achieving some evolutionarily relevant goals. These two senses are by no means identical. The first chapter went on at great length to show that commonly cited cases of irrationality in the first sense were not cases in the second sense.

5. Computational Requirements of the Rational Analysis

How can the mind do all the complex mathematics that your analyses imply? People find Bayesian mathematics very nonintuitive.
This remark reflects a fundamental misunderstanding of the enterprise in this book. The mathematics (opinions about its complexity vary) was done to determine what would be optimal under the assumptions described. In no way was the implication intended that the mind was engaged in Bayesian calculation. Each of the four central chapters ended with a consideration of how the mind could perform computations that approximated or realized the optimal ideal. In many cases, it was possible to show that quite plausible, neural-like computations could achieve these prescriptions.
It also needs to be stressed that there is no requirement that the mind exactly match the prescriptions of the rational analysis. Slight deviations from them will be without adaptive consequence. It is also the case that there were approximations and possible imperfections in the models assumed of the environment.[3] Therefore, the derivations may only approximate the true optimum. Thus, the claim was not that the mind had to exactly reproduce the prescriptions of the rational calculations. Rather, the claim was that it should approximate the prescriptions, and the typical empirical observation was that it did, within the accuracy of the available data.

6. Learning and Optimization

Humans, because of their powerful learning systems, will come to behave more or less optimally. If one wants to understand optimization, shouldn't one just study learning processes and not the environment?
Any learning system is optimal in some environments and only in some environments. One cannot speak about the power of a learning system independent of the structure of the environment. A learning system is basically a function that maps past experience onto future behavior. Because any future behavior is optimal in some environment (Question 2), any learning system is optimal in some environment. One often finds

---

[3]The grossest case of this was the wholesale simplifications of the problem-solving situation, depicted in Fig. 5-3, to make the situation analytically tractable.

learning systems preferred if they can induce more complex relationships. However, if those more complex relationships tend not to exist in the environment, then these systems are wasting their time and failing to find the true simple structure by postulating the complex structure. This is an important point that seems not to be appreciated in the literature of neural learning algorithms, machine learning algorithms, formal learning systems, and so on. Thus, considerations of learning do not eliminate the need to understand the environment; rather, they demand an environmental analysis for their justification. Much of what was in this book (particularly chapters 3 and 4) was concerned with laying forth the environmental assumptions that justified a particular learning algorithm.

7. Unified Theories of Cognition

This book offers a set of separate analyses for different aspects of cognition. Unlike a unified system like ACT* or SOAR, there is no discussion of how these things are integrated together. Are you advocating a separate solution to every aspect of cognition?

There is a lot of merit in this criticism. I have been attracted to unified theories of cognition, and I am convinced that any highly modular approach that goes so far as to propose a separate module for mathematics (Chomsky, 1980) has to be wrong. On the other hand, the mind is not simple. It consists of a great variety of components that are brought together to generate performance in any specific task domain like mathematics. It is not beyond belief that there are separate components for memory, categorization, causal inference, and problem solving. I have always disagreed with a SOAR-like approach (Newell, in press) with a single memory and felt that there had to be at least procedural and declarative systems. Maybe there are more.

Still, the issue arises as to how these systems work together. This book does not contain any answers to that question, although it may not be beyond rational analysis to offer some prescriptions for the integration of these aspects of cognition. However, trying to build a unified architecture that incorporates the prescriptions of rational analysis for single components is probably the quicker route to addressing these integration issues. Therefore, I have every intention of following up on the programmatic statements at the end of each chapter about implementation. Such an implementation effort would be the second step of Marr's research program.

8. Other Cognitive Abilities

Are there any cognitive abilities that remain to be addressed?
This depends, in part, on one's definition of cognitive. Issues of

perception have not been addressed here, although David Marr and others have made great progress in the domain of vision using a similar approach. There was a little discussion in the memory chapter and in the problem solving chapter on strategy selection, and that is a topic in need of greater treatment. The obvious major hole concerns language. Certainly more so than in 1983, I am willing to believe that the analysis of language might be different than that of other aspects of human cognition.

Under this topic of different aspects of cognition, it is worth repeating a point from the introductory chapter: We have to be prepared to find that some aspects of cognition lend themselves to a successful rational analysis, and others do not. Thus, there are many other interesting possibilities besides the extreme conclusion that all of cognition is optimized or none of it is.

9. Relationship to ACT*

What is the relationship between this theory and ACT*? Are you abandoning ACT*?

I still believe that ACT* is the best mechanistic model around, although this book and other work have certainly indicated places where it is wanting. As the implementation sections of this book indicated, I hope to be able to produce an update on ACT* in terms of another theory within the general ACT framework for architectural theories. I know I predicted in 1983 that ACT* was the last of the ACT theories, but this just goes to show that theory building is an empirical enterprise, and predictions about it turn out to be not always true. My own initial prediction about the new architecture is that it will not be so much different from ACT* as it will contain embellishments to reflect a broader conception of the problem situations that face humans than I had in 1983.

There is another relationship between the ACT framework and this rational analysis. The ACT framework has not been totally absent from the rational analysis. The rational analysis makes some general assumptions about the way the mind works in order to perform the rational analysis, and these tended to come from the ACT framework, if not the ACT* theory specifically. Thus, the memory analysis assumed a system in which memories were retrieved and tested for appropriateness. The problem-solving theory assumed that the system was focused on solving a particular goal. Categorization and causal inference assumed that objects and situations were held in some working memory and evoked generalizations from the past. These are very general processing assumptions that are not unique to the ACT framework, but it is certainly possible to imagine frameworks where such assumptions do not hold. Thus, certain aspects of the ACT framework served to identify the local domain over which the optimization was taking place. One of the sources of difference between the rational theory of categorization here and Shepard's theory of generalization (Shepard, 1987) turns on implicit architectural assumptions. These differences are not very consequential, but they do produce a rather different flavor to the resulting theory.

10. Individual Differences

What about individual differences? If human behavior is optimized, does this not imply that all people should behave the same, optimal way?
It is not true that adaptive optimization implies uniqueness of solution. There can be different solutions equivalent in their adaptativeness and solutions sufficiently close in adaptiveness not to be selected among. The mere fact of diversity is not a problem for the thesis of this book.

However, diversity of behavior may be a difficulty for the application of the thesis as it was practiced in this book. In every instance, the book tried to predict behavior by deriving a single solution. This is no different than attempts to apply single mechanistic models to human behavior. As in the case of mechanistic models, there are are at least two ways to accommodate diversity in a rational model. The first is to assume that there are different strategies for approaching a problem, and different subjects select differently among these strategies. As noted previously, some tentative stabs at strategy selection were made in this book, but that remains largely a topic for future rational analysis. This may be the most promising answer to the phenomenon of individual differences.

The second approach to individual differences is to assume that the same model applies to all individuals, but different individuals just differ in the the parameters of their models. First, there are two types of parameters in a rational model. There are computational parameters that describe things like cost of memory search. Individuals might differ on these parameters. This would view people as behaving optimally, given their different capabilities. Although this is the most obvious way to incorporate individual differences into a rational analysis, it poses difficulties. How can one argue that there is a force driving us to optimize our use of memories that does not also drive us to the optimal possible value of the memory retrieval parameter? The only possible answer that comes to mind is that there might be some countervailing cost, like metabolic expenditure, associated with faster memory retrieval. However, this takes me into domains about which I am hardly qualified to speculate.[4]

---

[4]Note that this is a problem for any theory of individual differences that claims that there are consequential differences in intellectual performance. If these differences are adaptively

The second sort of parameter in a rational model are those that represent the assumptions about the environment. It is conceivable that people differ in their assumptions about the environment. Their behavior would be optimized to different environments.[5] The case where I have thought most carefully about individual differences is memory and, particularly, the question of why some students show better memory for information in a classroom than do others. The rational model of memory does not predict good memory for classroom information. Rather, it predicts good memory for information to the extent that it is likely to prove useful in the future. The memory system tries to make available information that is likely to be needed. An individual should display poorer memory for classroom information to the extent that that type of information is not needed in the environment. It is interesting, in this regard, to note the criticisms that have been made of the relationship between what is learned in the classroom and real life. (Brown, Collins, & Duguid, 1988; Lave, 1988a, 1988b) It is argued that people naturally learn better in apprentice-like relationships with their instructor. This has led to recommendations to restructure instruction to produce better learning.

11. Role of Experimentation

Rational analysis seems to downplay the role of experimentation, just as traditional economics has downplayed experimentation. This book has largely been an exercise in postdicting. You have taken existing results and shown how a rational analysis can explain them. Isn't your attitude that experimentation is unnecessary because we know what behavior we will find from our analysis of the environment?

If (a) rational analysis were right and (b) we knew the right assumptions to make about the computational limitations and (c) if we knew how to characterize the environment, then we would be able to know what behavior to expect without experimentation. However, none of these premises has to be true. We need an experimental program to test a rational analysis just as we do in the case of a mechanistic theory. I have argued that there is more heuristic guidance in searching for a correct rational theory than a correct mechanistic theory. In the generate-and-test model of search, there is more guidance in generating rational theories than in generating mechanistic theories, but there is still the need for testing these candidates.

As in any theory-generation process, the knowledge of the data can play

---

consequential, why haven't the less adapted values been selected against? One seems forced to conclude that the differences are not adaptively consequential.

[5]Jay McClelland has pointed out to me that the human species is unique in creating so many different cultural niches in which people can specialize. For instance, in a world where there are farmers and fishermen, it behooves some to specialize as fishermen and others as farmers.

a critical role. I am sure that my knowledge of the empirical regularities in the domains of the previous chapters guided my construction of rational models, although I would be hard pressed to specify just how.

As to the issue of postdicting versus predicting, the strategy in this book has definitely been to take advantage of the wealth of empirical literature to test the theory. That seems an appropriate thing to do before beginning one's own empirical program. Nonetheless, there were a few new experimental tests reported. In well-researched domains like human memory, it is unclear how many robust phenomena remain to be discovered. We are left with weak predictions, such as that the serial position curve should not really be flat for long enough lists. In the case of domains like problem solving, this rational analysis has pointed us to largely unexplored regions, such as problem solving under uncertainty, where virtually any prediction of the theory is unique and untested. For instance, there were the predictions about when one would stop generating alternatives and satisfice (p. 215). As another example, there are other predictions about subgoal abandonment, such as that one will more readily abandon a subgoal in the face of frustration the more deeply embedded it is, and the more previous subgoals there are that have been tried and failed.

12. Implications for Practice

What are the implications of this approach for the practice of cognitive psychology?

I would hope to see three new practices in the field, one quite obvious from this book and two not quite so obvious. The obvious one is what I practiced in this book. This is that we would see more efforts to develop rational theories of various cognitive phenomena. The highly Bayesian approach of this book is not necessary, as Marr and Shepard have demonstrated in their work. However, it unavoidably requires getting serious about the nature of the information-processing demands imposed on us by the environment, the statistical character of those demands, and doing a little mathematics.

The second implication has already been stated herein, and this is that there should be empirical work on the actual structure of the environment. For instance, it would be informative to study how people use various routes in their environment to get statistics about information repetition (the memory chapter) and to see the frequency with which routes have unexpected obstacles (the problem solving chapter). To repeat, there is no reason why this is not as meritorious as empirical work on the structure of the brain.

The third implication has also been stated herein. This is that we buy into Marr's research program and try to guide our construction of mechanistic models with the outcome of a prior rational analysis.

None of these new practices is being advocated to the exclusion of existing practices. However, these existing practices would be more profitable if we took seriously the idea that there is a reason for the way the mind is. We are not trying to understand an arbitrary black box built out of billions of neurons.

REFERENCES

Anderson, J. A. (1973). A theory for the recognition of items from short memorized lists. *Psychological Review, 80,* 417–438.

Anderson, J. R. (1972). FRAN: A simulation model of free recall. In G. H. Bower (Ed.), *The psychology of learning and motivation* (Vol. 5, pp. 315–378). New York: Academic Press.

Anderson, J. R. (1974a). Retrieval of propositional information from long-term memory. *Cognitive Psychology, 5,* 451–474.

Anderson, J. R. (1974b). Verbatim and propositional representation of sentences in immedate and long-term memory. *Journal of Verbal Learning and Verbal Behavior, 13,* 149–162.

Anderson, J. R. (1976). *Language, memory, and thought.* Hillsdale, NJ: Lawrence Erlbaum Associates.

Anderson, J. R. (1978). Arguments concerning representations for mental imagery. *Psychological Review, 85,* 249–277.

Anderson, J. R. (1979). Further arguments concerning representations for mental imagery: A response to Hayes-Roth and Pylyshyn. *Psychological Review, 86,* 395–406.

Anderson, J. R. (1981a). *Cognitive skills and their acquisition.* Hillsdale, NJ: Lawrence Erlbaum Associates.

Anderson, J. R. (1981b). Effects of prior knowledge on memory for new information. *Memory and Cognition, 9,* 237–246.

Anderson, J. R. (1981c). Interference: The relationship between response latency and accuracy. *Journal of Experimental Psychology: Human Learning and Memory, 7,* 311–325.

Anderson, J. R. (1982). Acquisition of cognitive skill. *Psychological Review, 89,* 369–406.

Anderson, J. R. (1983). *The architecture of cognition.* Cambridge, MA: Harvard University Press.

Anderson, J. R. (1984). Spreading activation. In J. R. Anderson & S. M. Kosslyn (Eds.), *Tutorials in learning and memory* (pp. 61–90). San Francisco: Freeman.

Anderson, J. R. (1985). *Cognitive psychology and its implications (2nd ed.).* New York: W. H. Freeman & Company.

Anderson, J. R. (1986). Knowledge compilation: The general learning mechanism. In R. Michalski, J. Carbonell, & T. Mitchell (Eds.), *Machine learning* (Vol. 2, pp. 289–310). Los Altos, CA: Morgan Kaufmann.

Anderson, J. R. (1987a). Methodologies for studying human knowledge. *The Behavioral and Brain Sciences, 10,* 467–505.

Anderson, J. R. (1987b). Production systems, learning, and tutoring. In D. Klahr, P. Langley, & R. Neches (Eds.), *Production system models of learning and development* (pp. 437–458). Cambridge, MA: MIT Press.

Anderson, J. R. (1987c). Skill acquisition: Compilation of weak-method problem solutions. *Psychological Review, 94*(2), 192–210.

Anderson, J. R. (1989). A rational analysis of human memory. In H.L. Roedinger & F.I.M. Craik (Eds.), *Varieties of memory and consciousness* (pp. 195–210). Hillsdale, NJ:

Lawrence Erlbaum Associates.

Anderson, J. R. (in pressa). *Cognitive psychology and its implications, Third Edition*. New York: W. H. Freeman.

Anderson, J. R. (in pressb). The place of cognitive architectures in a rational analysis. In K. VanLehn (Ed.), *Architectures for intelligence*. Hillsdale, NJ: Lawrence Erlbaum Associates.

Anderson, J. R., & Bower, G. H. (1972). Configural properties in sentence memory. *Journal of Verbal Learning and Verbal Behavior, 11*, 594–605.

Anderson, J. R., & Bower G. H. (1973). *Human associative memory*. Washington, DC: Winston and Sons.

Anderson, J. R., Boyle, C. F., Corbett, A. T., & Lewis, M. W. (in press). Cognitive modelling and intelligent tutoring. *Artificial Intelligence*.

Anderson, J. R., Boyle, C. F., & Reiser, B. J. (1985). Intelligent tutoring systems. *Science, 228*, 456–462.

Anderson, J. R., Conrad, F. G., & Corbett, A. T. (1989). Skill acquisition and the LISP tutor. *Cognitive Science, 13*, 467–505.

Anderson, J. R., Kline, P. J., & Beasley, C. M. (1979). A general learning theory and its applications to schema abstraction. In G. H. Bower (Ed.), *The psychology of learning and motivation* (Vol. 13, pp. 277–318). New York: Academic Press.

Anderson, J. R., & Milson, R. (1989). Human memory: An adaptive perspective. *Psychological Review, 96*(4), 703–719.

Anderson, J. R., & Thompson, R. (1989). Use of analogy in a production system architecture. In S. Vosniadou & A. Ortony (Eds.), *Similarity and analogical reasoning* (pp. 267–297). Cambridge University Press.

Anzai, Y., & Simon, H. A. (1979). The theory of learning by doing. *Psychological Review, 86*, 124–140.

Arbib, M. A. (1987). Many levels: More than one is algorithmic. *Behavioral and Brain Sciences, 10*(3), 478–479.

Arkes, H. R., & Harkness, A. R. (1983). Estimates of contingency between two dichotomous variables. *Journal of Experimental Psychology: General, 112*, 117–135.

Atkinson, R., & Shiffrin, R. (1968). Human memory: A proposed system and its control processes. In K. Spence & J. Spence (Eds.), *The psychology of learning and motivation* (pp. 90–197). New York: Academic Press.

Atwood, M. E., & Polson, P. G. (1976). A process model for water jug problems. *Cognitive Psychology, 8*, 191–216.

Baddeley, A. (1986). *Working memory*. Oxford, England: Oxford University Press.

Baddeley, A. D., & Ecob, J. R. (1973). Reaction time and short-term memory: Implications of repetitions for the high-speed exhaustive scan hypothesis. *Quarterly Journal of Experimental Psychology, 25*, 229–240.

Bahrick, H. P. (1979). Maintenance of knowledge: Questions about memory we forget to ask. *Journal of Experimental Psychology: General, 108*, 296–308.

Balota, D., & Lorch, R. (1986). Depth of automatic spreading activation: Mediated priming effects in pronunciation but not in lexical decision. *Journal of Experimental Psychology: Learning, Memory, & Cognition, 12*, 336–345.

Battig, W. F. (1968). Paired-associate learning. In T. R. Dixon & D. L. Horton (Eds.), *Verbal behavior and general behavior theory* (pp. 146–171). Englewood Cliffs, NJ: Prentice-Hall.

Berge, C. (1971). *Principles of combinatonics*. New York: Academic Press.

Berger, J. O. (1985). *Statistical decision theory and Bayesian analyses*. New York: Springer-Verlag.

Berwick, R. C. & Weinberg, A. S. (1984). *The grammatical basis of linguistic performance*. Cambridge, MA: MIT Press.

Bookstein, A., & Swanson, D. R. (1974). Probabilistic models for automatic indexing.

Journal of the ASIS, 25, 312–318.

Bookstein, A., & Swanson, D. R. (1975). A decision theoretic foundation for indexing. *Journal of the ASIS, 26,* 45–50.

Bransford, J. D., Franks, J. J., Morris, C. D., & Stein, B. S. (1979). Some general constraints on learning and memory research. In L. Cermak & F. Craik (Eds.), *Levels of processing in human memory* (pp. 331–354). Hillsdale, NJ: Lawrence Erlbaum Associates.

Broadbent, D. (1985). A question of levels: Comment on McClelland and Rumelhart. *Journal of Experimental Psychology: General, 114,* 189–192.

Brooks, L. (1978). Nonanalytic concept formation and memory for instances. In E. Rosch & B. B. Lloyd (Eds.), *Cognition and categorization* (pp. 170–211). Hillsdale, NJ: Lawrence Erlbaum Associates.

Brown, J. S., Collins, A., & Duguid, P. (1988). *Situated cognition and the culture of learning* (Tech. Rep. No. 6886). Bolt, Beranek, & Newman, Inc.

Bruce, D. (1980). Single probes, double probes, and the structure of memory traces. *Journal of Experimental Psychology: Human Learning and Memory, 6,* 276–292.

Brunswick, E. (1956) Perception and the representative design of psychological experiments. Berkeley, CA: University of California Press.

Bullock, M., Gelman, R., & Baillargeon, R. (1982). The development of causal reasoning. In W. Friedman (Ed.), *The developmental psychology of time* (pp. 209–254). New York: Academic Press.

Burrell, Q. L. (1980). A simple stochastic model for library loans. *Journal of Documentation, 36,* 115–132.

Burrell, Q. L. (1985). A note on aging on a library circulation model. *Journal of Documentation, 41,* 100–115.

Burrell, Q. L., & Cane, V. R. (1982). The analysis of library data. *Journal of the Royal Statistical Society Series A, 145,* 439–471.

Buschke, H. (1974). Spontaneous remembering after recall failure. *Science, 184,* 579–581.

Campbell, D. T. (1974). Evolutionary epistemology. In P. A. Schilpp (Ed.), *The philosophy of Karl Popper.* La Salle, IL: Open Court.

Carbonell, J. G. (1985). *Derivational analogy: A theory of reconstructive problem solving and expertise acquisition* (Tech. Rep. No. 85-115). Pittsburgh, PA: Carnegie-Mellon University, Computer Science Department.

Chandler, P. J. (1965). *Subroutine STEPIT: An algorithm that finds the values of the parameters which minimize a given continuous function [Computer program].* Bloomington: Indiana University, Quantum Chemistry Program Exchange.

Chase, W. G. (1982). *Spatial representations of taxi drivers* (Tech. Rep. UPITT/LRDC/ONR/KBC-6). Pittsburgh: Carnegie Mellon.

Chase, W. G., & Ericsson, K. A. (1982). Skill and working memory. In G. H. Bower (Ed.), *The psychology of learning and motivation.* New York: Academic Press.

Chomsky, N. (1965). *Aspects of the theory of syntax.* Cambridge, MA: MIT Press.

Chomsky, N. (1980). Rules and representations. *Behavioral and Brain Sciences, 3,* 1–61.

Cohen, N., & Corkin, S. (1981, October). *The amnesiac patient H.M.: Learning and retention of a cognitive skill.* Paper presented at the 11th annual meeting of the Society for Neuroscience, Los Angeles, CA.

Cosmides, L. (1989). The logic of social exchange: Has natural selection shaped how humans reason? Studies with the Wason selection task. *Cognition, 31,* 187–276.

Crick, F. H. C., & Asanuma, C. (1986). Certain aspects of the anatomy and physiology of the cerebral cortex. In J. L. McClelland & D. E. Rumelhart (Eds.), *Parallel distributed processing: Exploration in the microstructure of cognition* (pp. 333–371). Cambridge, MA: Bradford Books.

Crocker, J. (1981). Judgment of covariation by social perceivers. *Psychological Bulletin, 90,* 272–292.

Crowder, R. G. (1976). *Principles of learning and memory*. Hillsdale, NJ: Lawrence Erlbaum Associates.

Crowder, R. G. (1982a). The demise of short-term memory. *Acta Psychologica, 50,* 291–323.

Crowder, R. G. (1982b). *The psychology of reading: An introduction*. New York: Oxford University Press.

Dawes, R. M. (1987). *Rational choice in an uncertain world*. New York: Harcourt, Brace, & Jovanovich.

Dawson, M. E., & Schell, A. M. (1982). Electrodermal responses to attended and nonattended significant stimuli during dichotic listening. *Journal of Experimental Psychology: Human Perception and Performance, 8,* 315–324.

de Groot, A. (1983). The range of automatic spreading activation in word priming. *Journal of Verbal Learning and Verbal Behavior, 22,* 417–436.

Deese, J. (1960). Frequency of usage and number of words on free recall: The role of association. *Psychological Reports, 7,* 337–344.

deKleer, J., & Brown, J. S. (1984). A physics based on confluences. *AI Journal, 24,* 7–83.

Dewey, J. (1910). *How we think*. Boston: Heath.

Donchen, E., McCarthy, G., Kutas, M., & Ritter, W. (1983). Event-related potentials in the study of consciousness. In G. E. Schwartz & D. Shapiro (Eds.), *Consciousness and self-regulation* (pp. 81–121). New York: Putnam.

Dupre, J. (1987). *The latest on the best*. Cambridge, MA: MIT Press.

Eddy, D. M. (1982). Probabilistic reasoning in clinical medicine: Problems and opportunities. In D. Kahneman, P. Stovic, & A. Tversky (Ed.), *Judgment under uncertainty: Heuristics and biases* (pp. 249–267). New York: Cambridge University Press.

Eich, J. M. (1982). A composite holographic associative recall model. *Psychological Review, 89,* 627–661.

Einhorn, H. J. & Hogarth, R. M. (1986). Judging probable cause. *Psychological Bulletin, 99*(1), 3–19.

Elio, R., & Anderson, J. R. (1981). The effects of category generalizations and instance similarity on schema abstraction. *Journal of Experimental Psychology: Human Learning and Memory, 7,* 397–417.

Elio, R., & Anderson, J. R. (1984). The effects of information order and learning mode on schema abstraction. *Memory and Cognition, 12,* 20–30.

Ericsson, K. A., & Simon, H. A. (1984). *Protocol analysis: Verbal reports as data*. Cambridge, MA: MIT Press.

Estes, W. K. (1986). Array models for category learning. *Cognitive Psychology, 18,* 500–549.

Estes, W. K., Cambell, J. A., Hatsopoulos, N., & Hurwitz, J. B. (1989). *Base-rate effects in category learning: A comparison of parallel network and memory storage-retrieval models. Journal of Experimental Psychology: Learning, Memory, and Cognition, 15,* 556–571.

Farah, M. J. (1988). Is visual imagery really visual? Overlooked evidence from neuropsychology. *Psychological Review, 95,* 307–317.

Fisher, D. H. (1987). Knowledge acquisition via incremental conceptual clustering. *Machine Learning, 2,* 139–172.

Flavell, J. H. (1977). *Cognitive development*. Englewood Cliffs, NJ: Prentice-Hall.

Foss, D. J., & Harwood, D. A. (1975). Memory for sentences: Implications for human associative memory. *Journal of Verbal Learning and Verbal Behavior, 14,* 1–16.

Fried, L. S., & Holyoak, K. J. (1984). Induction of category distributions: A framework for classification learning. *Journal of Experimental Psychology: Learning, Memory, and Cognition, 10,* 239–257.

Gelman, S. A. (1988). The development of induction within natural kind and artifact categories. *Cognitive Psychology, 20,* 65–95.

Gentner, D. (1983). Structure-mapping: A theoretical framework for analogy. *Cognitive Science, 7,* 155–170.

Gibson, J. J. (1966). *The senses considered as perceptual systems.* Boston: Houghton.

Gillund, G., & Shiffrin, R. M. (1984). A retrieval model for both recognition and recall. *Psychological Review, 91,* 1-67.

Glass, A. L. (1984). Effect of memory set on reaction time. In J. R. Anderson & S. M. Kosslyn (Eds.), *Tutorials in learning and memory* (pp. 119-136). New York: Freeman.

Glenberg, A. M. (1976). Monotonic and nonmonotonic lag effects in paired-associate and recognition memory paradigms. *Journal of Verbal Learning and Verbal Behavior, 15,* 1-16.

Glenberg, A. M., Bradley, M. M., Stevenson, J. A., Kraus, T. A., Tkachuck, M. J., Gretz, A. L., Fish, J. H., & Turpin, B. A. M. (1980). A two-process account of long-term serial position effects. *Journal of Experimental Psychology: Human Learning and Memory, 6,* 355-369.

Gluck, M. A., & Bower, G. H. (1988). From conditioning to category learning: An adaptive network model. *Journal of Experimental Psychology: General, 8,* 37-50.

Gluck, M. A., & Corter, J. E. (1985). *Information and category utility.* Stanford University.

Gould, S. J., & Lewontin, R. C. (1979). The Spandrels of San Marco and the Panglossian paradigm: A critique of the adaptationist program. *Proceedings of the Royal Society of London, 205,* 581-598.

Gregg, V. H., Montgomery, D. C., & Caslano, D. (1980). Recall of common and uncommon words from pure and mixed lists. *Journal of Verbal Learning and Verbal Behavior, 19,* 240-245.

Guthrie, E. R. (1952). *The psychology of learning.* New York: Harper and Row.

Guttman, N., & Kalish, H. J. (1956). Discriminability and stimulus generalization. *Journal of Experimental Psychology, 51,* 29-88.

Hayes, J. R., & Simon, H. A. (1974). Understanding written problem instructions. In L. W. Gregg (Ed.), *Knowledge and cognition* (pp. 167-200). Hillsdale, NJ: Lawrence Erlbaum Associates.

Hayes, J. R., & Simon, H. A. (1977). Psychological differences among problem isomorphs. In N. J. Castellan, D. B. Pisoni, & G. R. Potts (Eds.), *Cognitive theory.* Hillsdale, NJ: Lawrence Erlbaum Associates.

Hilton, D. J., & Slugoski, B. R. (1986). Knowledge-based causal attribution: The abnormal conditions focus model. *Psychological Review, 93,* 75-88.

Hintzman, D. L. (1986). Schema abstraction in a multiple-trace memory model. *Psychological Review, 93,* 411-428.

Hoffman, J., & Ziessler, C. (1983). Objectidentifikation in kunstlichen Begriffshierarcchien. *Zeitschrift fur Psychologie, 194,* 135-167.

Hogarth, R. M., & Reder, M. W. (1986). The behavior foundations of economic theory. *The Journal of Business, 59,* S181-S505.

Holland, J. H., Holyoak, K., Nisbett, R. E., & Thagard, P. R. (1986). *Induction: Processes of inference, learning, and discovery.* Cambridge, MA: MIT Press.

Holyoak, K. J., & Thagard, P. R. (1989). A computational model of analogical problem solving. In S. Vosniadou & A. Ortony (Eds.), *Similarity and analogical reasoning* (pp. 242-266). New York: Cambridge University Press.

Homa, D., & Cultice, J. (1984). Role of feedback, category size, and stimulus distortion in the acquisition and utilization of ill-defined categories. *Journal of Experimental Psychology: Learning, Memory, and Cognition, 10,* 83-94.

Homa, D., & Vosburgh, R. (1976). Category breadth and abstraction of prototypical information. *Journal of Experimental Psychology: Human Learning and Memory, 2,* 322-330.

Hume, D. (1938). *An abstract of a treatise of human nature.* London: Cambridge University Press. (Original work published 1740).

Ijiri, Y., & Simon, H. A. (1977). *Skew distributions and the sizes of business firms.* Amsterdam: North Holland.

James, W. (1892). *Psychology.* London: Macmillan.

Jaspars, J. M. F., Hewstone, M. R. C., & Fincham, F. D. (1983). The process of causal attribution in common sense. In J. M. F. Jaspars, M. R. C. Hewstone, & F. D. Fincham (Eds.), *Attribution theory: Essays and experiments* (pp. 3–36). London: Academic Press.

Jeffries, R. P., Polson, P. G., Razran, L., & Atwood, M. (1977). A process model for missionaries–cannibals and other river-crossing problems. *Cognitive Psychology, 9,* 412–440.

Jenkins, H. M., & Harrison, R. H. (1958). *Auditory generalization in the pigeons* (Tech. Rep. TN No. 58–443; Astia Document No. 158248). Washington, DC: Air Research and Development Command.

Jenkins, H. M., & Ward, W. C. (1965). Judgment of contingency between responses and outcomes. *Psychological Monographs: General and Applied, 79*(1, Whole No. 594), 1–17.

Johnson-Laird, P. N. (1983). *Mental models.* Cambridge, MA: Harvard University Press.

Jones, G. V. (1980). Interaction of intrinsic and extrinsic knowledge in sentence recall. In R. S. Nickerson (Ed.), *Attention and performance VIII.* Hillsdale, NJ: Lawrence Erlbaum Associates.

Kahneman, D., & O'Curry, S. (1988, November). *Surprise as an indication for spontaneous categorization.* Chicago Paper presented at the 29th annual meeting of the Psychonomics Society.

Kahneman, D., & Tversky, A. (1973). On the psychology of prediction. *Psychological Review, 80,* 237–251.

Kahneman, D., & Tversky, A. (1984). Choices, values, and frames. *American Psychologist, 39,* 341–350.

Kaiser, M. K., McCloskey, M., & Proffitt, D. R. (1986). Development of intuitive theories of motion: Curvilinear motion in the absence of external forces. *Developmental Psychology, 22,* 67–71.

Kaiser, M. K., & Proffitt, D. R. (1984). The development of sensitivity to causally relevant dynamic information. *Child Development, 55,* 1614–1624.

Kaiser, M. K., Proffitt, D. R., & McCloskey, M. (1985). The development of beliefs about falling objects. *Perception and Psychophysics, 38,* 533–539.

Karat, J. (1982). A model of problem solving with incomplete constraint knowledge. *Cognitive Psychology, 14,* 538–559.

Keenan, J. M., & Baillet, S. D. (1980). Memory for personally and socially significant events. In R. S. Nickerson (Ed.), *Attention and performance VIII.* Hillsdale, NJ: Lawrence Erlbaum Associates.

Kelley, H. H. (1973). The processes of causal attribution. *American Psychologist, 28,* 107–128.

Kelley, H. H. (1967). Attribution theory in social psychology. In D. Levine (Ed.), *Nebraska symposium on motivation* (pp. 192–238). Lincoln: University of Nebraska Press.

Kessler, C. M. (1988). *Transfer of Programming Skills in Novice LISP Learners.* Doctoral Dissertation, Carnegie-Mellon University, Pittsburgh.

Kintsch, W. (1970a). Models for free recall and recognition. In D. A. Norman (Ed.), *Models of human memory* (pp. 307–373). New York: Academic Press.

Kintsch, W. (1970b). *Learning, memory, and conceptual processes.* New York: Wiley.

Kline, P. J. (1983). *Computing the similarity of structured objects by means of a heuristic search for correspondences.* Unpublished doctoral dissertation, University of Michigan, Ann Arbor.

Kotovsky, K., & Fallside, D. (1988). Representation and transfer in problem solving. In D. Klahr & K. Kotovsky (Eds.), *Complex information processing* (pp. 69–108). Hillsdale, NJ: Lawrence Erlbaum Associates.

Kotovsky, K., Hayes, J. R., & Simon, H. A. (1985). Why are some problems so hard? Evidence from Tower of Hanoi. *Cognitive Psychology, 17*(2), 248–294.

Lave, J. (1988a). *Cognition in practice.* Boston, MA: Cambridge University Press.

Lave, J. (1988b). *Word problems: A microcism of theories of learning.* Paper presented at AERA annual conference, New Orleans, LA.

Lebowitz, L. (1987). Experiments with incremental concept formation: UNIMEM. *Machine Learning, 2,* 103–138.

Le Voi, M. E., Ayton, P. J., Jonckheere, A. R., McClelland, A. G. R., & Rawles, R. E. (1983). Unidimensional memory traces: On the analysis of multiple cued recall. *Journal of Verbal Learning and Verbal Behavior, 22,* 560–576.

Lewis, C. H. (1978). *Production system models of practice effects.* Unpublished doctoral dissertation, University of Michigan, Ann Arbor.

Lewis, C. H. (1988). Why and how to learn why: Analysis-based generalization of procedures. *Cognitive Science, 12,* 211–256.

Lipe, M. G. (1982). *A cross-study analysis of covariation judgments.* Unpublished manuscript, University of Chicago, Center for Decision Research, Graduate School of Business.

Loftus, G. R. (1972). Eye fixations and recognition memory for pictures. *Cognitive Psychology, 3,* 525–551.

Logan, G. D. (1988). Toward an instance theory of automatization. *Psychological Review, 95,* 492–527.

Lorch, R. F., Balota, D. A., & Stamm, E. G. (1986). Locus of inhibition effects in the priming of lexical decisions: Pre- or post-lexical access? *Memory & Cognition, 14,* 95–103.

MacKay, D. G. (1982). The problem of flexibility, fluency, and speed–accuracy trade-off in skilled behavior. *Psychological Review, 89,* 483–506.

Mandler, J. M., Bauer, P. J., & McDonough, L. (1988, November). Differentiating global categories. Paper presented at the 29th annual meeting of the Psychonomic Society, Chicago.

Marr, D. (1982). *Vision.* San Francisco: Freeman.

Mayr, E. (1983). How to carry out the adaptionist program? *American Naturalist, 121,* 324–334.

McClelland, J. L., & Rumelhart, D. E., (1986). *Parallel distributed processing: Explorations in the microstructure of cognition.* Cambridge, MA: Bradford Books.

McClelland, J. L., Rumelhart D. E., & Hinton, G. E. (1986). The appeal of parallel distributed processing. In D. E. Rumelhart & J. L. McClelland (Eds.), *Parallel distributed processing* (pp. 3–44). Cambridge, MA: Bradford Books.

McCloskey, M. (1983). Intuitive physics. *Scientific American, 248,* 122–130.

McKendree, J. E., & Anderson, J. R. (1987). Frequency and practice effects on the composition of knowledge in LISP evaluation. In J. M. Carroll (Ed.), *Cognitive aspects of human–computer interaction* (pp. 236–259). Cambridge, MA: MIT Press.

McNamara, T. P., & Altarriba, T. P. (1988). Depth of spreading activation revisited: Semantic mediated priming occurs in lexical decisions. *Journal of Memory and Language, 27,* 545–559.

Medin, D. L, Altom, M. W., Edelson, S. M., & Freko, D. (1982). Correlated symptoms and simulated medical classification. *Journal of Experimental Psychology: Learning, Memory, and Cognition, 8,* 37–50.

Medin, D. L., & Edelson, S. M. (1988). Problem structure and the use of base-rate information from experience. *Journal of Experimental Psychology: General, 117,* 68–85.

Medin, D. L., & Schaffer, M. M. (1978). Context theory of classification learning. *Psychological Review, 85,* 207–238.

Michalski, R. S., & Chilausky, R. L. (1980). Learning by being told and learning from examples: An experimental comparison of the two methods of knowledge acquisition in the context of developing an expert system for soybean disease diagnosis. *International Journal of Policy Analysis and Information Systems, 4,* 125–161.

Michotte, A. (1946). *La perception de la causalite.* Paris: Vrin.

Mill, J. S. (1843/1974). *A system of logic ratiocinative and inductive.* Toronto: University of Toronto Press.

Murdock, B. B., Jr. (1962). The serial-position effect of free recall. *Journal of Experimental Psychology, 64*(5), 482–488.

Murphy, G. L., & Medin, D. L. (1985). The role of theories in conceptual coherence. *Psychological Review, 92,* 289–316.

Murphy, G. L., & Smith, E. E. (1982). Basic level superiority in picture categorization. *Journal of Verbal Learning and Verbal Behavior, 21,* 1–20.

Neely, J. H. (1977). Semantic priming and retrieval from lexical memory: Roles of inhibitionless spreading activation and limited-capacity attention. *Journal of Experimental Psychology: General, 106,* 226–254.

Neisser, U. (1976). *Cognition and reality.* New York: W. H. Freeman.

Neisser, U. (Ed.). (1982). *Memory observed: Remembering in natural contexts.* New York: W. H. Freeman.

Nelson, K. E. (1974). Concept, word, and sentence: Interrelations in acquisition and development. *Psychological Review, 81,* 267–285.

Neumann, P. G. (1977). Visual prototype information with discontinuous representation of dimensions of variability. *Memory & Cognition, 5,* 187–197.

Newell, A. (1972). A theoretical exploration of mechanisms for coding the stimulus. In A. W. Melton & E. Martin (Eds.), *Coding processing in human memory* (pp. 373–434). Washington, DC: Winston.

Newell, A. (1980a). Physical symbol systems. *Cognitive Science, 4,* 135–183.

Newell, A. (1980b). Reasoning, problem-solving, and decision processes: The problem space as a fundamental category. In R. Nickerson (Ed.), *Attention and Performance VIII.* Hillsdale, NJ: Lawrence Erlbaum Associates.

Newell, A. (1982). The knowledge level. *Artificial Intelligence, 18,* 87–127.

Newell, A. (in press). *Unified theories of cognition.* Cambridge, MA: Harvard University Press.

Newell, A., & Rosenbloom, P. (1981). Mechanisms of skill acquisition and the law of practice. In J. R. Anderson (Ed.), *Cognitive skills and their acquisition* (pp. 1–55). Hillsdale, NJ: Lawrence Erlbaum Associates.

Newell, A., Shaw, J. C., & Simon, H. A. (1957). Empirical explorations of the logic theory machine: A case study in heuristics. In *Proceedings of the Joint Computer Conference* (pp. 218–230).

Newell, A., & Simon, H. A. (1961). GPS, a program that simulates human thought. In H. Billing (Ed.), *Lernende Automaten* (pp. 109–124). Munich: R. Oldenbourg.

Newell, A., & Simon, H. A. (1972). *Human problem solving.* Englewood Cliffs, NJ: Prentice-Hall.

Newell, A., & Simon, H. A. (1976). Computer science as empirical inquiry: Symbols and search. *Communications of the ACM, 19,* 113–126.

Nisbett, R. E., & Ross, L. (1980). *Human inference: Strategies and shortcomings of social judgment.* Englewood Cliffs, NJ: Prentice-Hall.

Nosofsky, R. (1988) Similarity, frequency, and category representation. *Journal of Experimental Psychology: Learning, Memory, and Cognition, 10,* 104–114.

Orvis, B. R., Cunningham, J. D., & Kelley, H. H. (1975). A closer examination of causal inference: The roles of consensus, distinctiveness, and consistency information. *Journal of Personality and Social Psychology, 32,* 605–616.

Paivio, A. (1971). *Imagery and verbal processes.* New York: Holt, Rinehart, & Winston.

Phelps, M. E. & Massiotta, J. E. (1985). Positron emission tomography: Brain function and biochemistry. *Science, 288,* 799–809.

Piaget, J. (1974). *Understanding causality.* New York: Norton.

Pinker, S., & Prince, A. (1988). On language and connectionism: analysis of a parallel distributed processing model of language acquisition. *Cognition, 28,* 73–193.

Posner, M. I., & Keele, S. W. (1968). On the genesis of abstract ideas. *Journal of Experimental Psychology, 77,* 353–363.

Posner, M. I., Peterson, S. E., Fox, P. T., & Racihle, M. E. (1988). Localization of cognitive operations in the human brain. *Science, 240,* 1627–1631.

Postman, L. (1970). Effects of word frequency on acquisition and retention under conditions of free-recall learning. *Quarterly Journal of Experimental Psychology, 22,* 185–195.

Pylyshyn, Z. W. (1980) Computation and cognition: Issues in the foundations of cognitive science. *Behavioral and Brain Sciences, 3,* 111–169.

Pylyshyn, Z. W. (1984). *Computation and cognition.* Cambridge, MA: MIT Press.

Raaijmakers, J. G. W., & Shiffrin, R. M. (1981). Search of associative memory. *Psychological Review, 88,* 93–134.

Ratcliff, R., & McKoon, G. (1988). A retrieval theory of priming in memory. *Psychological Review, 95,* 385–408.

Reder, L. M. (1987). Strategy selection in question answering. *Cognitive Psychology, 19,* 90–138.

Reder, L. M., & Ross, B. H. (1983). Integrated knowledge in different tasks: The role of retrieval strategy on fan effects. *Journal of Experimental Psychology: Learning, Memory, and Cognition, 9,* 55–72.

Reder, L. R., & Wible, C. (1984). Strategy use in question-answering: Memory strength and task constraints on fan effects. *Memory & Cognition, 12,* 411–419.

Rescorla, R. A. (1968). Probability of shock in the presence and absence of CS in fear conditioning. *Journal of Comparative and Physiological Psychology, 66,* 1–5.

Restle, F., & Greeno, J. G. (1970). *Introduction to mathematical psychology.* Reading, MA: Addison-Wesley.

Roberts, W. A. (1972). Free recall of word lists varying in length and rate of presentation: A test of total-time hypothesis. *Journal of Experimental Psychology, 92,* 365–372.

Roland, P. E., & Friberg, L. (1985). Localization of cortical areas activated by thinking. *Journal of Neurophysiology, 53,* 1219–1243.

Rosch, E., Mervis, C. B., Gray, W., Johnson, D., & Boyes-Braem, P. (1976). Basic objects in natural categories. *Cognitive Psychology, 7,* 573–605.

Rubin, D. C., & Wallace, W. T. (1989). Rhyme and reason: Analyses of dual retrieval cues. *Journal of Experimental Psychology: Learning, Memory, and Cognition, 15,* 698–709.

Rumelhart, D. E., Hinton, G. E., & Williams, R. J. (1986). Learning internal representations by error propogation. In D. E. Rumelhart & J. L. McClelland (Eds.), *Parallel distributed processing* (pp. 318–362). Cambridge, MA: MIT Press.

Rumelhart, D. E., & McClelland, J. L. Levels indeed! A response to Broadbent. *Journal of Experimental Psychology: General, 114,* 193–197.

Rumelhart, D. E., & McClelland, J. L., (1986). *Parallel distributed processing: Explorations in the microstructure of cognition.* Cambridge, MA: Bradford Books.

Rundus, D. (1971). Analysis of rehearsal processes in free recall. *Journal of Experimental Psychology, 89,* 63–77.

Salton, G., & McGill, M. J. (1983). *Introduction to modern information retrieval.* New York: McGraw-Hill.

Satyanarayanan, M. (1981). A study of file sizes and functional lifetimes. In *Proceedings of the Eighth Symposium on Operating Systems Principles.* Asilomar, CA.

Schustack, M. W., & Sternberg, R. J. (1981). Evaluation of evidence in causal inference. *Journal of Experimental Psychology: General, 110,* 101–120.

Seggie, J. L, & Endersby, H. (1972). The empirical implications of Piaget's concept of correlation. *Australian Journal of Psychology, 24,* 3–8.

Servan-Schreiber, E., & Anderson, J. R. (in press). Chunking as a mechanism of implicit learning. *Journal of Experimental Psychology: Learning, Memory, and Cognition.*

Shafer, G., & Tversky, A. (1985). Languages and designs for probability judgment. *Cognitive Science, 9,* 309–334.

Shaklee, H., & Tucker, D. (1980). A rule analysis of judgments of covariation between events. *Memory & Cognition, 8,* 459–467.

Shannon, C. E. (1949). Communications in the presence of noise. *Proceedings of the Institute of Radio Engineers, 37,* 10–21.

Shepard, R. N. (1984). Ecological constraints on internal representation: Resonant kinematics of perceiving, imagining, and dreaming. *Psychological Review, 91,* 417–456.

Shepard, R. N. (1987). Towards a universal law of generalization for psychological science. *Science, 237,* 1317–1323.

Shepherd, G. M. (1979). *The synaptic organization of the brain.* New York: Oxford University Press.

Shrager, J. C, Hogg, T., & Huberman, B. A. (1988). A dynamical theory of the power-law learning in problem-solving. In *Proceedings of the Tenth Annual Conference of the Cognitive Science Society* (pp. 468–474). Hillsdale, NJ: Cognitive Science Society.

Shultz, T. R. (1982). Rules for causal attribution. *Monographs of the Society for Research in Child Development, 47*(1, Serial No. 194).

Shultz, T. R., Fischer, G. W., Pratt, C. C., & Rulf, S. (1986). Selection of causal rules. *Child Development, 57,* 143–152.

Siegler, R. S. (1976). The effects of simple necessity and sufficiency relationships in children's causal inferences. *Child Development, 47,* 1058–1063.

Simon, H. A. (1955). A behavioral model of rational choice. *Quarterly Journal of Economics, 69,* 99–118.

Simon, H. A. (1972). Theories of bounded rationality. In C. B. Radner & R. Radner (Eds.), *Decision and organization* (pp. 161–176) Amsterdam: North-Holland.

Simon, H. A. (1981) The Sciences of the Artificial. *Second Edition.* Cambridge, MA: MIT Press.

Simon, H. A. (in press). Cognitive architectures and rational analysis: Comment. In K. Van Lehn (Ed.), *Architectures for Intelligence.* Hillsdale, NJ: Lawrence Erlbaum Associates.

Simon, H. A., & Hayes, J. R. (1976). The understanding process: Problem isomorphs. *Cognitive Psychology, 8,* 165–190.

Singely, K., & Anderson, J. R. (1989). *The transfer of cognitive skill.* Cambridge, MA: Harvard Press.

Smelslund, J. (1963). The concept of correlation in adults. *Scandinavian Journal of Psychology, 4,* 165–173.

Smith, E. E., Adams, N., & Schorr, D. (1978). Fact retrieval and the paradox of interference. *Cognitive Psychology, 10,* 438–464.

Stephens, D. W., & Krebs, J. R. (1986). *Foraging theory.* Princeton, NJ: Princeton University Press.

Sternberg, S. (1969). Memory scanning: Mental processes revealed by reaction time experiments. *American Scientist, 57,* 421–457.

Sternberg, S. (1975). Memory scanning: New findings and current controversies. *Quarterly Journal of Experimental Psychology, 27,* 1–32.

Stich, S. (in press). *The fragmentation of reason.*

Stigler, G. J. (1961). The economics of information. *Journal of Political Economy, 69,* 213–225.

Stritter, E. P. (1977). *File migration.* Unpublished doctoral dissertation, Stanford University, Stanford, CA.

Suppes, P. (1970). *A probabilistic theory of causality.* Amsterdam: North-Holland.

Theios, J., Smith, P. G., Haviland, S. E., Troupmann, J., & Moy, C. (1973). Memory scanning as a serial self-terminating process. *Journal of Experimental Psychology, 97,* 323–336.

Tolman, E. C. (1932). *Purposive behavior in animals and men.* New York: Appleton-Century-Crofts.

Townsend, J. T. (1974). Issues and models concerning the processing of a finite number of inputs. In B. H. Kantowitz (Ed.), *Human information processing: Tutorials in performance and cognition* (pp. 133–186). Hillsdale, NJ: Lawrence Erlbaum Associates.

Trabasso, T., Secco, T., & van den Broek, P. (1984). Causal cohesion and story coherence. In H. Mandl (Ed.), *Learning and comprehension of text.* Hillsdale, NJ: Lawrence Erlbaum Associates.

Tulving, E., & Watkins, M. J. (1975). Structure of memory traces. *Psychological Review, 82,* 261–275.

Walker, A., & Leakey, R. E. T. (1978). The hominids of East Turkana. *Scientific American, 238,* 54–66.

Wickelgren, W. A. (1976). Memory storage dynamics. In W. K. Estes (Ed.), *Handbook of learning and cognitive processes.* Hillsdale, NJ: Lawrence Erlbaum Associates.

Winston, P. H., Binford, T. O., Katz, B., & Lowry, M. (1983). Learning physical descriptions from functional definitions, examples, and precedents. In *Proceedings of AAAI-83* (pp. 433–439). Washington, DC: American Association of Artificial Intelligence.

Author Index

Adams, N., 70
Altarriba, T.P., 68
Altom, M.W., 115, 116, 130
Anderson, J.A., 40
Anderson, J.R., 2, 3, 10, 13, 17, 18, 21, 23, 24, 25, 31, 37, 39, 50, 55, 58, 62, 68, 69, 70, 71, 72, 73, 78, 79, 80, 83, 84, 85, 86, 92, 110, 113, 114, 130, 134, 137, 150, 179, 185, 201, 230, 248, 253
Anzai, Y., 223
Arbib, M.A., 6
Arkes, H.R., 157, 159
Asanuma, C., 14
Atkinson, R., 86
Atwood, M.E., 215, 216, 218, 219, 220, 221, 224, 226
Ayton, P.J., 79

Baddeley, A.D., 21, 87, 91
Bahrick, H.P., 59, 61
Baillargeon, R., 164, 165, 168
Baillet, S.D., 72
Balota, D.A., 67, 68
Battig, W.F., 73
Bauer, P.J., 99
Beasley, C.M., 110
Berge, C., 102
Berger, J.O., 51, 97, 105, 143, 163, 205
Berwick, R.C., 39
Binford, T.O., 179
Bookstein, A., 47
Bower, G.H., 2, 79, 80, 120, 121, 122, 124
Boyes-Braem, P., 95, 99
Boyle, C.F., 2
Bradley, M.M., 87
Bransford, J.D., 91
Broadbent, D., 11
Brooks, L., 99
Brown, J.S., 149, 255
Bruce, D., 79

Brunswik, E., 22
Bullock, M., 164, 165, 168
Burrell, Q.L., 49, 50
Buschke, H., 46

Cane, V.R., 49
Cambell, J.A., 125
Campbell, D.T., 22
Carbonell, J.G., 179
Caslano, D., 66
Chandler, P.J., 117, 160
Chase, W.G., 72
Chilausky, R.L., 106, 133
Chomsky, N., 8, 252
Cohen, N., 223
Collins, A., 255
Comsides, L., 22, 37
Conrad, F.G., 2, 3
Corbett, A.T., 2, 3
Corkin, S., 223
Corter, J.E., 125
Crick, F.H.C., 14
Crocker, J., 157, 159
Crowder, R.G., 18, 59
Cultice, J., 99, 111
Cunningham, J.D., 150

Dawes, R.M., 35, 199
Dawson, M.E., 25
Deese, J., 66
de Groot, A., 67
deKleer, J., 149
Dewey, J., 22
Donchen, E., 25
Duguid, P., 255
Dupre, J., 27

Ecob, J.R., 21
Eddy, D.M., 125
Edelson, S.M., 115, 116, 117, 118, 119, 130

Eich, J.M., 65
Einhorn, H.J., 161
Elio, R., 113, 114, 130
Endersby, H., 159
Ericsson, K.A., 21, 72
Estes, W.K., 94, 125
Fallside, D., 223
Farah, M.J., 25
Fincham, F.D., 150
Fischer, G.W., 164
Fish, J.H., 87
Fisher, D.H., 102, 130
Flavell, J.H., 84
Foss, D.J., 79, 80
Fox, P.T., 25
Franks, J.J., 91
Freko, D., 115, 116, 130
Friberg, L., 25
Fried, L.S., 99

Gelman, R., 164, 165, 168
Gelman, S.A., 93
Gentner, D., 179
Gibson, J.J., 6, 22
Gillund, G., 62, 65, 66, 86
Glass, A.L., 21
Glenberg, A.M., 59, 60, 87
Gluck, M.A., 120, 121, 122, 124, 125
Gould, S.J., 30
Gray, W., 95, 99
Greeno, J.G., 73
Gregg, V.H., 66
Gretz, A.L., 87
Guthrie, E.R., 192
Guttman, N., 177

Harkness, A.R., 157, 159
Harrison, R.H., 177
Harwood, D.A., 79, 80
Hatsopoulos, N., 125
Haviland, S.E., 21
Hayes, J.R., 223, 230
Hewstone, M.R.C., 150
Hilton, D.J., 150
Hinton, G.E., 94, 137
Hintzman, D.L., 111
Hoffman, J., 125, 127, 128, 129
Hogarth, R.M., 28, 161
Hogg, T., 58
Holland, J.H., 150, 173
Holyoak, K.J., 99, 150, 173, 179
Homa, D., 99, 111

Huberman, B.A., 58
Hume, D., 161, 165
Hurwitz, J.B., 125

Ijiri, Y., 73

James, W., 22
Jaspars, J.M.F., 150
Jeffries, R.P., 215, 216, 220, 221, 224, 226
Jenkins, H.M., 157, 177
Johnson, D., 95, 99
Johnson-Laird, P.N., 13
Jonckheere, A.R., 79
Jones, G.V., 79, 80

Kahneman, D., 35, 99, 196, 200, 201
Kaiser, M.K., 167, 168
Kalish, H.J., 177
Karat, J., 223
Katz, B., 179
Keele, S.W., 111
Keenan, J.M., 72
Kelley, H.H., 150
Kessler, C.M., 230
Kintsch, W., 36, 65, 66
Kline, P.J., 110, 130
Kotovsky, K., 223, 230
Kraus, T.A., 87
Krebs, J.R., 78, 201
Kutas, M., 25

Lave, J., 255
Leakey, R.E.T., 145
Lebowitz, L., 102, 130
Levoi, M.E., 79
Lewis, C.H., 58, 166, 182, 183
Lewis, M.W., 2
Lewontin, R.C., 30
Lipe, M.G., 157
Loftus, G.R., 73
Logan, G.D., 58
Lorch, R., 67, 68
Lowry, M., 179

Mackay, D.G., 58
Mandler, J.M., 99
Marr, D., 3, 7, 16, 246, 252, 253
Massiotta, J.E., 25
Mayr, E., 30
McCarthy, G., 25
McClelland, A.G.R., 79
McClelland, J.L., 11, 12, 13, 25, 94

McCloskey, M., 168
McDonough, L., 99
McGill, M.J., 42, 47, 62
McKendree, J.E., 230
McKoon, G., 67
McNamara, T.P., 68
Medin, D.L., 94, 98, 106, 108, 110, 115, 116, 117, 118, 119, 130
Mervis, C.B., 95, 99
Michalski, R.S., 106, 133
Michotte, A., 150, 163
Mills, J.S., 34
Milson, R., 55, 86, 92
Montgomery, D.C., 66
Morris, C.D., 91
Moy, C., 21
Murdock, B.B., 87, 88
Murphy, G.L., 98, 125, 126, 127

Neely, J.H., 67
Neisser, U., 22
Nelson, K.E., 95
Neumann, P.G., 114
Newell, A., 13, 14, 15, 18, 19, 56, 57, 58, 150, 203, 221, 223, 233, 252
Nisbett, R.E., 32, 34, 150, 173
Nosofsky, R., 94

O'Curry, S., 99
Orvis, B.R., 150

Paivio, A., 65
Peterson, S.E., 25
Phelps, M.W., 25
Piaget, J., 150
Pinker, S., 131
Polson, P.G., 215, 216, 218, 219, 220, 221, 224, 226
Posner, M.I., 25, 111
Postman, L., 66
Pratt, C.C., 164
Prince, A., 131
Proffitt, D.R., 167, 168
Pylyshyn, Z.W., 9, 10, 21

Raaijmakers, J.G.W., 86
Racihle, M.E., 25
Ratcliff, R., 67
Rawles, E., 79
Razran, L., 215, 216, 220, 221, 224, 226
Reder, M.W., 28
Reder, L.M., 69, 85

Reiser, B.J., 2
Rescorla, R.A., 173, 175, 177, 178
Restle, F., 73
Ritter, W., 25
Roberts, W.A., 89, 90
Roland, P.E., 25
Rosch, E., 95, 99
Rosenbloom, P., 56, 57, 58
Ross, B.H., 69
Ross, L., 32, 34
Rubin, D.C., 79, 80
Rulf, S., 164
Rumelhart, D.E., 11, 12, 13, 25, 94, 137
Rundus, D., 73

Salton, G., 42, 47, 62
Satyanarayanan, M., 39, 72
Schaffer, M.M., 94, 106, 108, 110
Schell, A.M., 25
Schorr, D., 70
Schustack, M.W., 159, 168
Secco, T., 150
Seggie, J.L., 159
Servan-Schreiber, E., 134
Shafer, G., 145, 146
Shaklee, H., 157
Shannon, C.E., 19
Shaw, J.C., 203
Shepard, R.N., 6, 22, 94, 97, 130, 254
Shepherd, G.M., 67
Shiffrin, R.M., 62, 65, 66, 86
Shrager, J.C., 58
Shultz, T.R., 161, 164
Siegler, R.S., 168, 169
Simon, H.A., 13, 18, 21, 32, 49, 73, 203, 214, 215, 221, 223, 230, 233, 248, 250
Singley, M.K., 230
Slugoski, B.R., 150
Smelslund, J., 157
Smith, E.E., 70, 125, 126, 127
Smith, P.E., 21
Stamm, E.G., 67
Stein, B.S., 91
Stephens, D.W., 78, 201
Sternberg, R.J., 159, 168
Sternberg, S., 11, 21, 40
Stevenson, J.A., 87
Stich, S., 31
Stigler, G.J., 215, 250
Stritter, E.P., 49, 53
Suppes, P., 150
Swanson, D.R., 47

Thagard, P.R., 150, 173, 179
Theios, J., 21
Thompson, R., 2, 179, 185
Tkachuck, M.J., 87
Tolman, E.C., 150
Townsend, J.T., 18, 24, 47
Trabasso, T., 150
Troupmann, J., 21
Tucker, D., 157
Tulving, E., 79
Turpin, B.A.M., 87
Tversky, A., 35, 145, 146, 196, 200, 201

van den Broek P., 150
Vosburgh, R., 111

Walker, A., 145
Wallace, W.T., 79, 80
Ward, W.C., 157
Watkins, M.J., 79
Weinberg, A.S., 39
Wickelgren, W.A., 55
Williams, R.J., 137
Winston, P.H., 179

Ziessler, C., 125, 127, 128, 129

Subject Index

Accuracy, see Probability of recall
Activation, 66–68, 82–84, 186–187, 231
ACT*, 2–3, 10, 20, 31, 46, 47, 67, 70,
   77–84, 85, 134–137, 186–187,
   230–231, 252, 253–254
Algorithm level, 9–13, 18–21, 134–138
Analogy, 177–186

Base rate effects, 34–37, 104, 112, 117–120
Basic-level categories, 125–130
Bounded rationality, 32, 249–250

Categorization, 93–148
   Causal inference, role in, 179–181
   Conditional probability, 104–105,
      142–145
   Environment, 96–100
   Goal, 95
   Ideal algorithm, 101–102, 138
   Implementation, 134–138
   Iterative algorithm, 102–103, 106–110
   Prior probability, 103–104, 138–142
Causal inference, 149–190
   Abstraction of causal laws, 177–186
   Causal estimation, 155–160
   Cues to causality, 161–168
   Discrimination of causal laws, 172–177
   Integration of cues, 168–172
Computational theory, see Rational level
Connectionism, 11–14
Contigency data, 157–160, 168–172
Contiguity, 161–165, 168–172
Correlated features, 114–117

Decision making, 194–201
Discrimination learning, 172–177

Environment, structure of, 29–30, 50–55,
   61–64, 96–100, 155–157, 161–168,
   207–214, 248–249

Evolutionary considerations, 26–28,
   246–247

Fan effects, 68–72, 84
Free Recall, 65–66, 85–90
Frequency, see Paradox of the expert, Prac-
   tice, Word frequency
Functional architecture, see Implementation
   level

Hierarchical structure, 99
Hill climbing, 215–221

Identifiability, 17–18, 23–26, 38–40
Individual differences, 254–255
Implementation level, 9–14, 17–18, 23–26
Implementation of rational analysis, 82–84,
   134–138, 186–187, 230–232, 251

Knowledge level, 9, 14–17
   see also Rational level

Labels in categorization, 95, 98, 99–100
Learning, 252–253
Levels of a cognitive theory, 3–31

Means-ends analysis, 221–228
Memory, 41–92
   Context factor, 48, 61–71
   History factor, 48–61
   Implementation, 82–84
   Latency of recall, 72–74, 77–78
   Probability of recall, 72–73, 74–76, 78–82
   Strategy effects, 66, 84–91

Paradox of the expert, 70–72
Power laws, see Practice, Retention
Practice, 51, 55–59, 74–76, 89

Priming, 66–68
Probability matching, 36–37, 120–125
  see also Base rate effects
Problem solving, 191–243
  Estimation of probability and cost,
    203–215
  Hill climbing, 215–221
  Implementation, 230–231
  Iterative plan-and-act structure, 201–207
  Means-ends analysis, 221–228
Production rules, 136, 186–187, 230–231
  see also ACT*, PUPS
PUPS, 2, 179, 185–186

Rational Level, 5–7, 22–23
  see also Knowledge level
Rationality, Principle of, 15, 26–31
Rationality, human, 31–38, 250–251

Recency, see Retention
Retention, 52, 55–59, 74–76, 86–89

Satisficing, 214–215, 247, 249–250
Serial position effects, 86–89
Short-term memory, 91–92, 202
Similarity, 34, 98, 105, 111–114, 165–168,
    207–214
Spacing, 53–55, 59–61
Spreading activation, see Activation
Strategy, 66, 84–91, 253
Symbols, 18–20
  see also Algorithm level

Theory-based categorization, 98

Word frequency, 64–66
Working memory, 91–92, 202